STRENGTHENING FAMILY COPING RESOL

Strengthening Family Coping Resources (SFCR) uses a skill-building, family framework to teach constructive resources to families who have a high exposure to stress and trauma. As an intervention for high-risk families, SFCR can cause a reduction in symptoms of traumatic distress and behavior problems and help families demonstrate higher functioning. The SFCR manual is based on a systemic, family approach and uses empirically supported trauma treatment that focuses on family ritual, storytelling, and narration, which improves communication and understanding among family members. The manual is organized into three accessible parts:

- Part I details the theoretical and empirical foundations of SFCR.
- Part II focuses on implementation and the clinical guidelines for conducting SFCR.
- Part III contains session guidelines focused on the multi-family group versions of SFCR.

Each session included in the intervention is structured according to specific guidelines, and instructions provide examples of what facilitators might say to a group.

Formed through the input of psychiatrists, psychologists, social workers, and anthropologists, *Strengthening Family Coping Resources* will help you reduce the symptoms of traumatic stress disorders and increase coping resources in children, adult caregivers, and the family system. It also provides a novel approach to addressing co-occurring traumatic reactions in multiple family members by including developmentally appropriate skill-building activities that are reinforced with family practice. For anyone working with families in a therapeutic capacity, this manual is a must-have resource.

Laurel Kiser, PhD, MBA, is a psychologist and an associate professor in the Department of Psychiatry at the University of Maryland School of Medicine. Her research focuses on the protective role of rituals and routines within families, schools, and neighborhoods, and the development of interventions to strengthen these to reduce the effects of trauma. Dr. Kiser was awarded an NIMH-mentored career development grant in support of this work and has also received funding from SAMHSA for dissemination and evaluation. Her articles appear frequently in the professional literature and she is a regular presenter and invited lecturer at national conferences.

STRENGTHENING FAMILY COPING RESOURCES

Intervention for Families Impacted by Trauma

LAUREL KISER

NEW YORK AND LONDON

First published 2015
by Routledge
711 Third Avenue, New York NY 10017

and by Routledge
27 Church Road, Hove, East Sussex BN3 2FA

Routledge is an imprint of the Taylor & Francis Group, an informa business

Library of Congress Cataloging-in-Publication Data
A catalog record for this book has been requested

ISBN: 978-1-138-83011-0 (hbk)
ISBN: 978-0-415-72953-6 (pbk)
ISBN: 978-1-315-83282-1 (ebk)

Typeset in Utopia
by Florence Production Ltd, Stoodleigh, Devon, UK

STRENGTHENING FAMILY COPING RESOURCES

Intervention for Families Impacted by Trauma

LAUREL KISER

Routledge
Taylor & Francis Group

NEW YORK AND LONDON

First published 2015
by Routledge
711 Third Avenue, New York NY 10017

and by Routledge
27 Church Road, Hove, East Sussex BN3 2FA

Routledge is an imprint of the Taylor & Francis Group, an informa business

Library of Congress Cataloging-in-Publication Data
A catalog record for this book has been requested

ISBN: 978-1-138-83011-0 (hbk)
ISBN: 978-0-415-72953-6 (pbk)
ISBN: 978-1-315-83282-1 (ebk)

Typeset in Utopia
by Florence Production Ltd, Stoodleigh, Devon, UK

STRENGTHENING FAMILY COPING RESOURCES

Intervention for Families Impacted by Trauma

LAUREL KISER

Routledge
Taylor & Francis Group

NEW YORK AND LONDON

First published 2015
by Routledge
711 Third Avenue, New York NY 10017

and by Routledge
27 Church Road, Hove, East Sussex BN3 2FA

Routledge is an imprint of the Taylor & Francis Group, an informa business

Library of Congress Cataloging-in-Publication Data
A catalog record for this book has been requested

ISBN: 978-1-138-83011-0 (hbk)
ISBN: 978-0-415-72953-6 (pbk)
ISBN: 978-1-315-83282-1 (ebk)

Typeset in Utopia
by Florence Production Ltd, Stoodleigh, Devon, UK

CONTENTS

ACKNOWLEDGMENTS

Strengthening Family Coping Resources would not have been imaginable without the contributions of many. The rituals and routines passed down in my family for many generations and practiced faithfully and joyfully by my husband, David, and my sons, Peter and AJ, convinced me of the value of this approach.

I am especially grateful to Dr. Linda Bennett, my friend and mentor, who introduced me to the study of family ritual and routines and who worked collaboratively to translate theory into clinical practice.

I would also like to acknowledge the contributions of colleagues who supported development and evaluation of SFCR through offering many wonderful suggestions for materials and activities, adapting them for SFCR, and trying them out with lots of families. The list is a long one and includes (but is not limited to) Barry Nurcombe, Maureen Black, Jerry Heston, Marilyn Paavola, Ewa Ostoja, Kay Connors, Vickie Beck, Barbara Baumgardner, Joyce Dorado, and Sharon Stephan.

I would also like to acknowledge support from the National Institute of Mental Health, the Substance Abuse & Mental Health Services Administration, and the Zanvyl and Isabel Krieger Fund.

Finally, to each of the families who has participated in *Strengthening Family Coping Resources*, I express my appreciation.

Cover art, SFCR logo, and session guideline design created by Communication Associates.

What is in the SFCR Manual?

The SFCR manual provides both a theoretical orientation to the intervention and detailed instructions for implementing it. The manual is presented in three parts.

Part I details the theoretical and empirical foundations of SFCR.

Chapter 1 provides a brief overview of the intervention, its development, and the multiple versions available.

Chapters 2 and 3 provide theoretical background related to the two primary goals of SFCR: reducing the symptoms of traumatic stress disorders and increasing coping resources in children, adult caregivers, and in the family system.

Chapter 2 presents a conceptual model for understanding how families adapt to living in traumatic contexts under chronic conditions of high stress.

Chapter 3 offers a unique perspective on family coping skills derived from multiple theories and models but with an emphasis on family ritual and routine theory. This chapter provides insight into the methods used in SFCR for translating theories of family coping to systemic trauma treatment strategies.

Chapter 4 provides a theoretical orientation to family storytelling and narration, as well as detailing with the use of these practice elements in SFCR.

Part II contains implementation and clinical guidelines for conducting SFCR.

Chapter 5 presents a multi-phased implementation process from exploration through sustainability. Each phase is described with detailed information regarding best practices for SFCR implementation.

Chapter 6 describes the clinical considerations and guidelines necessary for conducting SFCR. It includes background information and instructions for the more unique clinical strategies and practice elements that comprise the model.

Chapter 7 outlines the assessment processes integrated within the structure of SFCR, presents results of evaluation efforts to date, and reviews a research agenda for the future.

Part III includes the session guidelines specifically focused on the multi-family group versions of SFCR.

Supporting materials, including all of the handouts, discussion guides, homework, and posters needed for each session (along with recommendations for preparing them), are available on the SFCR website (sfcr.umaryland.edu).

PART I

THEORETICAL AND EMPIRICAL FOUNDATIONS

CHAPTER 1
INTRODUCTION TO SFCR

OVERVIEW

Strengthening Family Coping Resources (SFCR) is a manualized, skills-based, family-focused, and trauma-specific treatment. This empirically supported, clinic- and community-based intervention was developed using a participatory research methodology to assure acceptability and tolerability with populations living in traumatic contexts. Since most families living in traumatic contexts contend with multiple traumas, as well as ongoing stressors and threats, SFCR is designed to meet two primary goals: (1) to decrease the impact of chronic trauma on families and identified family members; and (2) to increase the protective function of the family by improving constructive coping.

As an intervention for families experiencing traumatic stress, SFCR provides accepted, empirically supported trauma treatment within a family format. The model includes work on family storytelling, which builds to a family trauma narrative, providing families with an opportunity to improve communication about, and understanding of, the traumas they have experienced.

In SFCR, trauma treatment strategies are coupled with skill building to increase coping resources in children, adult caregivers, and in the family system to support family protection and resilience. SFCR includes therapeutic strategies, based on family ritual and routine theory, to address the unpredictable and often uncontrollable nature of ongoing stress and threats of exposure faced by families. These strategies help families boost their sense of safety, function with stability, regulate their stress reactions, emotions, and behaviors, and make use of support resources.

In taking a systemic, family approach to addressing the effects of high stress and trauma, SFCR provides a fundamentally different intervention option. The majority of current empirically supported models of trauma prevention/treatment is focused either on individuals or dyads, and largely neglects the critical issue of how the family does or does not contribute to healing. The model of family treatment used in SFCR, which includes developmentally appropriate skill-building activities that are reinforced with family practice, provides a novel approach to addressing co-occurring traumatic reactions in multiple family members.

SFCR is being widely implemented by clinic- and community-based providers who are excited about a model that can address the needs of multi-problem families whose lives are permeated with stress and trauma. Practice-based evidence demonstrates that SFCR is feasible, tolerable, and effective. Children experience significant reductions in symptoms of PTSD and in behavior problems. In addition, families gain skills in coping and stress reduction, and demonstrate healthier functioning, which increases their capacity to serve as a source of support and protection.

SFCR INTERVENTION DEVELOPMENT

A multidisciplinary team of psychiatrists, psychologists, social workers, and anthropologists provided input into the formation of SFCR. Development of this family skill-building program was also greatly influenced by other successful prevention intervention programs.

The intervention development process comprised specification of content and treatment procedures in the form of a manual, creation of training materials, clinician competence and adherence measures, and determination of measures of change within an interactive process to assure cultural sensitivity and family engagement.

Using a context-specific, interactive intervention development model, a stakeholder group of population experts (community residents, opinion leaders, and community-based clinicians) provided input and feedback at all stages of the process. Stakeholder input was gathered around the following four issues: content and structure of the intervention, engaging families, measuring outcomes, and assessing family participation. Specific activities, materials, and methods created for SFCR were reviewed for sensitivity, readability, support of different family forms, and consistency with an approach that values the strengths within each family. Academic experts in family work and trauma also reviewed the manual and materials.

Initial versions of SFCR were implemented in a variety of settings using a multiple-baseline design to gather information on the manualized treatment and on the dynamics involved in the multi-family group (MFG) format. The outcomes of interest were the process measures indicating participation in the groups, cultural sensitivity and acceptability, clinician competence, and intervention integrity. The multiple-baseline design allowed for cycles of feedback, revision, and retesting.

SFCR VERSIONS

SFCR can be implemented using a variety of formats. The different formats allow the content of SFCR to be delivered in multiple settings using a variety of staffing patterns.

Multi-Family Groups

SFCR has primarily been delivered using an MFG format. Each SFCR MFG session is family-focused with everyone in the family encouraged to attend. In treating multiple families simultaneously, SFCR is an intervention with the reach necessary for addressing the public health needs of vulnerable families.

There are three versions of SFCR that use the MFG format. These include the trauma treatment MFG, the high-risk MFG, and the workshop MFG. The session guidelines in Part III of the manual provide instructions for implementing the trauma treatment and the high-risk MFGs.

Each MFG version is described briefly:

The *trauma treatment MFG* is a 15-session closed-enrollment intervention. This version of SFCR targets families impacted by traumas and ongoing threats as evidenced by one or more family members with symptoms of traumatic stress disorders. Families are recruited for enrollment, assessed for appropriateness, and asked to participate in weekly two-hour sessions. The trauma treatment MFG is conducted by a facilitator team primarily made up of professionals with clinical training and expertise.

The trauma treatment MFG focuses on symptom reduction and on improving family coping resources to increase protection and support recovery, resilience, and thriving. It is a phased intervention; concepts and skills introduced and practiced in early sessions are mastered and scaffolded in later sessions.

The 15-week trauma treatment MFG is divided into three modules. Module I introduces the families to the concept of family ritual, routine, and storytelling. Module II focuses on building constructive family coping resources for dealing with stress. Sessions in Module III engage families in narrative work either to build narrative skills or to talk explicitly about their trauma experiences. If a family is ready, their narrative work deals with specific traumatic events, helps them reconnect, reach shared meaning about their experiences, and move beyond their traumas.

The *high-risk MFG* is a 10-session intervention with closed enrollment. The high-risk version is most appropriate for families likely to experience trauma or families who have been exposed and are vulnerable to traumatic stress disorders. The high-risk MFG is also conducted by facilitator teams but does not require as many clinically trained team members.

This version of SFCR is divided into two modules covering all of the coping components of the trauma treatment MFG. The high-risk version includes sessions 1–9 and a final celebration session (a combination of sessions 14 and 15 of the trauma treatment MFG). The primary difference between the trauma treatment and the high-risk MFGs is that the high-risk version does not include the five-session module in which families engage in narrative.

The third MFG version is a workshop model. The *workshop MFG* is an open-enrollment group in which families can drop in for any number of sessions. The workshop MFG covers essentially the same content as the high-risk version with some adaptations made for the different format. For example, instead of asking families to complete homework between sessions, they are given tips for practicing at home what was learned during each session.

SFCR-Family Trauma Therapy (SFCR-FTT)

SFCR-FTT, a version of SFCR for individual families, provides trauma treatment using a family-driven approach. It includes many of the same therapeutic strategies used in the MFG models.

SFCR-FTT is delivered in weekly one-hour sessions. It uses the phased approach of the trauma treatment MFG and is comprised of three similar modules. The order and number of the sessions (especially those focused on coping skill development in Module II) can be customized to a certain degree to best reflect the needs of each family. SFCR-FTT requires a clinically trained professional to work with each family.

SFCR-Peer-to-Peer (SFCR-PP)

SFCR materials and strategies have also been adapted for use as a peer-to-peer group model. *SFCR-PP* involves one-hour weekly groups led by a peer facilitator. SFCR-PP groups are conducted using an open-enrollment model in which individuals can drop in for any number of sessions. SFCR-PP groups are typically conducted by trained and experienced peer mentors.

Along with their peer group leaders, participants focus on reconstructing intergenerational relationships whenever possible, "letting go" when reconciliation is not possible (or perhaps not desirable, as with family perpetrators of violence), interrupting the cross-generational transmission of trauma, violence, and substance abuse, and leaving a legacy of guidance based on their own experiences and learning. The groups support individuals in recovery to make connections between trauma, violence, substance abuse, and parenting practices. The desired outcomes for participants who attend these groups are twofold: (1) enhancing/strengthening an individual's own recovery; and (2) better positioning individuals in recovery to help family members with whom he or she has meaningful relationships avoid substance abuse, violence, and victimization.

Refer to Chapter 6 for additional information on the SFCR-FTT and SFCR-PP versions.

CHAPTER 2

CONCEPTUAL FOUNDATION FOR FAMILY TRAUMA

FAMILIES EXPOSED TO ACCUMULATED TRAUMATIC CONDITIONS[1]

As a field, we are just beginning to understand complex adaptations to trauma in families and to grapple with how best to provide treatment. We have been much more successful at understanding and treating individual psychopathology. As our understanding of complex trauma and developmental trauma disorder has improved, empirically derived treatments have been developed targeting the most distressing and debilitating symptoms. The well-developed complex trauma construct is now the foundation for such treatments as Attachment, Regulation, Competency (ARC; Kinniburgh, Blaustein, Spinazzola, & van der Kolk, 2005), Structured Psychotherapy for Adolescents Responding to Chronic Stress (SPARCS; DeRosa et al., 2006), and Trauma Affect Regulation: Guidelines for Education and Therapy for Adolescents and Pre-Adolescents (TARGET-A; Ford & Russo, 2006). All include a set of essential strategies or core components necessary for intervention with complex trauma.

In a similar fashion, describing the hallmark characteristics of complex adaptations to trauma in families has implications for organizing our clinical conceptualization of families who present for treatment. It provides a framework for looking at systemic adaptations in a way that is manageable and meaningful. As our understanding of how families adapt to chronic stress and trauma becomes more sophisticated, we can develop empirically derived treatments targeting the most pervasive family symptoms.

Because SFCR was developed specifically for families who have experienced chronically high levels of stress and multiple traumas related to living in a traumatic context, this chapter provides an in-depth look at the complex adaptations that families often make to survive so that SFCR facilitators can:

1. increase awareness of the contextual conditions or accumulated traumatic circumstances that influence families;
2. be familiar with adaptation processes that families use and appreciate the complex systemic maladaptations that result from living in a traumatic context;
3. recognize the clinical characteristics of such families and be able to adequately observe their concerns and strengths as they interact and react to the activities offered in SFCR; and
4. use this understanding to assist families in building new coping skills and resources.

DEFINITION

The family is one example of a "trauma membrane," the protective environment surrounding a trauma survivor (Martz & Lindy, 2010; Nelson Goff & Schwerdtfeger, 2004). Under the best of circumstances, the family provides extra support, structure, and coping resources for a family member who is traumatized, and, with such support, a healthy reaction and positive adjustment are more likely. However, under conditions of chronic, multiple, or ongoing trauma exposures, the family may lose the ability to serve its protective function. Repeated exposures are often associated with severe and persistent reactions in multiple family members and can also lead to systemic distress.

Efforts to define complex adaptations to trauma in families began in 2009 during an expert panel meeting conducted by the Family Informed Trauma Treatment (FITT) Center, a National Child Traumatic Network (NCTSN) Category II Center. The experts who took part in this meeting agreed on the following:

Too many families are exposed to accumulated traumatic circumstances. Complex adaptations to trauma in families are defined by the intensity, duration, chronicity, or toxicity of the accumulated trauma, and by the nature of the family's response. Those families whose strengths are overwhelmed by their accumulated traumatic stressors exhibit distress and disrupted family functioning.

EXPOSURE TO ACCUMULATED TRAUMATIC CIRCUMSTANCES

Family adaptation to trauma is related to the specifics of the family's context, making it essential to understand their experiences and circumstances. Complex adaptations to trauma are more likely to occur when families are dealing with accumulated traumatic circumstances.

Accumulated traumatic circumstances occur when a family's context contains high stress, traumatic exposures, associated secondary stressors, and continued threats. Unfortunately, for too many families these experiences of adversity and trauma are interdependent. Living with harsh circumstances increases overall stress levels and the risk of exposure to trauma. Once exposed to trauma, the risk of additional exposures grows. Exposure to trauma may also lead to a series of secondary or cascading stressors associated with the original

event or events. Finally, families living with accumulated traumatic circumstances deal with continuing unpredictable and uncontrollable threats.

Accumulated traumatic circumstances are related to five classes of family stressors, ranging from normative stressors to cataclysmic events or traumas (Baum & Davidson, 1986).

Normative stressors include all of the burdens associated with accomplishing the tasks of daily family life. We know that certain periods of the family life cycle (e.g., families with infants or toddlers) are associated with higher levels of normative stress. Normative stressors can feel overwhelming when families are also dealing with exposure to other stressors and traumas.

Families also experience *stress related to predictable individual and family developmental transitions*. With marriage comes the negotiation of new roles. When a child learns how to drive, new rules and routines are established. Although expected, these transitions create stress and require the family to adapt to the altered conditions (McGoldrick, Carter, & Garcia-Preto, 2011).

On top of normative and predictable transitions, many families experience *stress related to unpredictable transitions*. Divorce, separation, or removal of a child from the family would be examples of such transitions. Unpredictability creates more stress and typically requires more of the family's coping resources for successful adaptation.

Families also experience a variety of *contextual stressors* or hassles related to conditions in the community or society. Some family contexts are associated with multiple and chronic stressors. Consider families living in urban poverty. Often, these families encounter limited community resources, including crowded, substandard housing and disadvantaged schools, limited employment opportunities, hassles related to obtaining services from overwhelmed service systems, and stigma related to their underclass status in society. Military deployment during wartime is another example of a potentially stressful context for families (Park, 2011). Military families often experience financial instability and inadequate supports caused by extended separations and multiple deployments. Once reunited, changes caused by their service member's wartime experience may create additional stress. In addition, uncertainty about redeployment may raise further concerns for the family.

Finally, *overwhelming stressors*, often referred to as traumas or cataclysmic events, also impact families. As with individual responses to trauma, a family's response is in large part predicated by the nature of their traumatic exposure and with their experience of associated secondary stressors. One variable of importance to a family's response is the number of traumas experienced. Unfortunately for families exposed to accumulated traumatic circumstances, they often encounter multiple traumas over many years and across several generations.

Following cataclysmic events, families frequently have to contend with any number of related hassles (e.g., relocation following a hurricane or flood, legal proceedings following a rape or murder, separations following intra-familial abuse). Secondary or cascading stressors associated with the original event or events compound and extend the impact and require ongoing coping efforts.

Most families who live with accumulated traumatic circumstances are not dealing with post-traumatic reactions, but are faced with real and current dangers. "Episodes of actual danger are not the entire stressor. The chronic stressor at issue is the constant presence of the possibility of vulnerability to dangerous forces that cannot be controlled or avoided" (Wheaton, 1997, p. 57). Uncertainty about recurrence or continued threats of re-exposure increases the risk of maladaptations.

FROM CONTEXT TO RESPONSE: FAMILY ADAPTATION

Experiencing a stressor, by definition, requires a response (Selye, 1982). The magnitude of the response is dependent upon the *intensity, duration, chronicity, or toxicity of the stressor.* Over time, families who live with accumulated traumatic circumstances have to make significant adaptations to survive.

How do families adapt to accumulated traumatic circumstances? Many theories use a stage model to describe family adaptation to stress (Chaney & Peterson, 1989; McCubbin & McCubbin, 1993). These theories suggest that adaptation involves acute, transition, and long-term stages with distinct reactions characteristic of each stage.

The family enters the acute stage immediately following the trauma. As families make adjustments to deal with the demands of catastrophe, they move into the transition phase. This stage is distinguished by instability and may result in development of trauma-related distress. Symptoms of distress and diminished functioning may be present in individual family members, family subsystems, and the family unit, and may last for some time. After this period of adjustment, the family again establishes stable patterns of interaction. This is characteristic of the third phase or longer-term adaptation. The family may still experience symptoms of distress when faced with additional stressors or re-exposure to trauma (Peebles-Kleiger & Kleiger, 1994).

The typical stage model addresses family coping with discrete stressors. Adaptation to high stress, multiple traumas, and ongoing threats requires more complicated models:

Families, who are dealing with multiple events or situations involving on-going trauma, cycle through these stages multiple times and may be at different stages simultaneously related to separate exposures. The nature of chronic stressors, "typically open-ended, using up resources in coping, but not promising resolution" (Repetti & Wood, 1997, p. 53) obscures the adaptation process.

(Kiser & Black, 2005, p. 740)

Healthy adaption processes themselves may be vulnerable to overuse. First, family adaptation to ongoing stressors and traumas frequently involves adoption of coping and problem-solving strategies that work in the short-run but may create maladaptations long-term. Second, constant efforts to adapt require significant resources. This depletes coping resources for many families, increasing their vulnerability to new threats. Third, the constant need for adaptation makes families less efficient at responding and less flexible in choosing coping strategies that match stressor demands.

COMPLEX ADAPTATIONS TO ACCUMULATED TRAUMATIC CIRCUMSTANCES IN FAMILIES

Although most families are able to adapt successfully to enormous challenges and tremendous hardships, many are overwhelmed. Accumulated traumatic circumstances heighten vulnerability to traumatic distress for both individuals and families.

Families exposed to prolonged, repeated trauma often become "trauma-organized systems" (Bentovim, 1992). Such families can best be served by recognizing and appreciating consistencies in their clinical presentations.

Considering multiple frameworks for understanding complexly traumatized systems,[2] families exposed to accumulated traumatic circumstances often present with multilayered adaptations characterized by: (1) a family unit response commonly comprised of an anxious anticipatory coping style, systemic dysregulations, disturbed relations and supports, and altered schemas; (2) reciprocal distress reactions that disrupt family subsystem processes; and (3) increased rates of traumatic stress disorders among multiple family members that are likely dyssynchronous. The resultant lapses or declines in the family's ability to carry out their core functions often bring them into treatment. Figure 2.1 offers a schematic of the hallmark characteristics.

DISTURBANCES IN THE FAMILY UNIT

Anxious Anticipatory Coping Style

Anticipation or expectation of disturbing events creates a complex and dynamic condition characterized by alterations in individual and family unit functioning. When trauma is unpredictable or followed by uncertainty about recurrence, families must cope with feelings of fearfulness, suspiciousness, and an ongoing sense of threat. In response, they demonstrate heightened alert, anger and conflict, and silence.

Circumstances that create persistent feelings of not being safe and being unable to control situations challenge family-level coping. The chronic nature of anticipatory stress with ongoing attempts to cope with uncertainty may contribute to the development of dysfunctional coping mechanisms commonly associated with exposure to ongoing severe stressors. Adoption of these anxiety-reducing coping strategies may be healthy in the short-term but have longer-term negative consequences for family functioning (Dempsey, 2002). "These efforts [at coping with anticipatory anxiety] result in the development of new or more intense patterns of interaction within the family system. These patterns may temporarily reduce anxiety, but will likely make the family more

➡ **FIGURE 2.1** Model of Family Adaptation to Accumulated Traumatic Circumstances

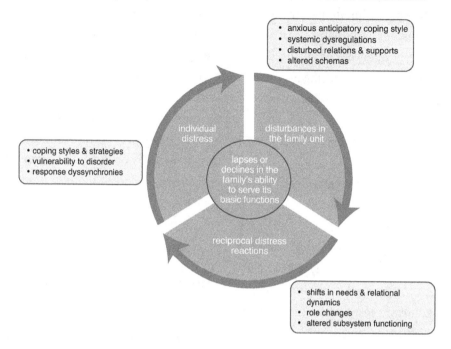

vulnerable and less adaptive to future stressors" (Harris & Topham, 2004, p. 289). Coping with chronic anticipatory anxiety alters the family unit.

As uncertainty persists, families tend to react with vigilance then shift to anger and increased aggression, or to avoidance. Either one reaction becomes the predominant family response or families alternate between the two.

Some families remain in a state of hyper-alert and reactivity. Threats immediately and automatically trigger anger or a fight response. These families focus on being tough, getting revenge or getting even, and often experience high levels of intra- and extra-familial conflict and violence. Family rules, patterns of interaction, and values may become distorted as this response set becomes ingrained.

For other families, avoidant coping (escape, distraction, or placating) becomes the dominant strategy to reduce anticipatory tension. Minimizing and avoidance lead to internalizing of pessimism, futurelessness, lowered expectations, cynicism,

hopelessness/helplessness, and a decreased sense of family efficacy (Diehl & Prout, 2002; Hobfoll, Spielberger, Breznitz, & Figley, 1991). At the extreme, avoidant coping can mean no active problem-solving, inaction, and passivity, and result in a cessation of family processes (Boss, Beaulieu, Wieling, Turner, & LaCruz, 2003). Families may stop communicating, spending time together, or working collaboratively to get things done.

Some families respond to certain situations aggressively yet avoid dealing with other similar stressful or catastrophic events. When families do not settle into a predictable style but alternate between hyper-alert/reactive and avoidant coping, it is difficult to know which response will be employed to deal with a new stressor or trauma. Such uncertainty adds to the anxiety experienced by individual family members who never know what to expect.

Dealing with unpredictable and uncontrollable events also affects a family's ability to plan and follow through on those plans. When daily routines are frequently disrupted, they stop serving their intended purpose. Families develop a sense of futility about their efforts to organize and structure daily family life. Instead, they focus on making it from day to day and crisis to crisis (Repetti, Taylor, & Seeman, 2002). They display diminished deliberateness characterized by low structure, chaotic family lifestyles, and crisis coping.

Systemic Dysregulations

Families play a significant role in regulation and regulation development. Families calibrate the regulation processes of individual family members, as well as set the tone for interpersonal interactions (see review by Morris, Silk, Steinberg, Myers, & Robinson, 2007). As regulatory systems, families typically interact within a comfort zone. The emotions and behaviors expressed by family members during shared family time are contained within this zone, neither too intense nor too subdued.

Families also assist younger family members in regulating their physiological, emotional, cognitive, and behavioral responses. The process of regulation development begins within the responsive inter-actions of the caregiver-child subsystem, but is shaped by the family's establishment of norms for acceptable affective and behavioral expression (McHale, Fivaz-Depeursinge, Dickstein, Robertson, & Daley, 2008).

Seeing the family as a regulatory unit is in keeping with research documenting associations between the regulatory processes of individual family members. Findings from both laboratory and home have demonstrated cortisol co-regulation between couples (Coan, Schaefer, & Davidson, 2006; Ditzen, Hoppmann, & Klumb, 2008; Johnson et al., 2013; Papp, Pendry, Simon, & Adam, 2013; Saxbe & Repetti, 2010). Linkages between family involve-ment and mother-adolescent cortisol synchrony have also been documented (Papp, Pendry, & Adam, 2009).

However, in the face of chronic exposure to high burden and uncontrollable life events, many families lose their ability to contain affect and behavior within the families' comfort zone. If multiple family members are experiencing arousal secondary to traumatic stress and the family unit as a whole is hyper-alert/reactive or avoidant, it is difficult for the family to experience well-modulated interactions and to assist individual family members in maintaining well-regulated responses. The family's inability to tolerate in-tense feelings engendered by their circumstances challenges their emotional and behavioral regu-lation capacities (Valiente, Fabes, Eisenberg, & Spinrad, 2004). Their capacity to regain regulated states becomes slower and more difficult to mobilize. This combination of intense feelings and dysregulation may further constrict the family's flexible use of coping strategies (Johnson, Feldman, Lubin, & Southwick, 1995). Thus, families may frequently and consistently lose control or become rigidly controlling of affective and behavioral expression.

Evidence regarding family context as a mod-erator of the stress response is based on reduc-tions in appraisals of threat when negative events are experienced within a social context. In these situations, lower threat appraisals lead to attenuated physiological responses. Again, findings have demonstrated diminished danger appraisals and stress reactions when couples who report close relationships view frightening videos together (Coan et al., 2006; Johnson et al., 2013). In addition, changes in circadian patterns of cortisol release in youth have been associated with severe familial neglect/abuse. When these youth were placed in less stressful family situations, cortisol patterns returned to normal (Fisher, Gunnar, Chamberlain, & Reid, 2000).

Disturbed Relations and Supports

The experience of accumulated traumatic circumstances strains the quality of interpersonal relations impacting intra- and extra-familial relationships, as well as support seeking. Within intra-familial relations, consequences include detachment and isolation, increased negativity, conflict and risk for violence, and disturbances in attachment and confidence in protection.

Families who expend significant resources dealing with high stress and multiple traumas have decreased energy for developing and maintaining familial relations (Donovan & Spence, 2000; Piotrkowski, Collins, Knitzer, & Robinson, 1994). Trauma-related symptoms, specifically avoidance and numbing, experienced by individual family members can disrupt family unity and effective communication (Faulkner & Davey, 2002). "Families who try to hide or minimize their trauma histories by maintaining silence, cutting off discussions about the trauma, or keeping family secrets experience detachment and distancing within family relations" (Kiser & Black, 2005, pp. 735–736).

Arousal symptoms, such as hyper-vigilance and irritability, and a family unit unable to regulate emotions increase the risk for harsh interactions and conflict. High levels of negative affect impact family communication, making it hard to talk about difficult topics or to solve tough problems. In addition, as family members struggle with their traumatic history, especially exposure to interpersonal violence, they may experience feelings of blame and a desire for retribution, feelings that raise the potential for further violence and aggression. Aggressive patterns of family interaction generate

sequences where violence serves simultaneously as additional trauma and a re-enactment of previous exposures (Kiser & Black, 2005; Kitzmann, 2000; Maughan & Cicchetti, 2002).

One of the most pernicious effects of high stress and trauma on family relations is related to disrupted attachments. Under high-stress conditions, committed relationships become difficult to maintain, which can lead to frequent changes in family membership. This is especially evident when intimate partner relationships become susceptible to tension, conflict, blame, and resentment and do not survive (Kiser, Ostoja, & Pruitt, 1998).

Changing family membership creates uncertainty about who is in the family and who will be there over the long haul. Often, changes in family membership are related to episodes of increased disorganization, anger, conflict, and violence (Heatherington, Cox, & Cox, 1982; Wallerstein & Corbin, 1996).

As family relations become strained and family members are unable to protect each other from danger, family relations become characterized by mistrust and relational insecurity. These negative representations of family relations become entrenched (Kiser & Black, 2005).

Adaptations to accumulated traumatic circumstances also impact the family's ability to interact with external supports. Family patterns of interaction and held beliefs about relationships influence how family members approach others. If intra-familial relationships are viewed as temporary and people are seen as not trustworthy, extrafamilial relations and support seeking will be difficult. Interpersonal conflict within the family will be mirrored in relationships outside the family.

Families who feel overwhelmed by or ashamed of their chronically traumatic circumstances may withdraw from extended family and friends. Interpersonal difficulties and social withdrawal may eliminate or significantly reduce resource seeking as well. In addition, "potential protective resources (e.g., familial and extrafamilial support networks) may themselves be compromised by chronically disadvantaged environments" (D'Imperio, Dubow, & Ippolito, 2000, p. 140).

Altered Family Schemas

Another characteristic of complex adaptations to trauma are altered family schemas. Family schemas are defined as stable, meaningful patterns of organizing information that allow efficient appraisal and response (Dattilio, 2005; Reiss, 1987). Family schemas develop through repeated interaction within the family unit—they shape cognitions, emotions, and behaviors related to family life. They translate into enduring values and views about the way the family understands and interacts with the world. They support the family's co-creation of meaning by defining beliefs about what is comprehensible, manageable, and meaningful (Antonovsky & Sourani, 1988; Bradley & Corwyn, 2000; Walsh, 2007).

Unpredictable conditions and recurring traumas shape family schemas. As families try to make sense of life events, they must evaluate them in the context of their shared beliefs and worldview. Uncontrollable traumatic events are often inconsistent with helpful family schemas and when these events occur repeatedly, family schemas end up changing to be more consistent with the traumatic exposures (Patterson, 2002). Accumulated traumatic circumstances can lead the family to develop schemas around distorted notions and beliefs:

- the world is dangerous and people are not trustworthy;
- things usually go wrong for our family and there is nothing that we can do to prevent the bad things from happening;

- our future will be much like our present, with nothing good happening;
- "rules" are for other families; even if we follow them, we don't get what we need; and
- we are not able to deal with the things that happen to us and never will be.

Two consequences of such altered schemas affect family adaptation. First, unhelpful or distorted schemas increase individual vulnerability to traumatic stress disorders following exposure (Weingarten, 2004). Second, as family schemas change in response to accumulated traumatic circumstances, healthy meaning-making processes are impacted. Altered schemas create problems with family meaning making, which can be critical to recovery from trauma. Negative family schemas create biases or distortions in family appraisal and inferencing, which can lead to misattributions of family members' behaviors. This exacerbates negative reactions and increases the risk of family conflict. Altered family schemas end up dictating how family members see themselves, each other, and their future. These negative schemas may end up restricting family members' view of the possibilities of how they can behave or take action in their lives (Dallos, 2004). Experiencing continued traumatic circumstances reinforces negative schemas and families find it more and more difficult to attach positive meaning to their experiences.

Implications for Working with Families in SFCR

Families make substantial adaptations in response to accumulated traumatic circumstances. Clinical vignettes help illustrate the necessity of considering the family unit response while working with families in SFCR.

An Anxious, Dysregulated Family System

This is the case of the Smalling family, a mother and her three sons presenting for treatment following exposure to significant community and domestic violence. The youngest, Alex, is 5 years old with problems regulating affect and behavior—he gets upset easily and acts out.

During a storytelling activity in SFCR, mother describes a stressful incident when Alex got mad while riding in the car. He repeatedly kicked the door, and then tried to open it. While telling about this episode, Alex becomes disruptive. The oldest, Brendon, tries to control him but quickly loses his cool and tries to strangle his brother and then acts like he is stabbing him. Mother ignores both the tantrum of the little one and the aggressive response of the oldest.

Anxiety in the family during the storytelling triggers the youngest, the oldest responds with threats and aggression re-enacting the violence he has seen, while the mother is passive and numb and unable to help regulate the interaction. The facilitator who is observing the family during the storytelling activity approaches the mother to encourage her to take a more active role in helping her boys modulate their emotions and behaviors. With coaching from the facilitator, the mother asks both boys to sit back down and to take a few deep breaths. She goes back to the storytelling activity and adds that she was really frightened that Alex might get hurt. She asks Alex to tell the story from his perspective.

Disrupted Family Relations

The Ciscos are a family coping with intra-familial abuse—it is the case of a 12-year-old boy, Walter, who was sexually molested over three to four years by his older brother. The brother, Johnny, is now staying with the maternal grandparents who live right down the street. Mr. Cisco has his own abuse history and was raised in foster care. The family is taking part in SFCR a couple of years following disclosure of the abuse; no one in the family has received therapy to date.

Walter describes how his mother is anxiously overprotective and worries about everything he does. This makes him feel that, on some level, his mother blames him for the sexual abuse. His father is extremely angry at Johnny about his abusive behavior and loses his temper any time the problem is discussed. Walter also believes that his mother and father are worried that he will be gay. He feels less and less able to converse with his parents about what happened, their altered living situation, and their strained family interactions. During the family sculpture activity, the young teen expresses concern about how the family's avoidance of addressing the sexual abuse caused him to see his grandparents less often and to lose an emotionally close and supportive relationship with them. The family was able to come up with a plan for Walter to spend some time with his grandparents while Johnny is not around.

RECIPROCAL DISTRESS REACTIONS

Accumulated traumatic circumstances create complicated shifts in relationships and roles affecting the functioning of subsystems. The reciprocal, goal-directed processes that distinguish relational dynamics are impacted. A discussion of the effects of trauma on the caregiving subsystem illustrates these reciprocal processes (Kiser & Black, 2005) (refer to Figure 2.2). Intergenerational, adult intimate partnership and sibling subsystems must be viewed through a similar lens.

First (Figure 2.2a), effects of accumulated traumatic circumstances on caregiving subsystems are related to how the caregivers' and children's stress reactions influence their functioning.

Trauma-related distress experienced by adults negatively impacts their caregiving; specific symptoms of PTSD, such as irritability and avoidance, undermine effective discipline and constrain caregiver-child interactions (Scheeringa & Zeanah, 2001). Harsh traumatic conditions are also associated with diminished caregiving capacity, often characterized by insensitivity, lack of responsiveness, low warmth, reactivity, negativity, and punitiveness (Kiser & Black, 2005).

Trauma-related distress experienced by children also impacts their caregiving needs. Increased fears and a decreased sense of safety may increase proximity seeking and need for attention, for instance. Anger may be expressed through acting out and tantrums, requiring firm limits.

Second (Figure 2.2b), caregiving subsystems are sensitive to how caregivers react to their child's trauma-related concerns and how children react to their caregiver's trauma-related distress. The concept of secondary stress is relevant here. Secondary stress results when traumatic distress symptoms in one family member disrupt family functioning (Figley, 1988). For instance, a child suffering with nightmares, a common symptom, may impact intimate partner and parental routines, resulting in loss of sleep for multiple family members. As the number of family members with trauma histories or traumatic stress symptoms increases, so does the risk of secondary stress.

Child symptoms, such as sleep disturbances, somatic complaints, new worries and fears, irritability, and developmental regression, necessitate responses from caregivers. In fact, caregivers describe making changes in family routines to accommodate their children's increased fears and problems with school and sleep (Kiser, Nurse, Luckstead, & Collins, 2008).

Children's perceptions of their parent's response also create shifts in relational processes. For example, when a caregiver is unavailable to their children due to withdrawal or avoidance or is disoriented due to flashbacks, it can create anxiety and fear. It is not uncommon, under such circumstances, to see children try to take over parental roles and responsibilities if they perceive their parent as unable to carry out caregiving obligations (Fitzgerald et al., 2008; Hooper, 2007). Equally likely is that children become disappointed, angry, frustrated, and disrespectful as their caregiver fails to meet their needs.

The mismatch between a caregiver with diminished capacities and a child, or children, with increased caregiving demands often creates a

→ **FIGURE 2.2 Reciprocal Effects of Trauma on Caregiving**

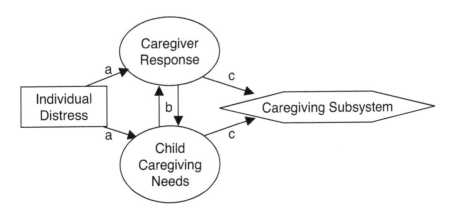

consistent sense of failure to meet role expectations. These new and dynamic changes in relating disrupt normal parent-child interactions and alter the caregiving subsystem in fundamental ways (Figure 2.2c).

Changes in subsystem dynamics and relations complicate family adaptation. A clinical vignette helps illustrate the necessity of considering the reciprocal interactional patterns that impact subsystem functioning while families are participating in SFCR.

The James family joined an SFCR MFG hoping to deal with their long and intergenerational history of neglect and child maltreatment. Alticia James was 29 years old and came to group with her four children, Calsandra (12 years old), Tyania (11 years old), Junior (6 years old), and Emmett (2 years old). Calsandra and Tyania lived with Alticia until Tyania was 9 months old and then were placed with Alticia's grandmother by social services. They were returned to Alticia's care about one year after Emmett was born and shortly before their grandmother passed away.

Alticia experienced severe poverty and neglect while growing up. She was also abused by several of her mother's partners. She suffers from PTSD and depression. She experienced post-partum depression following the birth of each of her children and found interacting with her babies frightening and painful.

Alticia is stable currently and trying hard to rebuild her relationships with her children. However, Calsandra does not trust her mother very much, puts her down a lot in subtle ways, and does not listen to much that she has to say. Tyania is more overtly angry and disrespectful toward her mother. The younger children are starting to pay attention to their sisters' attitudes and to approach their sisters rather than their mother for direction and nurturance.

During sessions, the facilitators took every opportunity to encourage Alticia to stay in charge of her children, to praise her for her parenting efforts, and to help her expand her parenting skills. The facilitators also redirected the younger children back to their mother when seeking assistance or reassurance from their sisters.

Through the narrative sessions, the girls were given the opportunity to tell their mother how they felt about their separation from her. They were able to express their anger and frustration and also their jealousy about the fact that the boys were not taken away. After saying all of this, their mother was able to acknowledge their feelings and talk about her own feelings of failure and self-blame. She was able to tell her children some (not too much) about the experiences that she had as a child and about her mental health problems. Toward the end of the narrative, the girls, armed with some new insights, were able to recognize that their mother was really trying and was doing a better job of caring for them. They were quick to point out that she still got too upset and was too mean, though.

INDIVIDUAL DISTRESS REACTIONS TO ACCUMULATED TRAUMATIC CIRCUMSTANCES

Traumatic distress and related illnesses in individual family members impact family functioning. Both vulnerability to and variability in individual responses to accumulated traumatic circumstances are significant factors in understanding the family unit response.

Vulnerability to Distress

Vulnerability to individual distress and disorder in response to accumulated traumatic circumstances is a significant factor in understanding family unit adaptation. Exposure to accumulated traumatic circumstances significantly increases the incidence of traumatic stress disorders among individual family members. Studies suggest that 0.5–24.6 percent of children and 8.8–23.6 percent of adults develop post-traumatic stress disorder (PTSD) following exposure to single events (Breslau, 2009; Breslau, Davis, Andreski, & Perterson, 1991; Breslau, Wilcox, Storr, Lucia, & Anthony, 2004; Copeland, Keeler, Angold, & Costello, 2007; Davis, Ressler, Schwartz, Stephens, & Bradley, 2008; Giaconia, Reinherz, Silverman, & Pakiz, 1995; Graham-Bermann & Levendosky, 1998; Kessler, Sonnega, Bromet, & Hughes, 1995; McCloskey & Walker, 2000). Higher rates of PTSD, up to 70 percent, have been noted in those victimized by violence (Carrion, Weems, Ray, & Reiss, 2002).

Females show higher rates of PTSD than males (Koenen, Moffitt, Poulton, Martin, & Caspi, 2007; Ozer, Best, Lipsey, & Weiss, 2003). As women often take the lead in organizing and maintaining family life and in parenting, this gender difference is noteworthy when focused on the family unit response.

Research on the rates of co-occurrence of PTSD within families is limited. However, one study examined the co-occurrence of PTSD in a sample of mother-child dyads exposed to domestic violence (Chemtob & Carlson, 2004). Of the 25 mother-child pairs, 10 children and 11 mothers met criteria for PTSD, with four cases in which both the mother and child met criteria. Other studies have also shown moderate correlations (Boyer, Knolls, Kafkalas, Tollen, & Swartz, 2000; Vila et al., 2001). A meta-analytic study exploring the correspondence between parental PTSD and child distress (including PTSD) produced a medium overall effect size (Lambert, Holzer, & Hasbun, 2014).

Furthermore, PTSD is not the only disorder that is likely to impact individual family members.

Studies indicate that many children and adults exposed to multiple traumas and interpersonal violence (i.e., family violence) develop a more complicated symptom presentation than PTSD. Complex trauma (Cook et al., 2005; Herman, 1992) and Type II trauma (Terr, 1991) have been used to describe this condition. Developmental trauma disorder (van der Kolk, 2005) is a formulation describing symptoms and distress following the experience of interpersonal traumas related to impaired caregiving. Affective, behavioral, and physiological dysregulations, attachment disturbances, changes in consciousness, self-perception, expectancies, and systems of personal meaning are common in individuals who have experienced chronic trauma and loss. Depression, generalized anxiety, and substance abuse are also widespread.

Finally, in addition to mental health concerns, studies of adverse childhood events (ACEs) document a high incidence of stress-related physical illnesses (diabetes, heart disease, obesity, and sleep disturbances) in adults with multiple ACEs (Clements & Burgess, 2002; Evans & Schamberg, 2009; Felitti & Anda, 2009). Imagine how irritability, sadness, detachment, lack of trust, dysregulations, substance abuse, and physical health problems interfere with family processes.

Variability in Response

With multiple family members likely to be experiencing traumatic distress, variability in the course of their illness becomes an issue for the family unit. Even when all members of a family are present during the traumatic event, their individual experiences and responses will be idiosyncratic. Family members will have different impressions of events while they are happening and will form personal appraisals in their aftermath.

Living with chronic stress and trauma alters the coping strategies and styles used by individual family members, and negotiation of the coping responses of individual family members is important for family-level coping (Salmon & Bryant, 2002). In response to chronic, unpredictable, and uncontrollable traumatic circumstances, situational appraisals are altered. Significant resources are expended attending to threat cues and appraisals of danger may be inflated. Flexibility in matching coping strategies with contextual circumstances is also diminished.

Family members will also almost certainly have varied reactions, as individual responses to trauma are best understood along intersecting continuums. Possible responses range from acute to delayed reactions and from thriving or surpassing pre-trauma levels of functioning to chronic impairments in level of functioning (Bonanno, 2004). Further, individual responses to trauma are not static and initial reactions do not necessarily predict later responses (Elliott & Carnes, 2001). Although individuals exposed to accumulated traumatic circumstances tend to respond more quickly to new exposures, experience greater distress, and recover more slowly (Carrion et al., 2002), they still show individual differences.

Such individual variability in family member responses complicates family adaptation. A clinical vignette helps illustrate the necessity of considering the individual's contribution to the familial response.

The Blake children experienced the murder of their parents during a home invasion. The four children, ranging in age from 3 to 12 years, were now living with their paternal aunt and uncle. Everyone in this newly formed family had different experiences of the event, reactions, symptoms, and triggers. As this family participated in SFCR, facilitators had to take into account the many varied responses demonstrated by each family member, including their stages of grief.

Different triggers and coping styles affected the family's response. For example, one of the children reacted by internalizing his feelings, expressing much sadness, and crying frequently. Seeing his sibling tearful, the oldest, who reported seldom seeing his father cry except during the invasion, responded with anger and aggression. For the aunt, the boys' fighting was a reminder of her lost sibling relationship and was quite painful. These differing individual responses undermined the aunt and uncle's attempts to bring this new family together.

SFCR facilitators helped this family recognize these different reactions, give each individual family member some space in which he or she could express him or herself while at the same time developing new family rules that provided some containment for the anger and grief. The family learned additional coping strategies, and although family members found some strategies more helpful than others, they were able to find ways to practice a variety and to appreciate what worked for each person.

LAPSES OR DECLINES IN THE FAMILY'S ABILITY TO SERVE ITS BASIC FUNCTIONS

These systemic adaptations (family unit, subsystem, and individual) compromise family functioning. What emerges at the family unit level is a slow erosion in the family's ability to carry out its primary purposes:

- Families have a difficult time meeting the basic needs of individual family members. They struggle, and often fail, to provide for basic needs (food and shelter), safety, and emotional security.

- Families often perceive diminished value in family and caregiving activities and find it hard to maintain stable roles, routines, and functional limits.

- Families have trouble creating a source of identification and a sense of belonging. They are not successful at developing and maintaining intimate patterns of interaction that create an emotional sense of home (Walsh, 2007).

- Families cannot provide the foundation necessary for socialization and for relating to the larger community. Family life typically provides experiences and lessons regarding how to get along with others and how to conduct oneself according to community standards. This is true except for isolated families with distorted rules, altered expectancies, and negative worldviews. Families with complex adaptations to trauma teach their children anxious coping strategies (characterized by anger and violence or silence and acceptance) and family schemas and narratives dominated by trauma and loss.

- Families have difficulty serving as a trauma membrane for family members when additional stress and trauma do occur. They are less likely to have the capacity to provide family members with support, empathy, consistency, a belief in their ability to cope, and hope.

- The family's struggle to serve in a protective capacity impacts the mechanisms for transmitting patterns of protection and attachment from one generation to the next. Disruptions and dysfunction created within the caregiving subsystem are passed along as enduring negative parenting styles and cycles of family violence.

CONCLUSION

SFCR addresses the needs of families with complex adaptations to accumulated traumatic circumstances. It was designed for those families who are struggling or failing to serve their primary functions. Consider specifically the strategies in SFCR to help families build preventive coping strategies to replace anxious coping strategies; develop skills for co-regulating emotions and behavior and have multiple experiences of safe, regulated interaction; strengthen interpersonal connectivity and seek support from others; and struggle with the meaning of their life circumstances with the goal of reaching a shared positive understanding of their past and present and a hopeful view of their future.

NOTES

1. I am grateful for contributions from the FITT Center team related to this conceptual model and clinical vignettes.
2. Multiple theories are fundamental to understanding the family's response to accumulated trauma, including systems theory (Howes, Cicchetti, Toth, & Rogosch, 2000; Shochet & Dadds, 1997), ecological and transactional models (Bronfenbrenner, 1979; Hill, Fonagy, Safier, & Sargent, 2003; Meyers, Varkey, & Aguirre, 2002), family stress (Hammack, Robinson, Crawford, & Li, 2004; McCubbin, 1995; Patterson, 2002), and resource models (Johnson, Palmieri, Jackson, & Hobfoll, 2007; Thornton, 1998).

REFERENCES

Antonovsky, A., & Sourani, T. (1988). Family sense of coherence and family adaptation. *Journal of Marriage and the Family, 50*, 79–92.

Baum, A., & Davidson, L. M. (1986). A suggested framework for studying factors that contribute to trauma in disaster. In B. J. Sowder, & M. Lystad (Eds.), *Disasters and mental health* (pp. 37–48). Washington, DC: American Psychiatric Press.

Bentovim, A. (1992). *Trauma organized systems: Physical and sexual abuse in families.* London: Karnac Books.

Bonanno, G. A. (2004). Loss, trauma, and human resilience: Have we underestimated the human capacity to thrive after extremely aversive events? *American Psychologist, 59,* 20–28.

Boss, P., Beaulieu, L., Wieling, E., Turner, W., & LaCruz, S. (2003). Healing loss, ambiguity, and trauma: A community-based intervention with families of union workers missing after the 9/11 attack in New York City. *Journal of Marital & Family Therapy, 29,* 455–467.

Boyer, B. A., Knolls, M. L., Kafkalas, C. M., Tollen, L. G., & Swartz, M. (2000). Prevalence and relationships of posttraumatic stress in families experiencing pediatric spinal cord injury. *Rehabilitation Psychology, 45,* 339–355.

Bradley, R. H., & Corwyn, R. F. (2000). Moderating effect of perceived amount of family conflict on the relation between home environmental processes and the well-being of adolescents. *Journal of Family Psychology, 14,* 349–364.

Breslau, N. (2009). The epidemiology of trauma, PTSD, and other posttrauma disorders. *Trauma, Violence, & Abuse, 10,* 198–210.

Breslau, N., Davis, G. C., Andreski, P., & Perterson, E. (1991). Traumatic events and posttraumatic stress disorder in an urban population of young adults. *Archives of General Psychiatry, 48,* 216–222.

Breslau, N., Wilcox, H. C., Storr, C. L., Lucia, V. C., & Anthony, J. C. (2004). Trauma exposure and post-traumatic stress disorder: A study of youths in urban America. *Journal of Urban Health, 81,* 530–544.

Bronfenbrenner, U. (1979). *The ecology of human development: Experiments by nature and design.* Cambridge, MA: Harvard University Press.

Carrion, V., Weems, C., Ray, R., & Reiss, A. (2002). Toward an empirical definition of pediatric PTSD: The phenomenology of PTSD symptoms in youth. *Journal of the American Academy of Child & Adolescent Psychiatry, 41,* 166–173.

Chaney, J., & Peterson, L. (1989). Family variables and disease management in juvenile rheumatoid arthritis. *Journal of Pediatric Psychology, 14,* 389–403.

Chemtob, C. M., & Carlson, J. G. (2004). Psychological effects of domestic violence on children and their mothers. *International Journal of Stress Management, 11,* 209–226.

Clements, P. T., & Burgess, A. W. (2002). Children's responses to family member homicide. *Family & Community Health, 25,* 32–42.

Coan, J. A., Schaefer, H. S., & Davidson, R. J. (2006). Lending a hand: Social regulation of the neural response to threat. *Psychological Science, 17,* 1032–1039. doi: 10.1111/j.1467-9280.2006.01832.x.

Cook, A., Spinazzola, J., Ford, J., Lanktree, C., Blaustein, M., Cloitre, M., et al. (2005). Complex trauma in children and adolescents. *Psychiatric Annals, 35,* 390–398.

Copeland, W. E., Keeler, G., Angold, A., & Costello, E. J. (2007). Traumatic events and posttraumatic stress in childhood. *Archives of General Psychiatry, 64,* 577–584.

Dallos, R. (2004). Attachment narrative therapy: Integrating ideas from narrative and attachment theory in systemic family therapy with eating disorders. *Journal of Family Therapy, 26,* 40–65.

Dattilio, F. M. (2005). The restructuring of family schemas: A cognitive-behavior perspective. *Journal of Marital and Family Therapy, 31,* 15–30.

Davis, R. G., Ressler, K. J., Schwartz, A. C., Stephens, K. J., & Bradley, R. G. (2008). Treatment barriers for low-income urban African Americans with undiagnosed posttraumatic stress disorder. *Journal of Traumatic Stress, 21,* 218–222.

Dempsey, M. (2002). Negative coping as mediator in the relation between violence and outcomes: Inner-city African American youth. *American Journal of Orthopsychiatry, 72,* 102–109.

DeRosa, R., Habib, M., Pelcovitz, D., Rathus, J., Sonnenklar, J., Ford, J., Sunday, S., Layne, C., Saltzman, W., Turnbull, A., Labruna, V. & Kaplan, S. (2006). Structured psychotherapy for adolescents responding to chronic stress. Unpublished manual.

Diehl, A. S., & Prout, M. F. (2002). Effects of posttraumatic stress disorder and child sexual abuse on self-efficacy development. *American Journal of Orthopsychiatry, 27,* 262–265.

D'Imperio, R. L., Dubow, E. F., & Ippolito, M. F. (2000). Resilient and stress-affected adolescents in an urban setting. *Journal of Clinical Child Psychology, 29,* 129–142.

Ditzen, B. Hoppmann, C., & Klumb, P. (2008). Positive couple interactions and daily cortisol: On the stress-protecting role of intimacy. *Psychosomatic Medicine, 70,* 883–889. doi: 883 0033-3174/08/7007-0883.

Donovan, C. L., & Spence, S. H. (2000). Prevention of childhood anxiety disorders. *Clinical Psychology Review, 20,* 509–531.

Elliott, A. N., & Carnes, C. N. (2001). Reactions of nonoffending parents to the sexual abuse of their child: A review of the literature. *Child Maltreatment, 6,* 314–331.

Evans, G. W., & Schamberg, M. A. (2009). Childhood poverty, chronic stress, and adult working memory. *PNAS, 106,* 6545–6549.

Faulkner, R., & Davey, M. (2002). Children and adolescents of cancer patients: The impact of cancer on the family. *The American Journal of Family Therapy, 30,* 81–91.

Felitti, V. J., & Anda, R. F. (2009). The relationship of adverse childhood experiences to adult medical disease, psychiatric disorders, and sexual behavior: Implications for healthcare. In R. Lanius & E. Vermetten (Eds.), *The hidden epidemic: The impact of early life trauma on health and disease* (pp. 77–87). Cambridge: Cambridge University Press.

Figley, C. R. (1988). Post-traumatic family therapy. In F. M. Ochberg (Ed.), *Post-traumatic therapy and victims of violence* (pp. 83–109). New York: Bruner/Mazel.

Fisher, P. A., Gunnar, M. R., Chamberlain, P., & Reid, J. B. (2000). Preventive intervention for maltreated preschool children: Impact on children's behavior, neuroendocrine activity, and foster parent functioning. *Journal of the American Academy of Child & Adolescent Psychiatry, 39,* 1356–1364.

Fitzgerald, M. M., Schneider, R. A., Salstrom, S., Zinzow, H. M., Jackson, J., & Fossel, R. V. (2008). Child sexual abuse, early family risk, and childhood parentification: Pathways to current psychosocial adjustment. *Journal of Family Psychology, 22,* 320–324. doi:10.1037/0893-3200.22.2.320.

Ford, J. D., & Russo, E. (2006). Trauma-focused, present-centered, emotional self-regulation approach to integrated treatment for posttraumatic stress and addiction: Trauma Adaptive Recovery Group Education and Therapy (TARGET). *American Journal of Psychotherapy, 60,* 335–355.

Giaconia, R. M., Reinherz, H. Z., Silverman, A. B., & Pakiz, B. (1995). Traumas and posttraumatic stress disorder in a community population of older adolescents. *Journal of the American Academy of Child & Adolescent Psychiatry, 34,* 1369–1380. doi:10.1097/00004583-199510000-00023

Graham-Bermann, S. A., & Levendosky, A. A. (1998). Traumatic stress symptoms in children of battered women. *Journal of Interpersonal Violence, 13,* 111–128. doi:10.1177/088626098013001007.

Hammack, P. L., Robinson, W. L., Crawford, I., & Li, S. T. (2004). Poverty and depressed mood among urban African-American adolescents: A family stress perspective. *Journal of Child and Family Studies, 13,* 309–323.

Harris, S. M., & Topham, G. (2004). Assessment and treatment of trauma from a Bowen Family Systems theory perspective. In D. R. Catherall (Ed.), *Handbook of stress, trauma, and the family* (pp. 283–306). New York: Bruner-Routledge.

Heatherington, E. M., Cox, M., & Cox, R. (1982). Effects of divorce on parents and children. In M. E. Lamb (Ed.), *Nontraditional families: Parenting and child development* (pp. 233–238). Hillsdale, NJ: Earlbaum.

Herman, J. (1992). *Trauma and recovery.* New York: Basic Books.

Hill, J., Fonagy, P., Safier, E., & Sargent, J. (2003). The ecology of attachment in the family. *Family Process, 42,* 205–221.

Hobfoll, S. E., Spielberger, C. D., Breznitz, S., & Figley, C. (1991). War-related stress: Addressing the stress of war and other traumatic events. *American Psychologist, 46*, 848–855.

Hooper, L. M. (2007). The application of attachment theory and family systems theory to the phenomena of parentification. *The Family Journal, 15*, 217–223. doi:10.1177/1066480707301290.

Howes, P. W., Cicchetti, D., Toth, S. L., & Rogosch, F. A. (2000). Affective, organizational, and relational characteristics of maltreating families: A systems perspective. *Journal of Family Psychology, 14*, 95–110.

Johnson, D. M., Palmieri, P. A., Jackson, A. P., & Hobfoll, S. E. (2007). Emotional numbing weakens abused inner-city women's resiliency resources. *Journal of Traumatic Stress, 20*, 197–206.

Johnson, D. R., Feldman, S. C., Lubin, H., & Southwick, S. M. (1995). The therapeutic use of ritual and ceremony in the treatment of post-traumatic stress disorder. *Journal of Traumatic Stress, 8*, 283–298.

Johnson, S. M., Moser, M. B., Beckes, L., Smith, A., Dalgleish, T., Halchuk, R., Hasselmo, K., Greenman, P. S., Merali, Z., & Coan, J. A. (2013). Soothing the threatened brain: Leveraging contact comfort with emotionally focused therapy. *PLoS ONE, 8*(11), e79314. doi:10.1371/journal.pone.0079314.

Kessler, R. C., Sonnega, A., Bromet, E., & Hughes, M. (1995). Posttraumatic stress disorder in the national comorbidity survey. *Archives of General Psychiatry, 52*, 1048–1060.

Kinniburgh, K. J, Blaustein, M., Spinazzola, J., & van der Kolk, B. A. (2005). Attachment, self-regulation, and competency. *Psychiatric Annals, 35*, 424–430.

Kiser, L. J., & Black, M. A. (2005). Family processes in the midst of urban poverty. *Aggression and Violent Behavior, 10*, 715–750.

Kiser, L. J., Ostoja, E., & Pruitt, D. B. (1998). Dealing with stress and trauma in families. In B. Pfefferbaum (Ed.), *Stress in children: Child and adolescent psychiatric clinics of North America, 7*, 87–104.

Kiser, L. J., Nurse, W., Luckstead, A., & Collins, K. S. (2008). Understanding the impact of traumas on family life from the viewpoint of female caregivers living in urban poverty. *Traumatology, 14*, 77–90.

Kitzmann, K. M. (2000). Effects of marital conflict on subsequent triadic family interactions and parenting. *Developmental Psychology, 36*, 3–13.

Koenen, K. C., Moffitt, T. E., Poulton, R., Martin, J., & Caspi, A. (2007). Early childhood factors associated with the development of post-traumatic stress disorder: Results from a longitudinal birth cohort. *Psychological Medicine, 37*, 181–192. doi:10.1017/S0033291706009019.

Lambert, J. E., Holzer, J., & Hasbun, A. (2014). Association between parents' PTSD severity and children's psychological distress: A meta-analysis. *Journal of Traumatic Stress, 27*, 9–17.

McCloskey, L. A., & Walker, M. (2000). Posttraumatic stress in children exposed to family violence and single-event trauma. *Journal of the American Academy of Child & Adolescent Psychiatry, 39*, 108–115.

McCubbin, M. (1995). The typology model of adjustment and adaptation: A family stress model. *Guidance & Counseling, 10*(4), 1–27.

McCubbin, M. A., & McCubbin, H. I. (1993). Families coping with illness: The resiliency model of family stress, adjustment, and adaptation. In C. B. Danielson (Ed.), *Families, health, & illness* (pp. 21–63). St. Louis, MO: Mosby-Year Book.

McGoldrick, M., Carter, B., & Garcia-Preto, N. (2011). *The expanded family life cycle: Individual, family, and social perspectives.* Upper Saddle River, NJ: Pearson Education.

McHale, J., Fivaz-Depeursinge, E., Dickstein, S., Robertson, J., & Daley, M. (2008) New evidence for the social embeddedness of infants' early triangular capacities. *Family Process, 47*, 445–463.

Martz, E., & Lindy, J. (2010). Exploring the trauma membrane concept. In E. Martz (Ed.), *Trauma rehabilitation after war and conflict* (pp. 27–54). New York: Springer.

Maughan, A., & Cicchetti, D. (2002). Impact of child maltreatment and interadult violence on children's emotion regulation abilities and socioemotional adjustment. *Child Development, 73,* 1525–1542.

Meyers, S. A., Varkey, S., & Aguirre, A. M. (2002). Ecological correlates of family functioning. *American Journal of Family Therapy, 30,* 257–273.

Morris, A. S., Silk, J. S., Steinberg, L., Myers, S. S., & Robinson, L. R. (2007). The role of the family context in the development of emotion regulation. *Social Development, 16,* 361–388.

Nelson Goff, B. S., & Schwerdtfeger, L. L. (2004). The systemic impact of traumatized children. In D. R. Catherall (Ed.), *Handbook of stress, trauma, and the family* (pp. 179–202). New York: Bruner-Routledge.

Ozer, E. J., Best, S. R., Lipsey, T. L., & Weiss, D. S. (2003). Predictors of posttraumatic stress disorder and symptoms in adults: A meta-analysis. *Psychological Bulletin, 129,* 52–73.

Papp, L. M., Pendry, P., & Adam, E. K. (2009). Mother-adolescent physiological synchrony in naturalistic settings: Within-family cortisol associations and moderators. *Journal of Family Psychology, 23,* 882–894.

Papp, L. M., Pendry, P., Simon, C. D., & Adam, E. K. (2013). Spouses' cortisol associations and moderators: Testing physiological synchrony and connections in everyday life. *Family Process, 52,* 284–298. doi:10.1111/j.1545-5300.2012.01413.x.

Park, N. (2011). Military children and families. *American Psychologist, 66,* 65–72.

Patterson, J. M. (2002). Integrating family resilience and family stress theory. *Journal of Marriage and the Family, 64,* 349–360.

Peebles-Kleiger, M. J., & Kleiger, J. H. (1994). Reintegration stress for Desert Storm families. *Journal of Traumatic Stress, 7,* 173–194.

Piotrkowski, C. S., Collins, R. C., Knitzer, J., & Robinson, R. (1994). Strengthening mental health services in Head Start: A challenge for the 1990s. *American Psychologist, 49,* 133–139.

Reiss, D. (1987). *The family's construction of reality.* Boston, MA: Harvard University Press.

Repetti, R. L., & Wood, J. (1997). Families accommodating to chronic stress: Unintended and unnoticed processes. In B. H. Gottlieb (Ed.), *Coping with chronic stress: The Plenum Series on stress and coping* (pp. 191–220). New York: Plenum Press.

Repetti, R. L., Taylor, S. E., & Seeman, T. E. (2002). Risky families: Family social environments and the mental and physical health of offspring. *Psychological Bulletin, 128,* 330–366.

Salmon, K., & Bryant, R. A. (2002). Posttraumatic stress disorder in children: The influence of developmental factors. *Clinical Psychology Review, 22,* 163–188.

Saxbe, D. E., & Repetti, R. L. (2010). For better or worse? Coregulation of couples' cortisol levels and mood states. *Journal of Personality and Social Psychology, 98,* 92–103. doi:10.1037/a0016959.

Scheeringa, M. S., & Zeanah, C. H. (2001). A relational perspective on PTSD in early childhood. *Journal of Traumatic Stress, 14,* 799–815.

Selye, H. (1982). History of the stress concept. In L. Goldberger & S. Breznitz (Eds.), *Handbook of stress: Theoretical and clinical aspects* (pp. 7–17). New York: The Free Press.

Shochet, I., & Dadds, M. (1997). When individual child psychotherapy exacerbates family systems problems in child abuse cases: A clinical analysis. *Clinical Child Psychology & Psychiatry, 2,* 239–249.

Terr, L. C. (1991). Childhood traumas: An outline and overview. *American Journal of Psychiatry, 148,* 10–20.

Thornton, M. C. (1998). Indigenous resources and strategies of resistance: Informal caregiving and racial socialization in black communities. In H. I. McCubbin & E. A. Thompson (Eds.), *Resiliency in African-American families. Resiliency in Families Series, Vol. 3* (pp. 49–66). Thousand Oaks, CA: Sage.

Valiente, C., Fabes, R. A., Eisenberg, N., & Spinrad, T. L. (2004). The relations of parental expressivity and support to children's coping with daily stress. *Journal of Family Psychology, 18,* 97–106.

van der Kolk, B. A. (2005). Developmental trauma disorder: Toward a rational diagnosis for children with complex trauma histories. *Psychiatric Annals, 35,* 401–408.

Vila, G., Witowski, P., Tondini, M. C., PerezDiaz, F., MourenSimeoni, M. C., & Jouvent, R. (2001). A study of posttraumatic disorders in children who experienced an industrial disaster in the Briey region. *European Child & Adolescent Psychiatry, 10,* 10–18.

Wallerstein, J. S., & Corbin, S. B. (1996). The child and the vicissitudes of divorce. In M. Lewis (Ed.), *Child and adolescent psychiatry* (pp. 1118–1127). Baltimore, MD: Williams & Wilkins.

Walsh, F. (2007). Traumatic loss and major disasters: Strengthening family and community resilience. *Family Process, 46,* 207–227.

Weingarten, K. (2004). Witnessing the effects of political violence in families: Mechanisms of intergenerational transmission and clinical interventions. *Journal of Marital & Family Therapy, 30,* 45–59.

Wheaton, B. (1997). The nature of chronic stress. In B. H. Gottlieb (Ed.), *Coping with chronic stress. The Plenum Series on stress and coping* (pp. 43–73). New York: Plenum Press.

CHAPTER 3

THEORETICAL FOUNDATION FOR FAMILY CONSTRUCTIVE COPING

As with most interventions addressing complex problems, SFCR's resource enhancement approach takes into account perspectives from multiple theories. Consistent with the two primary objectives of SFCR, this intervention is guided by theories related to: (1) the characteristics of traumatic distress evidenced by families (described in Chapter 2); and (2) a blend of ritual and routine theory with family stress and coping theories.

This chapter begins with a review of family ritual and routine theory. A brief description of relevant family process theories (including systems and relational theories, family stress and resource theories, and family resilience theory) follows and highlights each theory's application in SFCR. The final section describes six *protective family coping resources* derived from this theoretical base that are the focus of the therapeutic strategies that comprise SFCR.

> SFCR builds constructive family coping resources as a vehicle for strengthening a family's protective function potentially vulnerable to the effects of traumatic context and for accomplishing many of the treatment objectives outlined in the family trauma treatment literature.

FAMILY RITUALS AND ROUTINES AS COPING RESOURCES

SFCR is one of the first manualized clinical applications of family ritual and routine theory for improving adjustment to major life stresses or traumas. SFCR applies family ritual and routine theory in multiple ways, from the manner in which facilitators approach families, to the structure of each session, and including many of the therapeutic strategies employed. To successfully translate ritual and routine theory into effective intervention strategies, facilitators must:

1. recognize family ritual and routine practices;
2. accept that family rituals and routines are essential components of healthy family process and can serve as natural healing resources for families;
3. appreciate that functional family rituals and routines can be disrupted by experiences of accumulated traumatic circumstances;
4. enumerate the important dimensions of family ritual and routine that support constructive coping; and
5. be able to implement therapeutic strategies to increase a family's ritual and routine coping resources.

Defining Ritual and Routine

All families, regardless of culture, ethnicity, or stage in the family life cycle, practice rituals and routines. They are a ubiquitous part of family life.

Rituals and routines are patterned units of behaviors involving at least two family members. They are transactional in nature and are repeated over time. Most families practice a variety of rituals and routines (Spagnola & Fiese, 2007; Wolin & Bennett, 1984):

- celebrations (including holiday observances and graduations);
- traditions (including the specific way a family observes birthdays or anniversaries);
- patterned interactions or daily rituals (including shared family meals, greetings, and good-byes); and
- routines (including taking out the trash and getting the children ready for school).

Although distinct, rituals and routines often have blurred boundaries (Spagnola & Fiese, 2007). Bedtimes serve as a good example because they often comprise features of both. As a routine, bedtimes serve an instrumental function with the goal of preparing family members for sleep. Within a short and regularly scheduled period of time, family members change into pajamas and complete basic hygienic tasks to get ready for sleep. Bedtime routines can also include sharing of stories, prayers, reading books, or singing a favorite "night-night" song. These additional practices contain features of ritual in that they communicate symbolic meaning about what is important to the family.

Why Families Practice Rituals and Routines

Families practice rituals and routines for many reasons. Patterned interactions, daily rituals, and routines, those practices performed on a regular basis, serve the following purposes (Bennett, Wolin, & Reiss, 1988b; Fiese, 1992; Imber-Black, 1988; Pett & Lang, 1992; Roberts, 1988; Rogers & Holloway, 1991; Schuck & Bucy, 1997):

- accomplish tasks in order to meet basic needs;
- provide structure;
- clarify roles;
- stipulate rules;

- establish boundaries around who is part of the family;
- support family communication and cohesion; and
- establish an identity by denoting how things are done in this family.

Beyond the everyday significance, daily rituals and routines also contribute to coping in times of crisis. Although easily disrupted during times of transition and stress, families that return quickly to their ritual and routine practices show stability and positive adaptation (Fiese & Wamboldt, 2000; Imber-Black, Roberts, & Whiting, 2003).

Family rituals, including celebrations, traditions, and daily rituals, also serve a variety of purposes:

- communicate what is of central importance to the family;
- pass along traditions and heritage from one generation to the next;
- mark major events, both positive and negative, in the family life cycle;
- convey a shared meaning of life events; and
- add symbolism and beauty to family experience.

Links to Family Health and Well-Being

When families are able to practice rituals and routines, even under stressful circumstances, they function better and family members experience better psychosocial adjustment. Studies show evidence of this relationship in families coping with a wide variety of stressors. Early studies demonstrated that constructive use of family rituals was associated with better outcomes for families dealing with alcoholism (Bennett, Wolin, & Reiss, 1988a, 1988b; Wolin, Bennett, & Noonan, 1979). Later studies replicated this finding with families coping with chronic illness, especially asthma, and with psychiatric illness in youth (Fiese & Wamboldt, 2000; Kiser, Bennett, Heston, & Paavola, 2005). Family ritual and routine practice has also proven beneficial in families dealing with change in family memberships (Niska, Snyder, & Lia-Hoagber, 1998; Portes, Howell, Brown, Eichenberger, & Mas, 1992; Shapiro, 1994). According to results of the Add Health study, every health risk behavior, except pregnancy, was attenuated for youth whose parents were available and involved in daily routines (Resnick et al., 1997).

The Effect of Traumatic Contexts on Family Ritual and Routine

Family adaptations to high stress and trauma, as described in Chapter 2, are likely to impact the practice of ritual and routine. For many families, routines that are highly vulnerable to daily hassles and major family stressors will be disrupted frequently as families experience each new crisis (Fiese & Wamboldt, 2000). Such frequent interruptions diminish the effectiveness of ritual and routine practices, and over time families do not find them helpful anymore. Given the energy and resources required to carry out rituals and routine, if a family is under-resourced and rituals and routines are no longer serving their intended purpose, families stop practicing them.

From Theory to Practice

Given the solid connection between family ritual life and adjustment across such a wide variety of stressful family circumstances and the potential for erosion of ritual and routine practice due to high stressor conditions, SFCR focuses on building ritual and routine practices as an effective change mechanism for improving adjustment to major life

stresses or traumas (Fiese, 1997; Imber-Black, 1988; van der Hart, Witztum, & de Voogt, 1988; Wolin & Bennett, 1984). Effective use of family ritual and routine practices as intervention strategies requires an understanding of the ritual and routine dimensions related to protection and promotion of healthy family functioning. These dimensions are summarized in Table 3.1.

A foundational concept from family ritual and routine theory is deliberateness (Bennett, personal communication). In a series of studies, Wolin and Bennett defined deliberateness as: (1) planning the sort of family they wanted to have—including ritual activities—and then successfully following through on those plans; and (2) carrying out family rituals and routines regardless of problems that the family was facing (specifically alcohol abuse behavior). Couples high in deliberateness evidenced significantly less transmission of alcoholism into their family and their children showed fewer behavior problems than couples rated as low on deliberateness (Bennett et al., 1988a, 1988b; Wolin et al., 1979).

Additionally, continuity and change, two opposing dynamics, are critical to the practice of family rituals and routines (Fiese, 2006). When rituals and routines are adopted by a family, they are repeated in much the same manner time and time again. In this way, they become familiar and practiced. Family members know what to expect, what role they play, and what transactional rules they must follow. However, families are not static; family members grow and develop, times change. Rituals and routines must shift to meet the new needs of family members and to meet the needs of the family unit throughout the family life cycle. Importantly, families must work to maintain an appropriate balance between continuity and change.

→ TABLE 3.1 Protective and Promotive Dimensions of Family Rituals[1,2]

Dimension	Description
Routine Structure	Defined by the regularity of activity and the manner in which it is carried out (who, what, where, and when)
Ritual Meaning	Refers to the role of rituals and routines in understanding and communicating shared family values and beliefs
Deliberateness	Refers to having a clear idea about family life and successfully following through. Encompasses the family's capacity for carrying out rituals and routines despite obstacles. Often described on a continuum from disrupted (interrupted, avoided, missed, or lost) to distinctive (maintained in spite of stressors)
Adaptability or Flexibility	Indicates the family's ability to change ritual and routine practices over time in response to shifting individual and family needs
Preparation	Refers to the amount of groundwork needed to carry out the ritual or routine. Often described on a continuum from very elaborate and complex planning to nonexistent planning

Ritual and Routine as Intervention

Using ritual as a mechanism to create therapeutic change typically involves prescribed rituals (Fiese, 1997; Imber-Black, 1988; Johnson, Feldman, Lubin, & Southwick, 1995). In SFCR, however, the focus is on naturally occurring family rituals and routines. As opposed to prescribed rituals that are therapist-driven, naturally occurring rituals and routines are family-driven:

> Treatment techniques using naturally occurring rituals involve observing and assessing family life for disrupted rituals, for empty rituals that no longer serve the family's needs, for incomplete, avoided or missed rituals, and for lost rituals. Families are then encouraged to reinstate lost or disrupted rituals, to modify empty rituals to meet new family life cycle demands, or to construct new rituals (Bennett et al. 1988b; Rogers & Holloway, 1991; van der Hart et al. 1988).
>
> (Kiser et al., 2005, p. 218)

A few examples illustrate how SFCR incorporates ritual and routine theory in practice.

Shared Family Meals

Family mealtimes are a wonderful example of naturally occurring rituals and routines. On a day-to-day basis, family mealtimes accomplish a variety of purposes. In addition to meeting the basic need of family members for nutrition, mealtimes provide an opportunity for involving multiple family members in joint interaction and for sharing information necessary for organizing family life (Black & Hurley, 2007; Fiese, Foley, & Spagnola, 2006; Fulkerson, Neumark-Sztainer, & Story, 2006a; Wolin & Bennett, 1984). "For many families, dinnertime may be the only consistent time that all family members gather together. It is a time for updates about the day, discussions about family matters, and coordination of schedules" (Dickstein & Martin, 2002, p. 23).

Importantly, shared family meals are related to well-being. Studies of family mealtimes call attention to their protective functions. Eating meals together frequently has been associated with positive family processes such as cohesion, communication, and role modeling, and with individual outcomes in children and adolescents (Eisenberg, Olson, Neumark-Sztainer, Story, & Bearinger, 2004; Franko, Thompson, Affenito, Barton, & Striegel-Moore, 2008; Fulkerson et al., 2006a). Specifically, mealtime frequency has been linked to improved psychosocial development and lowered rates of eating disorders and high-risk behaviors (Fulkerson et al., 2006b; Neumark-Sztainer, Wall, Story, & Fulkerson, 2004).

Besides frequency, other dimensions of family mealtimes linked to well-being include deliberateness (i.e., limiting distractions), practice of meaningful rituals, regularity of shared activity, and quality of family relationships (Bennett, Wolin, Reiss, & Teitelbaum, 1987; Bennett et al, 1988a; Fiese & Wamboldt, 2000; Kiser et al., 2005; Markson & Fiese, 2000; Resnick et al., 1997). Direct communication and deliberate process during mealtimes have been related to fewer behavior problems in children (Fiese et al., 2006). Academic achievement and literacy have been predicted by mealtime experiences of narrative and explanatory discourse (Larson, Branscomb, & Wiley, 2006). Parental styles of conducting mealtimes have also been explored. A parent's role is to offer nourishment and direct the atmosphere of the meal (Black & Hurley, 2007). Finally, cultural differences in mealtime interactions and organization have been found (Larson et al., 2006).

Given the value of shared mealtimes to child and family functioning, helping families who are struggling to experience successful meals is an important goal. This may be especially relevant to low-income families who tend to eat fewer meals together than families in better economic circumstances (Eisenberg et al., 2004; Neumark-Sztainer, Hannan, Story, Croll, & Perry, 2003). As an intervention strategy, assisting families in changing their mealtime routine may be easier than altering more global family processes (Neumark-Sztainer et al., 2004). Thus, a variety of MFG interventions designed to strengthen family functioning, including SFCR, begin with a meal.

Using what we know about optimal mealtime experiences, SFCR facilitators deliberately structure shared mealtimes. The mealtime environment is arranged in advance to promote a positive experience. Families are coached to decrease distractions and conflict, co-regulate emotions and behavior, and engage in meaningful interaction (Black & Hurley, 2007; Cason, 2006). Dialogue is encouraged through the introduction of "conversation prompts," cards with questions or prompts designed to stimulate discussion on meaningful and playful topics.

Daily Routines (Especially Bedtimes)

SFCR sessions focus on deliberate performance of daily routines designed to increase predictability and stability in family functioning. Through a structured activity, caregivers/families are encouraged to develop a functional routine. This activity consists of helping caregivers/families build well-designed routines and to practice them deliberately. See Chapter 6 for more information about how families develop routines in SFCR.

In SFCR, families are encouraged to look for times during the day when their routines are not working or could be improved. Caregivers are often encouraged to focus on bedtime routines. With sleep problems a hallmark of traumatic stress disorders, bedtimes can be especially challenging and maintaining functional bedtime routines is often difficult. As bedtime approaches, family members are usually tired and often anxious about sleeping. Fears may be exacerbated. Anxiety, vigilance, and perceptions of threat are incompatible with sleep as the neural systems central to these processes are overlapping (Van Reeth et al., 2000).

Sleep hygiene, including regular bedtime routines, is related to overall health and well-being and is especially important for families coping with trauma-related distress (Sadeh, Gruber, & Raviv, 2003). Research demonstrates that having a regular bedtime is related to fewer behavior problems, and when caregivers establish a regular bedtime routine, behavior scores improve (Kelly, Kelly, & Sacker, 2013). Additionally, structured nighttime activities and a good night's sleep may be associated with stable and healthy 24-hour profiles of cortisol release and with regulation (e.g., emotional, behavioral) (Fisher, Stoolmiller, Gunnar, & Burraston 2007; Leproult & Van Cauter, 2010; Sadeh et al., 2003; Spiegel, Leproult, & Van Cauter, 1999; Steenari et al., 2003; Tininenko, Fisher, Bruce, & Pears, 2010).

If bedtimes are problematic, caregivers are encouraged to introduce a structured and feasible bedtime routine that can be practiced regularly. As caregivers share ideas about what might work, they are often introduced to new ideas for using calming activities to help down-regulate their children in preparation for sleep and about strategies that might work to calm nighttime fears and anxieties.

Importantly, regardless of whether the caregivers focus on bedtime routines, they are learning about how to structure successful routines and how to plan for deliberate follow-through. They apply this approach to developing routines again and again during SFCR sessions and hopefully generalize this knowledge and use it when faced with disrupted or unsuccessful routines in the future.

FAMILY SYSTEMS, COPING AND RESILIENCE THEORIES

Additional theories related to family process provide theoretical guidance for SFCR. These theories include systems and relational theories (including attachment and social network), family stress and resource theories, and family resilience theory. A brief review of these multiple theories allows SFCR facilitators to:

1. understand the theoretical foundations of the intervention;
2. recognize links between specific therapeutic activities and the theories that support their use; and
3. translate these connections between theories and activities into language that families will understand.

Systems and Relational Theories

Systems theory provides a foundation for many forms of family therapy and for understanding the impact of stress and trauma on the family (Boszormenyi-Nagy, 1987; Bronfenbrenner, 1979; Gelles & Maynard, 1987; Howes, Cicchetti, Toth, & Rogosch, 2000; Patterson, 1991; Shochet & Dadds, 1997). Building on general systems theory, *family systems theory* seeks to explain the interconnectedness of individual family members and family subsystems to better understand how their shared history, familial bonds, and collaborative coping strategies support family functioning.

Applying family systems theory to SFCR results in an emphasis on working with the family as a system, noting that if we create change at the multiple connected and interdependent levels within the family (individual members and multiple dyadic/multipartite subsystems), the whole family will change. In SFCR, a variety of activities are used to illustrate the basic tenets of systems theories for families. For example, families are asked to build a structure using gears to demonstrate that when something happens to one member of the family, the effects ripple through the entire family.

An important tenet of family systems theory is that families operate most effectively when in balance. However, high levels of stress and exposure to trauma events can be disruptive, throwing the system out of balance. Families who lose their balance must quickly try to "right" themselves. Depending upon the demands of the stressor or the extent of the trauma, this may be difficult and require significant effort. Families who have difficulty regaining balance may become distressed. Many of the therapeutic strategies in SFCR are designed to help families build the skills and garner the resources necessary to regain balance.

Another principle of systems theory important for understanding family functioning is that efficient functioning is related to anticipation of and preparation for what is likely to happen next, especially in the face of uncertain conditions (McEwen, 1998; Schulkin, 2011). Therapeutic strategies in SFCR emphasize planning, preparation, and anticipatory problem-solving as critical resources for dealing with accumulated traumatic circumstances.

Eco-transactional or developmental theories are important extensions of systems theory. They are crucial to understanding family trauma due to their emphasis on the role of larger systems and context in the lives of individuals and families (Bronfenbrenner, 1979; Hill, Fonagy, Safier, & Sargent, 2003; Kazak, 1989; Meyers, Varkey, & Aguirre, 2002). SFCR, developed using participatory research methods, places the importance of experience within context as central to the way in which facilitators respectfully work with families. SFCR facilitators value that families are rooted in neighborhoods or communities, in countries with laws and policies, and in a historical context, all of which impact the ways family react and interact.

Attachment theory explains the critical role of family relationships in human development. Attachment theory primarily focuses on the early bond between an infant and caregiver and the importance of this relationship in establishing a sense of safety and security (Bowlby, 1988; Sroufe & Waters, 1977). Confidence in protection is a concept basic to attachment theory. It describes the basic protective contract between caregiver and children (Goldberg, Grusec, & Jenkins, 1999). It is from this strong early bond that children are able to explore and learn.

Attachment researchers demonstrated that a secure attachment is internalized forming the basis for healthy and trusting relationships throughout life (Cicchetti, Rogosch, & Toth, 2006; Toth, Maughan, Manly, Spagnola, & Cicchetti, 2002). Alternatively, there is strong evidence that disruptions in attachment or impaired caregiving are associated with negative consequences in psychosocial development.

Increasing connection and trust between the caregivers and their children is emphasized in multiple SFCR intervention strategies. Activities promote attunement, co-regulation, and support seeking between caregivers and their children and among the family as a whole, thus promoting confidence in protection at the individual and family levels. Caregivers are encouraged to learn their children's distress/fear cues and to appreciate their efforts at protective parenting. Families create routines to ensure that family members act together to increase their sense of safety.

Attachment theory has far-reaching consequences for understanding patterns of relating within family relationships and within other social networks:

In the same way that infants form a working model of relationships from their responsive and caring interactions with their primary caregiver, family members develop family relationship schemas through consistent interactions with one another. These schemas provide guidelines that stipulate how family members react and interact with each other and are also extended to how family members relate to others.

(Figley & Kiser, 2013, p. 48)

Social support theories offer a variety of related paradigms exploring human behavior based on our nature as social beings. Theories, such as social learning and social network, postulate that our responses and the ways we cope with experience are transacted within a social context (Bandura, 1989; Cahill & Foa, 2007; Monson & Friedman, 2006). We operate within a social network described according to its specific characteristics (i.e., breadth, depth, integration), the types of support available to us (i.e., tangible, emotional), and various sources of support (i.e., family, friends, professional helpers). SFCR's focus on building people resources is predicated on the knowledge that: (1) our ability to receive and give support is related to both physical and mental health outcomes; and (2) positive outcomes are associated with connectedness in general and also with using social support resources during times of stress (Cohen & Wills, 1985; Hill & Herman-Stahl, 2002; Taylor, 2011; Uchino, 2009).

Family Stress and Resource Theories

Theories regarding individual *stress and coping* suggest that dealing effectively with stress includes "the ways in which individuals manage their emotions, think constructively, regulate and direct their behavior, control their autonomic arousal, and act on the social and nonsocial environments to alter or decrease sources of stress" (Compas, Connor-Smith, Saltzman, Thomsen, & Wadsworth, 2001, p. 127). Two critical aspects of coping are highlighted in this definition: (1) involuntary and voluntary efforts to manage one's internal stress response; and (2) efforts to modify the stressor condition to alter its impact. Individuals and families employ an assortment of strategies to accomplish these coping functions (Berg, Meegan, & Deviney, 1998; Park & Folkman, 1997; Winje, 1998).

Family stress management theories are often based on Hill's classic ABCX model (Hill, 1958). They postulate that family coping resources must meet the demands of the stressor faced. If the family's resources match the stressor demands, families adapt well. If, however, the family's resources do not match the stressor demands, the family experiences a crisis requiring significant changes in roles, responsibilities, and resources (Conger et al., 2002; Hammack, Robinson, Crawford, & Li, 2004; McCubbin, 1995; Patterson, 2002). Flexibility to choose coping resources or strategies that match the demands of the stressor leads to the most effective adaptation.

Consistent with the ABCX model of family stress, *resource theories* underscore the significance of resource loss during coping (Hobfoll, 1989; Hobfoll & Lilly, 1993; Hobfoll, Lilly, & Jackson, 1992; Johnson, Palmieri, Jackson, & Hobfoll, 2007). Coping with high stress and trauma requires individuals, and families, to expend significant resources (e.g., material goods, supports, interpersonal resources, time and energy). Thus, individuals and families need a variety of coping schemas or styles, including both individual and collaborative strategies, within their skill set (Peacock & Wong, 1996).

SFCR's emphasis on strengthening coping

resources is predicated on the theory that successful adaptation depends on the availability of sufficient resources and that conservation of resources is important for meeting the demands related to future hard times (Hobfoll, Johnson, Ennis, & Jackson, 2003). SFCR helps families build multiple coping resources, both individual and collaborative.

Table 3.2 summarizes common coping strategies (Berg et al., 1998; Figley, 1988; Figley & Kiser, 2013; Park & Folkman, 1997; Winje, 1998). Coping schemas such as cognitive coping or behavioral coping are less interdependent while strategies such as negotiation and perspective taking are more collaborative.

➡ **TABLE 3.2** Individual and Collaborative Coping Strategies

	Schema	Definition	Example
Individual	Problem-focused	Active attempts to alter the stressor conditions	Looking for a good solution, choosing a solution and enacting it
	Cognitive coping	Active attempts to change meaning of stressor so that it is congruent with self-knowledge and beliefs	Denial, distraction, need to know what happened
	Behavioral coping	Regulation of behavior associated with emotional experiences	Task completion, leaving, sleeping, hitting
	Emotional coping	Need for affective expression in response to stressor conditions	Crying, anger
	Social coping	Use of social resources	Seeking solace, altruism, withdrawal
	Preventive coping	Active attempts to alter the stressor conditions or the expected response prior to the event	Anticipation, planning, preparation
Collaborative	Negotiation	Attempts to find acceptable solutions to common problems	Compromise, interest-based negotiation, joint problem-solving, competition, manipulation
	Role clarity	Attempts to delineate how family members will participate in coping	Role change or adjustment, task realignment
	Balancing power	Attempts to spread influence and control among family members	Conflict resolution, power sharing
	Perspective taking	Figuring out what others think, feel or intend; ability to understand/accept different appraisals and reactions to stressor conditions	Reflection, empathy, cognitive flexibility

Additionally, SFCR focuses on helping families employ successful resource management tools. Often, families experiment with different combinations of individual members' efforts and family unit coping to find ways to manage the stressor demands (McCubbin & McCubbin, 1993). Families who maximize the use of both individual and collaborative coping resources matched to stressor demands adapt most successfully. Families are encouraged to manage their current resources, and to find or create new resources when needed. They are helped to prioritize how to use these resources and use them flexibly to meet the most critical demands.

Family Resiliency

SFCR strategies nurture the potential for resilience and growth in the context of accumulated trauma. *Resilience*, traditionally an individually based construct, is defined as the ability to adapt to significant adversity (Masten, 2001; Walsh, 2006). As research on resilience has matured, efforts to understand the concept within a broader systemic framework have highlighted its relational nature (Saltzman et al., 2011).

Family resilience research delineates family-level risk and protective factors that impede or support the ability of the family to carry out basic family functions (Carver, 1998; Delage, 2002; Hernandez, Gangsei, & Engstrom, 2007; Patterson, 2002). Characteristics that support resilience in families include (Fredrickson & Losada, 2005; Kiser, Ostoja, & Pruitt, 1998; Seligman & Csikszentmihalyi, 2000; Seligman, Steen, Park, & Peterson, 2005; Walsh, 2006):

- a strong commitment to the family and shared family experiences;
- parental leadership, good resource management skills, and clear role boundaries;

- family efficacy and celebration of successes;
- resolution of problems and conflicts before they become long-standing;
- maintenance of connectedness by seeking or offering support when needed;
- safely expressing a wide range of emotions, both positive and negative; and
- development of shared values, beliefs, and meaning.

As a strength-based intervention, SFCR includes multiple activities designed to help families reduce risk and enhance protective factors. For example, families are encouraged to mark even small successes and to find meaningful ways to make their celebrations special without overtaxing their resources.

Exploration of the potential for growth following exposure to catastrophic events also influenced the development of SFCR. The literature describing thriving and post-traumatic growth suggests important mechanisms through which individuals and families actually enhance their functioning and well-being following traumatic experiences (Calhoun & Tedeschi, 1998; Figley & Kiser, 2013; Tedeschi & Calhoun, 2004). Through the struggle to deal with traumatic distress, positive outcomes and thriving are real possibilities. Families participating in SFCR are encouraged to develop a new appreciation for, and commitment to, relationships and to look for meaning and purpose in their experiences and in their future.

PROTECTIVE FAMILY COPING RESOURCES

Derived from this theoretical backdrop, SFCR fosters six protective family coping resources: deliberateness, structure and a sense of safety, connectedness, resource seeking, co-regulation and crisis management, and positive affect, memories, and meaning. Each resource is described with the related coping schema and relevant theories indicated.

Deliberateness (coping schema: problem-focused, preventive; related theories: family ritual). Deliberateness strategies in SFCR support effective coping with anticipatory anxiety and help prevent additional exposures. As a problem-focused coping mechanism, deliberate planning and follow through helps family members focus attention on getting things done and creates positive feelings about successfully carrying out routines and rituals. It provides multiple opportunities for taking control of stressful or chaotic situations and demonstrating mastery. Deliberateness may also help families feel more positive about their future (Folkman & Moskowitz, 2000).

In SFCR, strategies used to reinforce deliberateness include planning, problem-solving, and follow-through as central aspects of effective stress management. The focus on deliberateness in multiple sessions includes the notions of forethought as to the possible course of family life, making life choices, intergenerational transmission, and future orientation. Finally, multiple sessions teach skills related to maintaining rituals and routines, regardless of what else is happening in the family, through anticipation and preventive planning. SFCR skill-building activities help families distinguish between disrupted and distinctive practices.

Structure and a sense of safety (coping schema: joint problem-solving, role clarity; related theories: family ritual and routine, attachment). Creating a predictable and stable social ecology within the family is critical for the treatment of trauma-related symptoms related to chronic exposure to high stress and trauma. Structure entails insulation from danger, rapid stabilization of family functioning, and establishing order and regularity in daily family

life. Skill-building activities teach families to effectively use daily routines that help family members understand what to expect and establish rules and limits for day-to-day life. "There is a feeling of safety and trust in knowing that the same thing will happen every day" (Butterfield, 2002, p. 30). "Through repetition, daily routines provide structure and meaning, maintain order and regularity in contrast to disorder or chaos (Driver, 1991). For children, this translates into a sense of security (Parker, 1999)" (Kiser, 2006, p. 219).

Since "the stress potential of life events is most clearly seen in its ability to disrupt family routines and add to daily hassles" (Fiese & Wamboldt, 2000, pp. 410–411), SFCR skill-building strategies enlist families in establishing order and regularity in daily family life. Families are encouraged to effectively use daily routines to establish limits and rules, to build routines that insulate the family from danger, and to invest in preventive routines that allow a degree of control over otherwise uncontrollable circumstances. Over time and with predictable, regular practice of daily stress management and safety routines, family members gain a sense of confidence in protection. In addition, SFCR strategies reinforce attunement with, and communication of, safety needs to prevent further trauma exposure.

Connectedness (coping schema: social, collaborative; related theories: family ritual, attachment, resilience). Fostering close connections among family members is important for families whose relations have been threatened by conflict and violence, frequent changes in membership, and intergenerational transmission of under-protection (refer back to Chapter 2). Connectedness and cohesion involve close, stable relationships and commitment to building a sense of belonging. Connectedness involves healthy attachments, confidence in protection, positive emotional bonds, healthy communication, and shared beliefs and values. It encompasses setting family as a priority and maintaining this commitment even in the face of adversity (Brodsky, 1999). Themes of nurturing and taking care of are also integrated.

SFCR's emphasis on family rituals and routines and collaborative coping increases interdependencies that foster family connectedness (Kiser et al., 2005). In each session, families work together on activities designed to increase closeness, trust, and enjoyment of shared experience. "Family ritual life, including celebrations, can provide each member with multiple opportunities to participate in planning and sharing responsibilities, thus communicating a belief in the competence and worth of the family and of individual members" (Kiser, 2006, p. 220).

Resource seeking (coping schema: social, collaborative; related theories: social support, resource). Social support buffers the impact of trauma. Strong positive relationships with extended family and friends are important indicators of well-being and family resilience. A strong social support network can make valuable contributions to a family that is struggling to cope with high stress and chronic trauma (Dubow, Edwards, & Ippolito, 1997; Figely & Kiser, 2013).

SFCR intervention strategies are directed at helping the family identify who they can rely on and increasing the availability of resources they can access when encountering threats. SFCR encourages families to involve others in their family life, especially in times of stress, accept assistance when needed, and also give to others when the opportunity arises. The MFG models incorporate many strategies to build community and to use the power of the group as a healing resource.

Co-regulation and crisis management (coping schema: cognitive, emotional, behavioral; related theories: family stress, resource). When triggered

responses of threat and negative affect are frequent, family members' emotions and behavior are driven by fight, flight, or freeze reactions, and families struggle to modulate their interactions. Dysregulation among multiple family members reduces the capacity to provide co-regulation.

Throughout, SFCR therapeutic strategies support family coping practices that encourage collective experiences of regulation. First, joint family activities in SFCR provide multiple opportunities for families to define their comfort zone during interactions. During these activities, family members learn to read each other cues, listen to each other, and contain emotional expression within a safe range. Second, SFCR introduces anxiety management training within a family context to improve regulation of the stress reaction. Third, the symbolic nature of ritual expression and storytelling allows individuals to maintain a distance from the real "danger" while still being involved emotionally (Driver, 1991; Johnson et al., 1995).

> The experience of safety, predictability and "fun" is essential to establish the capacity to observe what is going on, to put it into a larger context and initiate appropriate physiological and motoric responses.
>
> (Streeck-Fisher & van der Kolk, 2000, p. 914)

In keeping with family stress management and resource models, during SFCR, families are coached to build and use a variety of skills/resources to improve the chances that they will have sufficient resources to prevent new stressors and cope with ongoing threats without moving into crisis responding. They are encouraged to remain flexible in how they appraise crises and match coping strategies as needed to the demands of current stressors.

Positive affect, memories, and meaning (coping schema: cognitive, emotional, collaborative; related theories: resilience). In opposition to interactions characterized as negative and threatening, positive experiences reduce vigilance and support slower, more deliberate information processing, problem-solving, choice of coping response, and follow-through. SFCR includes multiple opportunities for positive exchanges to compensate for the predominately negative encounters that many families remember related to their exposure to chronic stress and multiple traumas (Folkman & Moskowitz, 2000).

SFCR appreciates current coping and resilience theories that value positivity, including helping families make memories of shared experience filled with expressions of laughter and positive affect (Folkman & Moskowitz, 2000). In SFCR, enacting rituals and storytelling, through joining metaphor with symbolic action, play, touch, and stimulation of the senses, provides a vehicle for creating such lasting memories.

Meaning-making processes within families depend upon a shared belief system and worldview. In support of the associations between religiosity/ spirituality and coping with adversity, SFCR activities help families talk about their spiritual beliefs and develop a shared understanding of trauma(s) within the context of their spiritual life (Donahue & Benson, 1995; Evans, Boustead, & Owens, 2008; Haight, 1998; Meyer & Lausell, 1996). Finally, SFCR includes practices, such as storytelling and narration, to help families build and clearly communicate a coherent and hopeful understanding of life events.

NOTES

1. Adapted from Kiser (2006).
2. Fiese and Wamboldt (2000) and Schuck and Bucy (1997).

REFERENCES

Bandura, A. (1989). Regulation of cognitive processes through perceived self-efficacy. *Developmental Psychology, 25*, 729–735.

Bennett, L. A., Wolin, S. J., & Reiss, D. (1988a). Cognitive, behavioral, and emotional problems among school-aged children of alcoholics. *American Journal of Psychiatry, 145*, 85–90.

Bennett, L. A., Wolin, S. J., & Reiss, D. (1988b). Deliberate family process: A strategy for protecting children of alcoholics. *British Journal of Addiction, 82*, 821–829.

Bennett, L. A., Wolin, S. J., Reiss, D., & Teitelbaum, M. A. (1987). Couples at risk for transmission of alcoholism: Protective influences. *Family Process, 26*(1), 111–129.

Berg, C. A., Meegan, S. P., & Deviney, F. P. (1998). A social-contextual model of coping with everyday problems across the lifespan. *International Journal of Behavioral Development, 22*, 239–261.

Black, M. M., & Hurley, K. M. (2007). *Helping children develop healthy eating habits.* Montreal, QC: Centre of Excellence for Early Child Development.

Boszormenyi-Nagy, I. (1987). *Foundations of contextual therapy: Collected papers of Ivan Boszormenyi, M.D.* Philadelphia, PA: Brunner/Mazel.

Bowlby, J. (1988). *A secure base: Parent-child attachment and healthy human development.* New York: Basic Books.

Brodsky, A. E. (1999). "Making it": The components and process of resilience among urban, African American, single mothers. *American Journal of Orthopsychiatry, 59*, 148–150.

Bronfenbrenner, U. (1979). *The ecology of human development.* Cambridge, MA: Harvard University Press.

Butterfield, P. M. (2002). Child care is rich in routines. *Zero to Three, 22*, 29–32.

Cahill, S. P., & Foa, E. B. (2007). Psychological theories of PTSD. In M. J. Friedman, T. M. Keane, & P. A. Resick (Eds.), *Handbook of PTSD: Science and practice* (pp. 55–77). New York: The Guilford Press.

Calhoun, L., & Tedeschi, R. (1998). Beyond recovery from trauma: Implications for clinical practice and research. *Journal of Social Issues, 54*, 357–371.

Carver, C. S. (1998). Resilience and thriving: Issues, models, and linkages. *Journal of Social Issues, 54*, 245–266.

Cason, K. L. (2006). Family mealtimes: More than just eating together. *Journal of the American Dietetic Association, 106*, 532–533. doi:10.1016/j.jada.2006.01. 012.

Cicchetti, D., Rogosch, F. A., & Toth, S. L. (2006). Fostering secure attachment in infants in maltreating families through preventive interventions. *Developmental Psychopathology, 18*, 623–650.

Cohen, S., & Wills, T. A. (1985). Stress, social support, and the buffering hypothesis. *Psychological Bulletin, 98*, 310–357. doi:10.1037/0033-2909.98.2.310.

Compas, B. E., Connor-Smith, J. K., Saltzman, H., Thomsen, A. H., & Wadsworth, M. E. (2001). Coping with stress during childhood and adolescence: Problems, progress, and potential in theory and research. *Psychological Bulletin, 127*, 87–127.

Conger, R. D., Wallace, L. E., Sun, Y., Simons, R. L., McLoyd, V., & Brody, G. H. (2002). Economic pressure in African American families: A replication and extension of the family stress model. *Developmental Psychology, 38*, 179–193.

Delage, M. (2002). Strengthening family resilience in traumatic situations. *Therapie Familiale, 23*, 269–287.

Dickstein, S., & Martin, S. (2002). What's for dinner? Family functioning, maternal depression, and early childhood outcomes. *Zero to Three, 22*(4), 21–28.

Donahue, M. J., & Benson, P. L. (1995). Religion and the well-being of adolescents. *Journal of Social Issues, 51*, 145–160.

Driver, T. F. (1991). *The magic of ritual: Our need for liberating rites that transform our lives and our communities.* New York: HarperCollins.

Dubow, E. F., Edwards, S., & Ippolito, M. F. (1997). Life stressors, neighborhood disadvantage, and resources: A focus on inner-city children's adjustment. *Journal of Clinical Child Psychology, 26*, 130–144.

Eisenberg, M. E., Olson, R. E., Neumark-Sztainer, D., Story, M., & Bearinger, L. H. (2004). Correlations between family meals and psychosocial well-being among adolescents. *Archives of Pediatrics & Adolescent Medicine, 158*, 792–796. doi:10.1001/archpedi.158.8.792.

Evans, C. J., Boustead, R. S., & Owens, C. (2008). Expressions of spirituality in parents with at-risk children. *Families in Society, 89*, 245–252.

Fiese, B. H. (1992). Dimensions of family rituals across two generations: Relation to adolescent identity. *Family Process, 31*, 151–152.

Fiese, B. H. (1997). Family context in pediatric psychology from a transactional perspective: Family rituals and stories as examples. *Journal of Pediatric Psychology, 22*, 183–196.

Fiese, B. H. (2006). *Family routines and rituals.* New Haven, CT: Yale University Press.

Fiese, B. H., & Wamboldt, F. S. (2000). Family routines, rituals, and asthma management: A proposal for family-based strategies to increase treatment adherence. *Families, Systems & Health, 18*, 405–418.

Fiese, B. H., Foley, K. P., & Spagnola, M. (2006). Routine and ritual elements in family mealtimes: Contexts for child well-being and family identity. *New Directions for Child and Adolescent Development, 111*, 67–89.

Figley, C. R. (1988). Post-traumatic family therapy. In F. M. Ochberg (Ed.), *Post-traumatic therapy and victims of violence* (pp. 83–109). New York: Bruner/Mazel.

Figley, C. R., & Kiser, L. J. (2013) *Helping traumatized families* (2nd ed.). New York: Routledge.

Fisher, P. A., Stoolmiller, M., Gunnar, M. R., & Burraston, B. O. (2007). Effects of a therapeutic intervention for foster preschoolers on diurnal cortisol activity. *Psychoneuroendocrinology, 32*, 892–905.

Folkman, S., & Moskowitz, J. T. (2000). Positive affect and the other side of coping. *American Psychologist, 55*(5), 547–554.

Franko, D. L., Thompson, D., Affenito, S. G., Barton, B. A., & Striegel-Moore, R. H. (2008). What mediates the relationship between family meals and adolescent health issues. *Health Psychology: Official Journal of the Division of Health Psychology, American Psychological Association, 27*(2 Suppl), S109–117. doi:10.1037/0278–6133.

Fredrickson, B. L., & Losada, M. F. (2005). Positive affect and the complex dynamics of human flourishing. *American Psychologist, 60*, 678–686.

Fulkerson, J. A., Neumark-Sztainer, D., & Story, M. (2006a). Adolescent and parent views of family meals. *Journal of the American Dietetic Association, 106*, 526–532. doi:10.1016/j.jada.2006.01.006.

Fulkerson, J. A., Story, M., Mellin, A., Leffert, N., Neumark-Sztainer, D., & French, S. A. (2006b). Family dinner meal frequency and adolescent development: Relationships with developmental assets and high-risk behaviors. *The Journal of Adolescent Health: Official Publication of the Society for Adolescent Medicine, 39*, 337–345. doi:10.1016/j.jadohealth.2005.12.026.

Gelles, R. J., & Maynard, P. E. (1987). A structural family systems approach to intervention in cases of family violence. *Family Relations, 38*, 270–275.

Goldberg, S., Grusec, J. E., & Jenkins, J. M. (1999). Confidence in protection: Arguments for a narrow definition of attachment. *Journal of Family Psychology, 13*, 475–483. doi:10.1037/0893-3200.13.4.475.

Haight, W. (1998). "Gathering the spirit" at First Baptist Church: Spirituality as a protective factor in the lives of African American children. *Social Work, 43*, 213–221.

Hammack, P. L., Robinson, W. L., Crawford, I., & Li, S. T. (2004). Poverty and depressed mood among urban African-American adolescents: A family stress perspective. *Journal of Child and Family Studies, 13*, 309–323.

Hernandez, P., Gangsei, D., & Engstrom, D. (2007). Vicarious resilience: A new concept in work with those who survive trauma. *Family Process, 46*, 229–241.

Hill, J., Fonagy, P., Safier, E., & Sargent, J. (2003). The ecology of attachment in the family. *Family Process, 42*, 205–221.

Hill, N. E., & Herman-Stahl, M. A. (2002). Neighborhood safety and social involvement: Associations with parenting behaviors and depressive symptoms among African-American and Euro-American mothers. *Journal of Family Psychology, 16*, 209–219.

Hill, R. (1958). Generic features of families under stress. *Social Casework, 49*, 139–150.

Hobfoll, S. E. (1989). Conservation of resources: A new attempt at conceptualizing stress. *The American Psychologist, 44*, 513–524.

Hobfoll, S. E., & Lilly, R. S. (1993). Resource conservation as a strategy for community psychology. *Journal of Community Psychology, 21*, 128–148.

Hobfoll, S. E., Lilly, R. S., & Jackson, A. P. (1992). Conservation of social resources and the self. In H. O. F. Veiel & U. Baumann (Eds.), *The meaning and measurement of social support* (pp. 125–141). Washington, DC: Hemisphere.

Hobfoll, S. E., Johnson, R. J., Ennis, N. E, & Jackson, A. P. (2003). Resource loss, resource gain, and emotional outcomes among inner-city women. *Journal of Personality and Social Psychology, 84*, 632–643.

Howes, P. W., Cicchetti, D., Toth, S. L., & Rogosch, F. A. (2000). Affective, organizational, and relational characteristics of maltreating families: A systems perspective. *Journal of Family Psychology, 14*, 95–110.

Imber-Black, E. (1988). Ritual themes in families and family therapy. In E. Imber-Black, J. Roberts, & R. Whiting (Eds.), *Rituals in families and family therapy* (pp. 47–83). New York: W. W. Norton & Co.

Imber-Black, E., Roberts, J., & Whiting, R. (Eds.) (2003). *Rituals in families and family therapy* (2nd ed.). New York: W. W. Norton & Co.

Johnson, D. M., Palmieri, P. A., Jackson, A. P., & Hobfoll, S. E. (2007). Emotional numbing weakens abused inner-city women's resiliency resources. *Journal of Traumatic Stress, 20*, 197–206.

Johnson, D. R., Feldman, S. C., Lubin, H., & Southwick, S. M. (1995). The therapeutic use of ritual and ceremony in the treatment of post-traumatic stress disorder. *Journal of Traumatic Stress, 8*, 283–298.

Kazak, A. E. (1989). Families of chronically ill children: A systems and social-ecological model of adaptation and challenge. *Journal of Consulting and Clinical Psychology, 57*, 25–30.

Kelly, Y., Kelly, J., & Sacker, A. (2013). Changes in bedtime schedules and behavioral difficulties in 7-year-old children. *Pediatrics, 132*, 1184–1193. doi:10.1542/peds. 2013-1906.

Kiser, L. J. (2006). Protecting children from the dangers of urban poverty. *Clinical Psychology Review, 27*, 211–225.

Kiser, L. J., Ostoja, E., & Pruitt, D. B. (1998). Dealing with stress and trauma in families. In B. Pfefferbaum (Ed.). *Stress in Children*. Child and Adolescent Psychiatric Clinics of North America, 7, 87–104.

Kiser, L. J., Bennett, L., Heston, J. D., & Paavola, M. (2005). Family ritual and routine: Comparing clinical and non-clinical families. *Journal of Child and Family Studies, 14*, 357–372.

Larson, R. W., Branscomb, K. R., & Wiley, A. R. (2006). Forms and functions of family mealtimes: Multi-disciplinary perspectives. *New Directions for Child and Adolescent Development, 111*, 1–15.

Leproult, R., & Van Cauter, E. (2010). Role of sleep and sleep loss in hormonal release and metabolism. *Endocrine Development, 17*, 11–21. doi:10.1159/000262524.

McCubbin, M. (1995). The typology model of adjustment and adaptation: A family stress model. *Guidance & Counseling, 10*(4), 1–27.

McCubbin, M. A., & McCubbin, H. I. (1993). Families coping with illness: The resiliency model of family stress, adjustment, and adaptation. In C. B. Danielson (Ed.), *Families, health, & illness* (pp. 21–63). St. Louis, MO: Mosby-Year Book.

McEwen, B. S. (1998). Stress, adaptation, and disease: Allostasis and allostatic load. *Annals of the New York Academy of Science, 840*, 33–44. doi:10.1111/i.1749-6632.1998.tb09546.x.

Markson, S., & Fiese, B. H. (2000). Family rituals as a protective factor for children with asthma. *Journal of Pediatric Psychology, 25*, 471–480.

Masten, A. (2001). Ordinary magic: Resilience processes in development. *American Psychologist, 56*, 227–238.

Meyer, A. L., & Lausell, L. (1996). The value of including a higher power in efforts to prevent violence and promote optimal outcomes during adolescence. In R. L. Hampton & P. Jenkins (Eds.), *Preventing violence in America: Issues in children's and families' lives, Vol. 4* (pp. 115–132). Thousand Oaks, CA: Sage.

Meyers, S. A., Varkey, S., & Aguirre, A. M. (2002). Ecological correlates of family functioning. *American Journal of Family Therapy, 30*, 257–273.

Monson, C. M., & Friedman, M. J. (2006). Back to the future of understanding trauma: Implications for cognitive-behavioral therapies for trauma. In V. M. Follette & J. I. Ruzek (Eds.), *Cognitive behavioral therapies for trauma* (pp. 1–13). New York: The Guilford Press.

Neumark-Sztainer, D., Hannan, P. J., Story, M., Croll, J., & Perry, C. (2003). Family meal patterns: Associations with sociodemographic characteristics and improved dietary intake among adolescents. *Journal of the American Dietetic Association, 103*, 317–322. doi:10.1053/jada.2003.50048.

Neumark-Sztainer, D., Wall, M., Story, M., & Fulkerson, J. A. (2004). Are family meal patterns associated with disordered eating behaviors among adolescents? *The Journal of Adolescent Health: Official Publication of the Society for Adolescent Medicine, 35*, 350–359. doi:10.1016/j.jadohealth.2004.01.004.

Niska, K., Snyder, M., & Lia-Hoagber, B. (1998). Family ritual facilitates adaptation to parenthood. *Public Health Nursing, 15*, 329–337.

Park, C. L., & Folkman, S. (1997). Meaning in the context of stress and coping. *Review of General Psychology, 2*, 115–144.

Parker, R. J. (1999). The art of blessing: Teaching parents to create rituals. *Professional School Counseling, 2,* 218–225.

Patterson, J. M. (1991). A family systems perspective for working with youth with disability. *Pediatrician, 18,* 129–141.

Patterson, J. M. (2002). Integrating family resilience and family stress theory. *Journal of Marriage and Family, 64,* 349–360.

Peacock, E. J., & Wong, P. T. P. (1996). Anticipatory stress: The relation of locus of control, optimism, and control appraisals to coping. *Journal of Research in Personality, 30,* 204–222.

Pett, M., & Lang, N. (1992). Late-life divorce. *Journal of Family Issues, 13,* 525–552.

Portes, P. R., Howell, S. C., Brown, J. H., Eichenberger, S., & Mas, C. A. (1992). Family functions and children's postdivorce adjustment. *American Journal of Orthopsychiatry, 52,* 513–517.

Resnick, M. D., Bearman, P. S., Blum, R. W., Bauman, K. E., Harris, K. M., Jones, J., Tabor, J., Beuhring, T., Sieving, R. E., Shew, M., Ireland, M., Bearinger, L. H., & Udry, J. R. (1997). Protecting adolescents from harm: Findings from the national longitudinal study on adolescent health. *Journal of the American Medical Association, 278,* 823–832.

Roberts, J. (1988). Setting the frame: Definition, functions, and typology of rituals. In E. Imber-Black, J. Roberts, & R. Whiting (Eds.), *Rituals in families and family therapy* (pp. 3–45). New York: W. W. Norton & Company.

Rogers, J. C., & Holloway, R. L. (1991). Family rituals and the care of individual patients. *Family System Medicine, 9,* 249–259.

Sadeh, A., Gruber, R., & Raviv, A. (2003). The effects of sleep restriction and extension on school-age children: What a difference an hour makes. *Child Development, 74,* 444–455.

Saltzman, W. R., Lester, P., Beardslee, W. R., Layne, C. M., Woodward, K., & Nash, W. P. (2011). Mechanisms of risk and resilience in military families: Theoretical and empirical basis of a family-focused resilience enhancement program. *Clinical Child and Family Psychology Review, 14,* 213–230. doi:10.1007/s10567-011-0096-1.

Schuck, L. A., & Bucy, J. E. (1997). Family rituals: Implications for early intervention. *Early Childhood Special Education, 17,* 477–494.

Schulkin, J. (2011). Social allostasis: Anticipatory regulation of the internal milieu. *Frontiers in Evolutionary Neuroscience, 2,* 1–15. doi:10.3389/fnev0.2010.00111.

Seligman, M., & Csikszentmihalyi, M. (2000). Positive psychology: An introduction. *American Psychologist, 55,* 5–14.

Seligman, M., Steen, T. A., Park, N., & Peterson C. (2005). Positive psychology progress: Empirical validation of interventions. *American Psychologist, 60,* 410–421.

Shapiro, E. R. (1994). *Grief as a family process.* New York: The Guilford Press.

Shochet, I., & Dadds, M. (1997). When individual child psychotherapy exacerbates family systems problems in child abuse cases: A clinical analysis. *Clinical Child Psychology & Psychiatry, 2,* 239–249.

Spagnola, M., & Fiese, B. (2007). Family routines and rituals: A context for development in the lives of young children. *Infants & Young Children, 20,* 284–299.

Spiegel, K., Leproult, R., & Van Cauter, E. (1999). Impact of sleep debt on metabolic and endocrine function. *Lancet, 354,* 1435–1439.

Sroufe, L. A., & Waters, B. (1977). Attachment as an organizational construct. *Child Development, 49,* 1184–1199.

Steenari, M., Vuontela, V., Paavonen, J., Carlson, S., Fjallberg, M., & Aronen, E. T. (2003). Working memory and sleep in 6- to 13-year-old schoolchildren. *Journal of the American Academy of Child & Adolescent Psychiatry, 42,* 85–92.

Streeck-Fischer, A., & van der Kolk, B. A. (2000). Down will come baby, cradle and all: Diagnostic and therapeutic implications of chronic trauma on child development. *Australian & New Zealand Journal of Psychiatry, 34,* 903–918.

Taylor, S. E. (2011). Social support: A review. In M. S. Friedman (Ed.), *The handbook of health psychology* (pp. 189–214). New York: Oxford University Press.

Tedeschi, R. G., & Calhoun, L. G. (2004). Posttraumatic growth: Conceptual foundations and empirical evidence. *Psychological Inquiry, 15*, 1–18.

Tininenko, J. R., Fisher, P. A., Bruce, J., & Pears, K. C. (2010). Sleep disruption in young foster children. *Child Psychiatry & Human Development, 41*, 409–424. doi:10.1007/s10578-010-0177-2.

Toth, S. L., Maughan, A., Manly, J. T., Spagnola, M., & Cicchetti, D. (2002). The relative efficacy of two interventions in altering maltreated preschool children's representational models: Implications for attachment theory. *Developmental Psychopathology, 14*, 877–908.

Uchino, B. (2009). Understanding the links between social support and physical health: A life-span perspective with emphasis on the separability of perceived and received support. *Perspectives on Psychological Science, 4*, 236–255.

van der Hart, O., Witztum, E., & de Voogt, A. (1988). Myths and rituals: Anthropological views and their application in strategic family therapy. *Journal of Psychotherapy & the Family, 4*, 57–80.

Van Reeth, O., Weibel, L., Spiegel, K., Leproult, R., Dugovic, C., & Maccari, S. (2000). Interactions between stress and sleep: from basic research to clinical situations. *Sleep Medicine Reviews, 4*, 201–219.

Walsh, F. (2006). *Strengthening family resilience* (2nd ed.). New York: The Guilford Press.

Winje, D. (1998). Cognitive coping: The psychological significance of knowing what happened in the traumatic event. *Journal of Traumatic Stress, 11*, 627–643.

Wolin, S. J., & Bennett, L. A. (1984). Family rituals. *Family Process, 23*, 401–420.

Wolin, S. J., Bennett, L. A., & Noonan, D. L. (1979). Family rituals and the recurrence of alcoholism over generations. *American Journal of Psychiatry, 135*(4B), 589–593.

CHAPTER 4
STORYTELLING AND NARRATIVE IN SFCR

The world, the human world, is bound together not by protons and electrons, but by stories. Nothing has meaning in itself: all the objects in the world would be shards of bare mute blankness, spinning wildly out of orbit, if we didn't bind them together with stories.

(Brian Morton, *Starting Out in the Evening*, in Schoemperlen, 2000, p. 141)

Storytelling is a notable part of normal family ritual and routine life. Storytelling also provides a natural healing resource for families who have experienced trauma (Figley & Kiser, 2013). In SFCR, we make use of this valuable resource as families explore and hone their storytelling capacities throughout the intervention, leading, for many families, to the co-construction of a family trauma narrative.

BACKGROUND FOR FAMILY STORYTELLING AND NARRATIVE[1]

As a foundation for incorporating storytelling and narration in therapy, SFCR facilitators need to:

1. understand the functions and benefits of family storytelling;
2. be familiar with the skills that family members use in the act of telling stories;
3. be aware of the impact of traumatic experience on family stories and on the family's capacity to engage in storytelling; and
4. be familiar with the use of narrative as a core therapeutic strategy in trauma treatment.

An important *note* for SFCR facilitators is the distinction between family storytelling, narrative, and family trauma narrative. In SFCR, storytelling or storying is the routine process that families use to share experiences, while narrative implies a facilitated sharing of experiences. Family trauma narrative involves a co-constructed story with a specific focus on the family's experience of trauma. All forms can be part of the healing process.

Functions and Benefits of Family Storytelling

Families tell stories for so many reasons:

- Family stories are a vehicle for translating individual experience into a jointly held version of life events. As each family member shares his or her individual perspective about what happened, how it felt, and why it happened, individual moments become intertwined and lose their separateness. As family stories unfold, family members get to know one another intimately.

- The act of telling family stories has important benefits for processing shared experiences. Family stories improve memory for events, help fill in gaps in the story, and correct misinformation. Sharing family stories helps with joint appraisal and interpretation of events. Family storytelling is linked with co-regulating emotional reactions tied to events and with experiencing empathy and support for any pain the story reveals. Finally, telling family stories involves joint problem-solving and implementing collaborative coping strategies (Habermas & Bluck, 2000; Lantz & Gyamerah, 2002; Salmon & Bryant, 2002).

- Families construct and share stories to create an identity as a unit. Family stories pass along information about who the family is and the way the family acts. For example, family stories teach children about family roles and relationships. Stories shared with children about their early years teach them about their place and emotional value in the family, fostering a sense of belonging. If individual narrative is important to autobiographical understanding, in other words, tying memory to self-understanding, family stories serve a similar purpose by tying shared remembrances to a sense of belonging (Vollmer, 2005).

- Families tell stories to record their history and preserve the memories of previous generations. This family history, as recorded in story, chronicles significant events in the family's past and preserves the legacies of notable (famous and infamous) ancestors.

- Family stories create shared meaning (Hill, Fonagy, Safier, & Sargent, 2003). Through storying, family members strive to reach a common explanation, based on their values and beliefs, for why things happen. As family members process experiences as a unit, they develop a shared or joint frame of reference. They begin to interpret experiences and their meaning in a manner that is congruent with this family identity.

- Families tell stories to communicate their beliefs, values, aspirations, and life lessons (Fiese & Wamboldt, 2003). Through retelling stories, families pass their core beliefs from generation to generation.

- Families use this testimony of their history to anticipate their future. Stories allow families to look beyond their past and present experience. They allow families to interpret events based upon the past while at the same time envisioning a shared future.

Research affirms the longer-term value of both telling and knowing family stories (Bohanek et al., 2009; Fivush, Bohanek, & Zaman, 2010; Fivush, Duke, & Bohanek, 2010; Marin, Bohanek, & Fivush, 2008; Sales & Fivush, 2005). Children and adolescents who participate in family storytelling and who know the information contained in family stories have higher self-esteem, higher internal locus of control, and are better able to articulate and regulate emotions than youth from families less engaged in storytelling. In terms of mental health, youth demonstrate lower levels of anxiety and fewer behavior problems when they participate in family storytelling compared to youth who have fewer experiences with storying. Further, these same youth engage in fewer risky behaviors and experience better outcomes when faced with stressors.

Families who engage in storytelling and whose members are knowledgeable about their family's history report more family traditions and better functioning. Since storytelling is also a relational process, positive caregiver-child relations and family cohesion are reported.

FAMILY STORYTELLING SKILLS

Sharing family stories happens as a routine part of daily family life. Families tell stories to each other as they sit together at meals, as they share leisure time, and as they come together for special family events. Even so, family storytelling is a fairly complex process requiring many interdependent skills. With repetition, families develop their storytelling abilities.

Families tell stories throughout SFCR. Facilitators have the great honor of hearing these stories. Facilitators also use the storytelling activities as opportunities for observing the family's storytelling skills. Facilitators then help families build upon these skills and use them in the healing process. While helping families gain skills in storying, it is necessary to consider the narrative abilities and styles of each family member, the interactive style of multiple family subsystems, and also the family as a whole. A review of family storytelling skills will direct SFCR facilitators' attention to those skills of central importance.

Family storytelling comprises practicing characteristics and representing characteristics (Pratt & Fiese, 2004). Both characteristics involve complex skill sets for the family to practice.

Practicing characteristics involve the act of storytelling, such patterns of practice as who tells which parts of the story and the rules that the family has for listening. Practicing characteristics differ from family to family. They may also change depending on the content of the story being told (Pratt & Fiese, 2004).

Practicing characteristics involve: (1) the form that a story takes; (2) the listening skills used; and (3) the rules for co-construction.

First, the story being told has to communicate enough information in a recognizable form, that of a typical family story and that of a family story that belongs to a particular family. Family narratives, just as personal narratives, must include referential elements (characters, plots), context with enough orienting information, temporal sequencing, and relevant information that ties the story in important or interesting ways to the family. To be of interest, most family stories include a plot twist along with efforts to reach a resolution that is consistent with the family's beliefs and hopes for the future.

A recognizable family story requires a *sense of autobiographical coherence*—in other words, it must be obvious to the family how the main characters, the context, and the plot of the story are part of a normal family story (Habermas & Bluck, 2000).

Not only do family members need to be familiar with the form of the story, but, as the story is being told, it must be obvious who the main characters are and why they are being included in the story or, alternatively, the main events need to be understood as pertinent to the family. This is the *evaluative component* (Dallos, 2004).

The recognizable form of the family story provides a way to attach *semantic meaning* to experiential memories. As the family talks about what occurred, they are able to label and name the experience. They are converting memories into words.

Second, the family must practice various listening skills, including synoptic, credulous, and empathic listening (Nwoye, 2006).

Synoptic listening allows family members to hear and appreciate multiple perspectives. It involves acceptance of the fact that every family member will have different perceptions and points of view about events, even those events experienced together.

When family members use *credulous listening*, they are able to listen to the story without criticizing, judging, or correcting. Two aspects of credulous listening are important. One involves giving the orator the floor and letting him or her tell the story without interruption. Credulous listening also allows the storyteller to proceed with the belief that those hearing the story will accept it as accurately representing his or her perspective, even if they do not see things in exactly the same way.

Empathic listening also supports family storytelling. When family members use empathic listening, the storyteller has permission to express feelings with the expectation that those listening will accept them and will also help him or her manage them.

Third, family storytelling occurs within a relational context that requires that the stories are co-constructed, not simply told by one family member. This process requires an additional set of skills, including a collaborative style, a coordinated perspective, collaborative problem-solving, co-regulation of affect, and reflectivity.

One important aspect of family storytelling is the style used by the family (Bohanek, Marin, Fivush, & Duke, 2006). When families use a *collaborative style*, they can co-construct a story that joins together the voices of all family members and allow a shared meaning to emerge. A collaborative style requires managing the storytelling process so that all voices are heard.

As families seek to reach a *coordinated perspective*, each family member determines what part of his or her lived experience is pertinent to the family story. Family members then decide together which moments of their personal experiences fit with and help define their family. "Several perspectives are taken, and most important, parents structure and integrate these different perspectives for a more complex understanding of one's own perspective, the perspective of others, and the integration of the self with others" (Bohanek et al., 2006, p. 48).

Co-constructing a story that belongs to the whole family necessitates *collaborative problem-solving*. Using skills such as balancing power, influence, control, and negotiation, the family can structure the storytelling process so that all voices are heard, not just the most influential, and multiple points of view are negotiated to reach a shared perspective (Besley, 2002).

Co-construction also demands *co-regulation of affect*. As emotional expression is incorporated into the storyline, family members work together to make sure that the affect is consistent with the content of the story, that the intensity of the affect expressed is tolerable, and that it remains within the bounds of familial/cultural norms.

Finally, achieving a co-constructed story involves reflective processes. *Reflectivity* implies how each individual feels about the story being told while at the same time considering how others in the family might have experienced the situation, how they might have felt, and why they felt or acted the way they did (Singer & Rexhaj, 2006).

Representing characteristics involve the meaning-making aspects of storytelling. This includes how family members make sense of the content and their understanding of how the story relates to the family's beliefs and values. Through representing characteristics, families communicate messages about what is important and about their worldview (Pratt & Fiese, 2004). "Meaning is not a stable entity but an outcome of relational negotiations in a particular context" (Penn, 2001, p. 44). Family storytelling provides a platform for conveying meaning but also for reaching agreement about the meaning. Through storytelling, families often develop a dominant theme that becomes central to their family identity.

As with practicing characteristics, making meaning through storytelling involves a set of skills and abilities, including a joint frame, coherence, and storytelling agility.

Families use a *joint frame* or established family schemas to make sense of their stories. The shared frame involves "the interpretations and views that have been collectively constructed by family members as they interact with each other; as they share time, space, and life experience, and as they talk about these experiences" (Patterson, 2002, p. 355). The joint frame is not owned by an individual family member; rather, it "is a characteristic of the 'system' that has established them" (Hill et al., 2003, p. 210). The shared frame provides a shorthand for appraising and interpreting the events or situations being storied within the context of the beliefs, values, and important life lessons of the family system and of the larger sociocultural context. Joint frame develops through (Hill et al., 2003):

- past experience with each other in similar situations;
- individual appraisals of events;
- observing the reactions of other family members; and
- considering the effect of one's own responses on others.

To achieve *coherence*, family stories need to possess a goal structure, explanatory significance, thematic consistency, and causal coherence.

Part of the meaning that is made of family stories reflects a *goal structure*. The goal structure helps family members understand how the story fits within the hopes and the ambitions that the family holds.

To achieve *explanatory significance*, the story needs to include details about:

> why events happened to the family, or how an event is similar/dissimilar to other experiences in the family's history, and how the storied event links with other events along the family timeline. By making these connections, the family ties together discrete scenes across the family cycle to explain who they are (Dimaggio & Semerari, 2001).
>
> (Kiser et al., 2010, p. 245)

Thematic consistency is also necessary for coherence and ensures that the story's message is compatible with the family's beliefs and values (Habermas & Bluck, 2000). Family stories typically reveal certain themes that are reflective of the family's identity. The themes that family stories relate to are often fairly constant over time.

Family storytelling allows the family to add their explanations for why things happen. Typically, these explanations are based on what has happened in the past, the family's worldview, and the family's basic belief system. A story with *causal coherence* provides sufficient explanation for how the story is consistent with the family's views or how it reflects changes in family meaning making (Habermas & Bluck, 2000).

Finally, *storytelling agility* encourages the family to think beyond their dominant theme when necessary. When families use storytelling agility, they remain open to supposing what else might have happened, how else they might have acted, or how else they may have felt. "Agility allows family members to hear or imagine the untold stories, the different possible versions of the stories being told, the options that are not included as the story unfolds, or the alternative endings (Hester, 2004)" (Kiser et al., 2010, p. 245).

EMERGING CAPACITIES AND FAMILY STORYTELLING[2]

Since family storytelling must include the voices of family members of all ages, helping families develop storytelling skills involves negotiating the capacities of family members at various skill levels and appreciating how older and younger family members work together to co-create their story. Importantly, these are interdependent processes as, for instance, the narrative style of the family influences the developing narrative abilities of the children.

The ability to tell a story emerges from a relational context. Secure attachment between an infant and his or her primary caregivers fosters many storytelling skills, including experiential learning, referencing and perspective, empathy, language development, reasoning, and reflectivity, and shapes a child's ability to regulate (Kagan & Herschkowitz, 2005). Joint attention, which matures gradually within the attachment relationship during the first 16–20 months of life, provides a foundation for co-constructing stories. Consider the four fundamental components of joint attention and their significance for storytelling: (1) interacting with a social partner; (2) to share an experience; (3) through coordinated attention to an object (or event); (4) with mutual affect (Carpenter, Nagell, Tomasello, Butterworth, & Moore, 1998; Liszkowski, Carpenter, Henning, Striano, & Tomasello, 2004).

Children rely on conversations with adults to learn storytelling skills. Children as young as two years old begin to talk about past events (Hudson, 1990). Caregivers and older siblings play a role in scaffolding these narrative productions by asking questions that prompt young orators, for example, to add needed context or to sequence events from beginning to end.

Within another year or two, by age 3 or 4 years, young children are often able to talk about events using the practicing components of storytelling, such as the setting, salient events, unexpected complications, and outcomes (Templeton & Wilcox, 2000). The stories of children this age sometimes seem to lack cohesion and chronology but rather provide insight into what is of interest to the child. However, these very early stories are heavily influenced by the jointly held frame of the caregivers. Children learn to tell stories that get their caregivers' attention.

The stories of young children illustrate their developing cognitive strategy of selectively attending to, or shifting attention away from, experience. Such selective attention makes important contributions to individual emotional organization and regulation (Oppenheim, Nir, Warren, & Emde, 1997).

At the next stage of development, the young elementary schoolchild is able to include the who, what, when, and where of the story. The stories of 5–7-year-old children move toward a goal with a reasoned progression of events and are set within a place and time. Children of this age also typically add some range of emotion vocabulary beyond the feelings of good and bad to their stories.

By the time children reach middle elementary age, 8–10 years, they usually understand more complex emotions and understand how to tell their story to another person by taking into account what they might want or need to know to make sense of the story.

After the age of 10 years, most children have attained cognitive and linguistic competence to effectively narrate a story at essentially an adult skill level. Children of this age demonstrate the ability to organize complex narrative material and to communicate it effectively to different audiences (Wigglesworth, 1997).

UNDERSTANDING THE IMPACT OF TRAUMA ON FAMILY STORIES

Utilizing a trauma-informed approach to working on family storytelling requires an understanding of how traumatic experiences can modify both the way families tell stories as well as the stories that they tell. Recall the adaptations that families make to chronic stress and repeated trauma and imagine how these adaptations might impact family stories. In trauma-organized family systems, both the practicing and representing characteristics of family storytelling are altered. A couple of examples illustrate the potential repercussions.

Families with complex trauma histories often cope with their anticipatory anxiety through avoidance. These families have likely given up on talking about or working through their traumas.

Unaddressed traumas impact *synoptic listening, reflectivity,* and *storytelling agility* (Briere & Scott, 2006). Being stuck in their own traumatic memories limits the capacity of family members to hear another's perspective, to think about how others might think or feel, or to imagine a different ending to the story. Without these critical skills and faced with painful reminders when retelling, some families stop sharing stories altogether.

Following exposure to accumulated traumatic circumstances, families often struggle to serve their regulatory function. Families who are dysregulated find storytelling difficult as they struggle with the skills related to co-construction. If the caregivers in the family have their own traumatic pasts and struggle to be attuned and regulated, they have difficulty helping their children learn these skills and structuring well-modulated family storytelling opportunities (Cook, Blaustein, Spinazzola, & van der Kolk, 2005; Green et al., 1991; Haden, 1998; Kinniburgh, Blaustein, Spinazzola, & van der Kolk, 2005; Laible & Thompson, 2000; Schechter et al., 2007; Valiente, Fabes, Eisenberg, & Spinrad, 2004).

Dealing with the affect contained in family stories is also particularly challenging. When family members are hyper-reactive, they have a hard time with *empathic listening* and with *co-regulation of affect.* As a result, family stories are often either devoid of affect or the emotions expressed are so extreme that they are overwhelming.

When family schemas or worldview are transformed by chronic, repeated, multigenerational patterns of exposure to stress and trauma, meaning making is also changed. Trauma often becomes the dominant theme or the *joint frame* and families see everything that happens to them through a trauma lens (Dallos, 2004). Negative worldviews and victim mentalities dictate the family understanding of what happens and why it happens (*explanatory significance*). "The dominance of a (post) traumatic identity can then be consolidated at personal and social levels, as it functions as an interpretive framework for integrating subsequent life experiences and relating and enacting them with others" (Neimeyer, Herrero, & Botella, 2006, p. 132).

Finally, when a family experiences trauma, their usual explanations for why things happen may not fit or be sufficient for understanding the catastrophic consequences of the event(s). *Causal coherence* can be threatened when the family experiences events that are so horrific that major changes in their beliefs, worldview, and life course are required for adaptation and explaining these changes in the family story may be too difficult and painful.

NARRATIVE: A THERAPEUTIC APPROACH[3]

In terms of faith, what brings meaning and integration to one's experience, the facts are quite secondary. It's the story (and not the facts) that grips the imagination, impregnates the heart, and animates the spirit within.

(Diarmuid O'Murchu, *Quantum Theology,* in Schoemperlen, 2000, p. 304)

Narrative therapeutic strategies are incorporated in evidenced-based practices in multiple areas of mental health, not just in trauma. Although the evidence supports the use of trauma-specific narrative work in supporting recovery from exposure to catastrophic events, curative effects can be achieved by narrative work that does not directly address trauma (Besley, 2002; Pennebaker, 1993).

The healing effects of *non-trauma-specific family narrative* might include:

- improving communication processes;
- relationship building and repair;

- increasing tolerance for affective expression;
- ability to talk about difficult issues;
- collaborative problem solving; and
- reflectivity.

For example, narrative therapy is based on the assumption that identity is socially constructed, co-created in relationships with others, and by one's culture (Bakhtin, 1981; Hermans & Dimaggio, 2004; Neimeyer et al., 2006). "We come to see ourselves by looking into the mirrors that other people hold up for us" (Sween, 1998, p. 5). So, by engaging in work to build narrative skills (both practicing and representing characteristics), families can better understand and appreciate each other. As family stories unfold, family members subtly influence each individual's identity while at the same time creating a stronger sense of belonging to the family.

A goal of family narrative is helping the family appreciate that each family member will have a different memory for what happened, even for an experience that was shared by all family members:

> Our lives are multistoried. There are many stories occurring at the same time and different stories can be told about the same events. No single story can be free of ambiguity or contradiction and no single story can encapsulate or handle all the contingencies of life.
>
> (Morgan, 2000)

With increased ability to tolerate different perspectives, families build capacity for tackling difficult and unresolved issues.

Multiple theories support the use of a *trauma-specific narrative* but often emphasize different functions:

- gradual exposure (approach versus avoid);
- desensitization/co-regulation;
- cognitive processing;
- reconstruction of the story; and
- integration of experience into coherent identity.

What is healing about constructing a trauma narrative? Is it telling the story to a sympathetic listener? Is it the cathartic effect of retelling? Is it finding meaning in the retelling? The answer depends on which theory or approach is used to structure the narrative work.

For example, trauma-focused cognitive behavioral therapy (TF-CBT), an evidence-based treatment for children and adolescents with trauma-related disorders, incorporates a trauma narrative as a technique for gradual exposure with response prevention (Cohen, Mannarino, & Deblinger, 2006). For gradual exposure to be effective, it is important for the individual to provide as many details of the trauma as possible within the safety of the therapy context, and to tell the story repeatedly, including writing down the details. Following construction of the detailed narrative, the therapist facilitates cognitive processing to correct errors and distortions.

Using a trauma narrative to promote gradual exposure is a technique that was developed and is best suited to address a single trauma, or at least a worst trauma, about which a single story can be told. For many families, multiple, chronic traumas are woven throughout their lives, so that it is not possible to isolate the worst trauma, but rather the trauma and the expectation of future trauma become central to the family storyline. For other families, who must continue to live in traumatic circumstances, the ongoing sense of threat makes detailing previous trauma(s) too frightening. In these situations, adaptations to using narrative as gradual exposure may be necessary.

Narrative work is also helpful for dealing with high levels of arousal when reminded of the trauma.

Individuals and entire families can become easily triggered if they think about or start to talk about traumatic experiences. The inability to tolerate thoughts and reminders is linked to physiological dysregulation or an automatic activating of the fight/flight/freeze response (McKeever & Huff, 2003). Narrative therapy allows the individual or family to tell the story of the trauma within a safe and modulated space. The narrative therapist serves as a co-regulator, aiding the speakers in maintaining a safe distance from the confusion, fear, and terror provoked by the actual experience.

Other theorists suggest that trauma narrative work may be helpful when the family is stuck and has come to view themselves as defined by their trauma story. In other words, their family identity is so linked to their trauma story that it ends up dictating how they view themselves, their future, and the world. Unable to see themselves as separate from their traumatic experiences, families may feel restricted in their view of the possibilities that lie ahead and may be uncertain of their ability to handle the future any differently than they have handled the past (Dallos, 2004). Their family story becomes dominated by trauma, by feeling overwhelmed and victimized.

In this case, trauma narrative therapy provides the curative opportunity for the teller to rework the experience. "Telling the story of the trauma pain allows the other family members to help you continue the story while changing the story line in a way that results in a better ending" (Lantz & Raiz, 2003, p. 169). Described as "intervention fantasies" by Pynoos, Steinberg, and Aronson (1997), re-working the trauma in story can "represent mental efforts to contend with or counter traumatic helplessness and injurious outcome" (p. 279). Additionally, as the family processes their trauma story, the narrative therapist works to elicit alternate stories that help explore coping, endurance, and survival.

Turning toward therapy approaches that emphasize meaning making, Pierre Janet asserted that consciousness is made up of "a unified memory of all psychological facets related to a particular experience: sensations, emotions, thoughts, and actions" (van der Kolk & van der Hart, 1989, p. 1532, citing Janet). Normally, a person integrates an experience into his or her memory system by cognitively interpreting the experience and verbally representing it as a cohesive personal narrative. However, frightening and novel events may not fit into existing cognitive schemas (van der Kolk & van der Hart, 1989; van der Kolk, Brown, & van der Hart, 1989). If an event is so overwhelming that the person becomes too upset to tell the story of what happened and to transform the event into a "neutral narrative," the trauma cannot be synthesized into the person's memory system or placed in context alongside other life experience.

This is central to understanding the use of narrative in meaning-making approaches. Attaching language to traumatic events helps to transform traumatic memories into narrative memories that can be integrated into the survivor's personal identity and into a coherent sense of self (van der Kolk & van der Hart, 1989; van der Kolk et al., 1989; Vollmer, 2005). "Embedding experience in a narrative is a fundamental way of making sense of it" (Habermas & Bluck, 2000, p. 749). From a family perspective, telling the story provides a means for reaching a collective sense of meaning and a coherent sense of family.

FACILITATING STORYTELLING AND NARRATIVE IN SFCR

To facilitate family storytelling and narration, SFCR facilitators need to:

1. monitor family storytelling capacities and assist each family in strengthening them when necessary;
2. plan a therapeutic narrative process with each family; and
3. conduct family narrative sessions in a safe manner that permits healing.

Overview of Storytelling in SFCR

SFCR incorporates storytelling as a natural resource for healing. Families have multiple opportunities to tell stories throughout the treatment. Storytelling activity begins in the earliest sessions with families asked to share simple stories about their family life. Such storytelling activities require families to think about their relevant experiences or their memory bank of stories in order to agree on a story to tell. Families then have the opportunity to practice either constructing or telling a story.

In the very first SFCR-MFG session on storytelling, the practice of storytelling is made universal by introducing families to a myth about how stories were brought to earth from the gods. Facilitators share the story of Ananse, the Spider Man (*A Story, A Story*, by Gail E. Hailey). All stories belonged to the sky god who kept them safely in a golden box beside his throne. Ananse had to make a deal with the sky god to bring them to earth. After successfully meeting the three challenges that the sky god posed, Ananse brought all stories back to earth to share.

Examples of the storytelling activities in SFCR include:

Positive Family Story

Facilitator. I am willing to bet that each and every family here has some great stories to tell. Tonight, we are going to get a chance to hear some of those stories. Please gather your families around and get comfortable. Now spend a few minutes thinking about something good that the whole family experienced together in the past few years. Once you have decided on something good that happened to your family, discuss this event. Just pretend that you were sitting around and someone brought it up.

Mildly Stressful Family Story

Facilitator. Tonight, we are going to get a chance to hear some more family stories. Please gather your families around and get comfortable. Now spend a few minutes thinking about a time that something a little bit scary or mildly stressful happened to your family over the past two to three years. Once you have decided on something to talk about, just pretend that you were sitting around and someone brought it up.

Visioning Family Story

Facilitator. To end the session, let's tell another story. Tell a story that represents a "vision statement" for your family. Remember, this is what you imagine and can plan for yourselves in the future.

Importantly, as families practice telling stories, facilitators take note of the storytelling skills that they are using. As they become familiar with the family's narrative style, facilitators may offer suggestions or make recommendations designed to improve the family's ability to tell stories.

Planning for Family Narrative Work

Module III of SFCR comprises narrative therapy sessions. Having practiced storytelling in multiple sessions and built a number of new coping skills, families participate in co-constructing narratives.

In the MFG format, all families begin the narrative phase at the same time. However, each family will be at a somewhat different point in their readiness to engage in the narrative process.

A careful planning process is necessary to make sure that the narrative work done in SFCR meets the needs of the family and can be done safely. This planning process involves several steps. First, the facilitator reviews the family case, taking into account their knowledge of the family's trauma history and their observations of the family's storytelling skills demonstrated in earlier sessions. Completion of the "Family Narrative Guide for Facilitators" provides a framework for this review. Case conferences with the treatment team can be an important part of this step.

Between Modules II and III, a treatment conference should be held to discuss each family who will be co-constructing a narrative. This meeting is important for planning the family work involved in Module III, including timing of the narrative, strategies for working with the family and with each individual family member, and communication of potential issues that might arise as the family moves through creation of a shared family trauma story. Facilitators should discuss this information as a team as they plan the sessions in Module III. Inclusion of input from other clinicians or case managers who are working with the family is often helpful.

Once the facilitator has this basic formulation completed, it is time to engage the family in a shared decision-making process about how to proceed. The facilitator begins by reminding the family of the importance of the narrative process in healing. After explaining what other families have found helpful, the facilitator helps the family identify their own goals for the family narrative process.

Designing a Safe Narrative Experience

The Family Narrative Planning Decision Tree helps direct the design of a safe, therapeutic experience (see Figure 4.1). The first decision that the facilitator and family must make is whether the narrative work will focus on storytelling skill building or on specific discourse about trauma.

This decision involves consideration of the following:

- Are the family's storytelling skills able to support a trauma narrative process?
- Where are family members in their reactions or course of recovery?
- Is there dyssynchrony that will affect the narrative process? Is everyone in the family ready to talk about the trauma?
- Are there triggered reactions that could create crisis for the family?

Storytelling Skill Building

Because both practicing characteristics and representing characteristics are affected by trauma, working with families to bolster their skills may, in and of itself, be curative and may serve them well in dealing with potential new traumas (Bohanek et al., 2006). If the family is not ready to, or does not have the requisite skills to, co-construct a trauma narrative safely and therapeutically, the narrative sessions should focus on building storytelling skills.

If this is the case, choosing storytelling skill-building activities is next. The facilitator joins with the family to decide on a set of skills that will build the family's capacity for talking about difficult and unresolved issues and will prepare the family to deal more effectively with stressful and traumatic situations that might arise in the future. Families can work on practicing skills, such as perspective

➜ FIGURE 4.1 Family Narrative Decision Tree

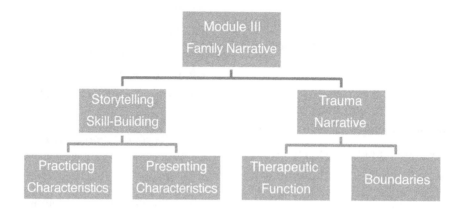

taking or listening. They can also build representing skills by engaging in therapeutic activities such as chronicling their family history, completing values clarification exercises, discussing moral dilemmas, or sharing stories about family heroes and villains.

Trauma Narrative

If the family is going to proceed with a trauma narrative, determining the therapeutic function and boundaries of the trauma narrative process is a major step, critical to doing this work without causing harm.

Making decisions about function and boundaries requires considering questions such as:

Function

- To what extent is the family avoidant or aroused when thinking or talking about what happened?
- What processing of the trauma has the family already done?
- In what ways has the trauma significantly changed the family?

Boundaries

- Which traumatic event(s) need to be incorporated in the narrative?
- Which trauma to begin with and how to sequence the discussion?
- Whether all family members are aware of the details of the event(s)?
- Whether discussion of certain specifics should be limited?
- Whether there are family secrets related to the trauma and what purpose the secrets are filling?
- What developmental differences, readiness issues, and dyssynchronies will need to be addressed?

A typical trauma narrative process might proceed in following manner. The family begins by talking about a trauma. As the family talks about what happened, they improve their memories of the event by filling in any missing pieces and by correcting any misinformation. The family continues this process by clarifying interpretations and attributions. The family works to jointly appraise what happened and to bring each individual family member's perceptions of the trauma into alignment with the shared family story. As they add affect to their storyline, they have the opportunity to hear each other's pain and to develop empathy for how each family member felt. After telling the story, the family explores their beliefs about why the trauma happened to them and comes to a shared sense of meaning. They conclude their narrative process by finding ways to work through the trauma and build an understanding of how their experience has changed their family for better and for worse.

But each family's narrative may emphasize a different part of this process. By determining the therapeutic function of the trauma narrative process that is most consistent with the family's objectives, trauma history, and previous treatment, the facilitator and family can make the best decisions about what to emphasize.

Establishing appropriate boundaries is necessary to prevent vicarious traumatization. Vicarious trauma occurs when family members become distressed hearing the trauma survivor tell about the trauma as the experience becomes incorporated into the family story (Figley, 1988). To protect family members, families decide what traumatic event(s) they can talk about safely, how much detail about these events will be shared, and who will be included in hearing about which traumas.

Once the narrative planning is complete, facilitators can begin the narrative work knowing how best to meet the family's needs. They can outline specific storytelling skills that will increase the family's ability to communicate effectively. If the family is proceeding with a trauma narrative, the facilitator begins with a clearer appreciation about how to help the family co-construct their trauma story safely. The facilitator, as well as the family, will be aware of the specific function of the narrative and also the necessary boundaries.

Conducting Narrative Sessions in SFCR

Use of narrative therapy is an accepted component of individual trauma treatments (Silverman et al., 2008; Wethington et al., 2008). However, in SFCR, we apply this therapeutic approach with families impacted by trauma. Facilitating the co-construction of a family narrative is a complex process. It requires many of the same skills used when assisting individuals with narrative, but must be approached from a systemic framework. When working with a family, the facilitator must recognize and harness the varied skills and multiple perspectives of each individual family member, honor the boundaries and hierarchies that support family subsystem functioning, and monitor for dyssynchronous individual reactions or stages of recovery.

Facilitators conducting narrative sessions in SFCR utilize the following strategies and techniques:

- Deal with the potential for the family to avoid the narrative phase

Avoidance is a hallmark symptom of traumatic stress disorders. Many families will participate actively in Modules I and II, but when faced with the task of telling their story they may start missing sessions. Facilitators should directly address the potential for avoidance by providing psychoeducation about it, anticipating that families may feel some avoidance, assuring families that they are now prepared for the narrative work, and problem-solving how to overcome their avoidance.

- Review and use each family's new skill sets

Families have learned new skills during Modules I and II that prepare them to engage in the narrative process. For example, families have practiced co-regulation strategies in many sessions and hopefully developed a regulation routine that they carry out regularly at home. The facilitator will want to review the stress inoculation techniques that each family has used successfully at the beginning of the narrative process. This helps to assure them that the narrative work can be accomplished without family members becoming overwhelmed. It also helps to reinforce the shared responsibility of the caregivers and the facilitator for their co-regulation function.

The families have also had practice with storytelling during early sessions. Facilitators scaffold and bolster the family's natural storytelling capacities to support their co-construction efforts. Structuring communication processes during the narrative helps the family stay on track and well modulated. During the initial narrative session, the family develops a list of communication rules that they will practice. This list could detail turn-taking guidelines, use of listening skills conducive to a healthy narrative process, inclusion of all family members, respect for individual perspectives, no name calling or verbally abusive language, etc. Families may need frequent reminders of the rules that they have established, especially if their communication style is drastically different during typical interactions.

- Help the family titrate experience so it is not too overwhelming

The facilitator constantly monitors the cues expressed by all family members for indications of dysregulation. Attention to both verbal and non-verbal communications increases the likelihood of attuned and regulated interactions. Adults are typically more focused on verbalizations and may miss significant nonverbal cues from their children, especially the youngest family members. The facilitator helps the caregivers both recognize and respond appropriately to these cues. This

co-regulation function is incorporated throughout the narrative process.

In response to either externalizing and internalizing cues, the facilitator and the caregivers employ strategies to match, either calming, soothing techniques (down-regulating) to help family members who have become aroused, or activating, energizing techniques (up-regulating) for family members who have withdrawn or shut down (Kinniburgh et al., 2005).

The facilitator helps the family titrate the narrative experience in several other ways. First, he or she sets the pace for sharing. Sometimes families have been waiting for weeks, or even years, to talk about what happened. They are in a rush to tell about it all at once. The facilitator works with the family to take their time and to proceed at a pace that is not too intense. Second, the facilitator monitors what details are being shared. As family members become immersed in telling their story, they may lose track of how much detail they are including. Sometimes the facilitator needs to ask for a break and remind everyone of the safety boundaries that were established.

Making sure that the family is well modulated is especially pertinent at the conclusion of each narrative session. Families should leave each session in a state of affective and behavioral regulation so that they are able to resume normal family routines and activities.

- Change the way family members relate to one another

Setting up new rules about communication and helping the family maintain interactions within their affective and behavioral comfort zone changes relational dynamics. This may open space for family members to view each other differently and to develop altered expectations about how they can interact with each other. Facilitators encourage repetition of and consistency in these new ways of relating and point out how family members are able to respond differently to each other when they trust each other to follow the new communication rules and when the reactions that they get are not harmful or scary.

The facilitator uses a variety of strategies to encourage direct communication among members. He or she quickly takes him or herself out of the role of communication hub.

- Get the facts straight

As the family retells the story of their experiences, some family members may have faulty, distorted, or even missing memories of the way events unfolded. Sometimes in the retelling, memory can be reinstated, facts can be corrected, and missing information can be filled in.

In other families, some family members may not know all of the facts about what happened. As the family tells their story, facilitators help family members make decisions about who needs to know what and how to correct or fill in missing information without sharing too much.

- Elicit pieces of story from each family member realizing that there are multiple truths to be told

The new communication rules established for the family's narrative work encourage the family to use a collaborative storytelling style. Powerful voices are still heard but so are the quiet ones. As the family practices taking turns and family members alternately take the role of telling the story and listening to the story of others, acceptance of many differing perspectives is possible. It is often the role of the facilitator to remind the family of the multiple

realities that are possible even when family members are describing the same event. The goal is not for everyone in the family to agree on one set of facts, but to appreciate that others may have differing viewpoints and may be responding to the situation based on this alternate way of looking at it.

- Integrate the individual perspectives into a family story

Once the family has told their story, including everyone's version and the pertinent facts, the facilitator assists the family in reaching a shared and coherent narrative. This shared version moves the story from an individual to a family narrative. This shared version may have pieces of each individual's experience but represents the collective experience of the family. As the family joins their voices together to work toward a shared trauma story, the problems and consequences become less tied to any individual family member. This distance helps family members think about the situation differently and from several different angles. In doing so, family members may be able to let go of any blame and guilt that has been unresolved. Coming to this shared version "can help weave the family together, improving cohesion while at the same time allowing space for individual growth and development" (Kiser et al., 2010, p. 247).

- Create a healthy, coherent family narrative that can change the framework through which life experiences are interpreted

Through exploring the trauma story and the meaning that the family ascribes to their experience, the facilitator can help discern what is most meaningful to the family. In helping the family find what is of greatest importance, they can demonstrate their refusal to allow the trauma to overpower their strongest convictions.

- Seek out open spaces in the story to discover new possibilities

Through reflective questions, the facilitator can help the family look for parts of the story that have not yet been told, unforeseen possibilities, alternate endings, and silver linings (Freedman & Combs, 1996; Levy, 2006; Sween, 1998; White, 2005). Facilitators query for *unique outcomes* that show how family members overcame the traumas and how they were active in resisting the effects of the traumas. In response, the family can contemplate what they wish might have happened and how they could have acted differently. Through such reflections, they might gain a sense of mastery over the traumatic event while also finding new confidence concerning how they might react to future traumatic events. Ultimately, the facilitator helps the family recover a sense of personal and family agency and efficacy.

In addition to developing verbal mastery over the event, telling the trauma story allows the family to get some distance from the stresses, challenges, and catastrophes they have experienced (Besley, 2002). Part of the work of interventions with families who have experienced trauma is problem-solving and implementing new coping strategies (Lantz & Gyamerah, 2002; Salmon & Bryant, 2002). Through exploring new possibilities and trying on new solutions, families separate themselves from the "disqualifying story" of the dominant trauma narrative and begin to experience their past as more validating and their future as more promising.

NOTES

1. For a more complete review of the theoretical and conceptual framework that underlies storytelling and narration in SFCR, see Kiser, Baumgardner, and Dorado (2010).

2. My thanks to Barbara Baumgardner for her thoughtful contributions to this section.

3. My thanks to Joyce Dorado and Barbara Baumgardner for their thoughtful contributions to this section.

REFERENCES

Bakhtin, M. M. (1981). *The dialogic imagination: Four essays.* M. Holquist M. (Ed.). C. Emerson, M. Holquist (Trans.). Austin, TX: University of Texas Press.

Besley, A. C. (2002). Foucault and the turn to narrative therapy. *British Journal of Guidance and Counselling, 30,* 125–143.

Bohanek, J. G., Marin, K. A., Fivush, R., & Duke, M. (2006). Family narrative interaction and children's sense of self. *Family Process, 45,* 39–54.

Bohanek, J. G., Fivush, R., Zaman, W., Lepore, C. E., Merchant, S., & Duke, M. P. (2009). Narrative interaction in family dinnertime conversations. *Merrill-Palmer Quarterly, 55,* 488–515.

Briere, J., & Scott, C. (2006). *Principals of trauma therapy: A guide to symptoms, evaluations, and treatment.* Thousand Oaks, CA: Sage.

Carpenter, M., Nagell, K., Tomasello, M., Butterworth, G., & Moore, C. (1998). Social cognition, joint attention, and communicative competence from 9 to 15 months of age. *Monographs of the Society for Research in Child Development, 63*(4), i–174.

Cohen, J. A., Mannarino, A. P., & Deblinger, E. (2006). *Treating trauma and traumatic grief in children and adolescents.* New York: Guilford Press.

Cook, A., Blaustein, M., Spinazzola, J., & van der Kolk, B. (2003). *Complex trauma in children and adolescents: White Paper from the National Child Traumatic Stress Network Complex Trauma Task Force.* Los Angeles, CA: National Child Traumatic Stress Network.

Dallos, R. (2004). Attachment narrative therapy: Integrating ideas from narrative and attachment theory in systemic family therapy with eating disorders. *Journal of Family Therapy, 26,* 40–65.

Dimaggio, G., & Semerari, A. (2001). Psychopathological narrative forms. *Journal of Constructivist Psychology, 14,* 1–23.

Fiese, B. H., & Wamboldt, F. S. (2003). Coherent accounts of coping with a chronic illness: Convergences and divergences in family measurement using a narrative analysis. *Family Process, 42,* 439–451.

Figley, C. R. (1988). Post-traumatic family therapy. In F. M. Ochberg (Ed.), *Post-traumatic therapy and victims of violence* (pp. 83–109). New York: Bruner/Mazel.

Figley, C., & Kiser, L. J. (2013) *Helping traumatized families* (2nd ed.). New York: Routledge.

Fivush, R., Bohanek, J. G., & Zaman, W. (2010). Personal and intergenerational narratives in relation to adolescents' well-being. In T. Habermas (Ed.), *The development of autobiographical reasoning in adolescence and beyond* (pp. 45–57). *New Directions for Child and Adolescent Development, 131,* 45–57.

Fivush, R., Duke, M., & Bohanek, J. G. (2010, February 23). "Do You Know...?" The power of family history in adolescent identity and well-being. *Journal of Family Life.* Retrieved from www.journaloffamilylife.org (accessed August 20, 2013).

Freedman, J., & Combs, G. (1996). *Narrative therapy: The social construction of preferred realities.* New York: W. W. Norton & Company.

Green, B. L., Korol, M., Grace, M. C., Vary, M. C., Leonard, A. C., Gleser, G. C., et al. (1991). Children and disaster: Age, gender, and parental effects on PTSD symptoms. *American Academy of Child and Adolescent Psychiatry, 30,* 945–951.

Habermas, T., & Bluck, S. (2000). Getting a life: The emergence of the life story in adolescence. *Psychological Bulletin, 12,* 748–769.

Haden, C. A. (1998). Reminiscing with different children: Relating maternal stylistic consistency and sibling similarity in talk about the past. *Developmental Psychology, 34,* 99–114.

Hailey, G. E. (1988). *A story, a story.* New York: Simon & Schuster.

Hermans, H. J. M., & Dimaggio, G. (2004). The dialogical self in psychotherapy: An introduction. In H. J. M. Hermans, & G. Dimaggio (Eds.), *The dialogical self in psychotherapy* (pp. 13–28). New York: Brunner-Routledge.

Hester, R. L. (2004). Early memory and narrative therapy. *Journal of Individual Psychology, 60*(4), 338–347.

Hill, J., Fonagy, P., Safier, E., & Sargent, J. (2003). The ecology of attachment in the family. *Family Process, 42,* 205–221.

Hudson, J. A. (1990). The emergence of autobiographic memory in mother-child conversations. In R. Fivush & J. A. Hudson (Eds.), *Knowing and remembering in young children* (pp. 166–196). New York: Cambridge University Press.

Kagan, J., & Herschkowitz, V. (2005). *A young mind in a growing brain.* New York: Lawrence Erlbaum.

Kinniburgh, K. J., Blaustein, M., Spinazzola, J., & van der Kolk, B. A. (2005). Attachment, self-regulation, and competency. *Psychiatric Annals, 35,* 424–430.

Kiser, L. J., Baumgardner, B., & Dorado, J. (2010). Who are we, but for the stories we tell: Family stories and healing. *Psychological Trauma: Theory, Research, and Practice, 2,* 243–249.

Laible, D. J., & Thompson, R. A. (2000). Mother-child discourse, attachment security, shared positive affect, and early conscience development. *Child Development, 71,* 1424–1440.

Lantz, J., & Gyamerah, J. (2002). Existential family trauma therapy. *Contemporary Family Therapy: An International Journal, 24,* 243–255.

Lantz, J., & Raiz, L. (2003). Play and art in existential trauma therapy with children and their parents. *Contemporary Family Therapy: An International Journal, 25,* 165–177.

Levy, J. (2006). Using a metaperspective to clarify the structural-narrative debate in family therapy. *Family Process, 45,* 55–73. doi:10.1111/j.1545-5300.2006.00080.x.

Liszkowski, U., Carpenter, M., Henning, A., Striano, T., & Tomasello, M. (2004). Twelve-month-olds point to share attention and interest. *Developmental Science, 7*, 297–307. doi:10.1111/j.1467-7687.2004.00349.x.

McKeever, V. M., & Huff, M. E. (2003). A diathesis-stress model of posttraumatic stress disorder: Ecological, biological, and residual stress pathways. *Review of General Psychology, 7*, 237–250.

Marin, K. A., Bohanek, J. G., & Fivush, R. (2008). Positive effects of talking about the negative: Family narratives of negative experiences and preadolescents' perceived competence. *Journal of Research on Adolescence, 18*, 573–593.

Morgan, A. (2000). What is narrative therapy? Retrieved from www.dulwichcentre.com.au/what-is-narrative-therapy.html (accessed August 22, 2013).

Neimeyer, R., Herrero, O., & Botella, L. (2006). Chaos to coherence: Psychotherapeutic integration of traumatic loss. *Journal of Constructivist Psychology, 19*, 127–145.

Nwoye, A. (2006). A narrative approach to child and family therapy in Africa. *Contemporary Family Therapy, 28*, 1–23.

Oppenheim, D., Nir, A., Warren, S. L., & Emde, R. N. (1997). Emotion regulation in mother-child narrative co-construction: Associations with children's narratives and adaptation. *Developmental Psychology, 33*, 284–294.

Patterson, J. M. (2002). Integrating family resilience and family stress theory. *Journal of Marriage and the Family, 64*, 349–360.

Penn, P. (2001). Chronic illness: Trauma, language, and writing: Breaking the silence. *Family Process, 40*, 33–52.

Pennebaker, J. W. (1993). Putting stress into words: Health, linguistic, and therapeutic implications. *Behaviour Research and Therapy, 31*, 539–548.

Pratt, M. W., & Fiese, B. H. (2004). Family stories and the life course. In M. W. Pratt, & B. H. Fiese (Eds.), *Family stories and the life course* (pp. 1–24). Mahwah, NJ: Lawrence Erlbaum Associates.

Pynoos, R., Steinberg, A., & Aronson, L. (1997). Traumatic experiences: The early organization of memory in school-age children and adolescents. In P. Appelbaum, M. Elin, & L. Uyehara (Eds.), *Trauma and memory: Clinical and legal controversies* (pp. 272–289). New York: Oxford University Press.

Sales, J. M., & Fivush, R. (2005). Social and emotional functions of mother-child reminiscing about stressful events. *Social Cognition, 23*, 70–90.

Salmon, K., & Bryant, R. A. (2002). Posttraumatic stress disorder in children: The influence of developmental factors. *Clinical Psychology Review, 22*, 163–188.

Schechter, D. S., Zygmunt, A., Coates, S. W., Davies, M., Trabka, K. A., McCaw, J., Kolodji, A., & Robinson, J. L. (2007). Caregiver traumatization adversely impacts young children's mental representations on the MacArthur Story Stem Battery. *Attachment & Human Development, 9*, 187–205.

Schoemperlen, D. (2000). *Our lady of the lost and found.* New York: Penguin Books.

Silverman, W. K., Ortiz, C. D., Viswesvaran, C., Burns, B. J., Kolko, D. J., Putnam, F. W., & Amaya-Jackson, L. (2008). Evidence-based psychosocial treatments for children and adolescents exposed to traumatic events. *Journal of Clinical Child & Adolescent Psychology, 37*, 156. doi:10.1080/15374410701818293.

Singer, J. A., & Rexhaj, B. (2006). Narrative coherence and psychotherapy: A commentary. *Journal of Constructivist Psychology, 19*, 209–217.

Sween, E. (1998). The one-minute question: What is narrative therapy? Some working answers. *Gecko, 2*, 3–6.

Templeton, L. M., & Wilcox, S. A. (2000). A tale of two representations: The misinformation effect and children's developing theory of mind. *Child Development, 71*, 402–416.

Valiente, C., Fabes, R. A., Eisenberg, N., & Spinrad, T. L. (2004). The relations of parental expressivity and support to children's coping with daily stress. *Journal of Family Psychology, 18*, 97–106.

van der Kolk, B. A., & van der Hart, O. (1989). Pierre Janet and the breakdown of adaptation in psychological trauma. *The American Journal of Psychiatry, 146*, 1530–1540.

van der Kolk, B. A., Brown, P., & van der Hart, O. (1989). Pierre Janet on post-traumatic stress. *Journal of Traumatic Stress, 2,* 365–378.

Vollmer, F. (2005). The narrative self. *Journal for the Theory of Social Behavior, 35,* 189–205.

Wethington, H. R., Hahn, R. A., Fuqua-Whitley, D. S., Sipe, T. A., Crosby, A. E., Johnson, R. L., Liberman, A. M., Moscicki, E., Price, L. N., Tuma, F. K., Kalra, G., & Chattopadhysy, S. K. (2008). The effectiveness of interventions to reduce psychological harm from traumatic events among children and adolescents: A systematic review. *American Journal of Preventive Medicine, 35,* 287–313. doi:10.1016/j.amepre.2008.06.024.

White, M. (2005). Children, trauma and subordinate storyline development. *The International Journal of Narrative Therapy and Community Work, 3/4,* 10–21.

Wigglesworth, G. (1990). Children's narrative acquisition: A study of some aspects of reference and anaphora. *First Language, 10,* 105–125.

PART II

THE PRACTICE OF SFCR

CHAPTER 5

IMPLEMENTING SFCR

Putting a new intervention into practice involves multiple phases: an exploration phase, an installation or preparation phase, initial implementation with consultation and learning objectives, a full implementation phase, and program sustainability (Fixsen, Naoom, Blasé, Friedman, & Wallace, 2005). Each phase builds upon the other and achieving sustainability of the practice is dependent on successful completion of each. SFCR is best implemented following such a process.

Providers interested in implementing SFCR will:

1. become knowledgeable about the factors that need to be considered before implementation;
2. make informed decisions regarding implementation that are consistent with organizational needs; and
3. recognize specific practices and supports necessary for successful execution in their setting.

EXPLORATION PHASE OR PRE-IMPLEMENTATION PLANNING

A pre-planning phase is recommended for new providers interested in implementing SFCR. This phase is designed to make sure that SFCR is an appropriate model for the provider organization and for the target population. It is also designed to determine that the provider agency has sufficient organizational capacity to implement SFCR successfully. The foundations for sustainability of the model are established through careful consideration of implementation issues in the exploration phase.

During the pre-planning phase, providers are encouraged to consider such questions as:

- What challenges are you hoping to address through implementing SFCR?
- Who are the consumers, or clients, that you want to reach through this model?
- There are multiple versions of SFCR currently available (e.g., trauma treatment (15-week), high-risk (10-week), peer-to-peer). Which version(s) are you planning on employing?
- SFCR, especially the MFG versions, utilizes facilitator teams. Clinicians who have experience with clients who have been impacted by trauma are required. Who in your organization will deliver the service and what is their clinical training and experience?
- Providers of SFCR have used several fee-for-service methods to bill clients for SFCR. Do you propose to bill for these services? If so, have you considered how?
- What barriers will you face when putting this model into practice in your setting? How will you handle these barriers?

Is SFCR Right for Us?

Organizations considering implementing SFCR need to decide whether it will meet the needs of their client or patient population. SFCR is an intervention designed for a specific population of families, families who are living in circumstances involving exposure to chronic stress, adversity, and trauma. Families who are struggling or failing to survive such circumstances and organizations working with families to boost their chances of survival are appropriate for SFCR.

Families Appropriate for SFCR

Understanding which families are appropriate for SFCR is critical to making the decision about adopting the model. Families who have participated in SFCR have been recruited from multiple types of organizations, including, for example, community mental health and health clinics, schools and school mental health programs, domestic violence and homeless shelters, transitional living facilities, and service systems such as human services and justice, and Veteran Administrations. These organizations are frequently challenged to meet the needs of families who have made complex adaptations to the traumatic circumstances they face. SFCR has been used successfully with families who have experienced a wide variety of trauma types.

SFCR is appropriate for families who have a variety of structures—biological two-parent families, single-parent families, stepparent families, multigenerational families, kinship care families, and foster and adoptive families.

Staffing SFCR

As an active therapeutic intervention, SFCR can only be implemented with qualified facilitators. SFCR MFGs are conducted using facilitator teams. These teams usually comprise experienced clinicians along with additional staff. All facilitators require training in SFCR (described in the next section).

FAQ: Who Should Take Part in SFCR?

The selection criteria for SFCR vary with the model chosen. As a reminder, versions of SFCR currently available include the trauma treatment MFG, the high-risk MFG, the workshop MFG, SFCR-Family Trauma Therapy (SFCR-FTT), and SFCR-Peer-to-Peer (SFCR-PP). For all versions, the family has been exposed to high stress and trauma, is struggling or failing to cope, and their functioning is impaired.

For the 15-week *trauma treatment MFG* or *SFCR-FFT*, exposure to trauma and associated traumatic stress symptoms are a requirement for eligibility. More specifically, at least one member in the family must have experienced multiple traumatic events. In addition, an identified family member(s) must also meet criteria for a full or partial diagnosis of a stressor-related disorder.

The selection criteria for the *high-risk MFG* are less stringent. It is common for families who participate in this version to have experienced traumatic events or live in environments where the risk for exposure to trauma is high. Additionally, multiple family members may be experiencing stress- or trauma-related distress or be at risk for related disorders.

The *workshop MFG* is typically offered by organizations serving families at high risk for trauma exposure. These organizations typically either select or recruit families to participate by advertising and inviting any interested family to drop in.

Individuals in recovery from mental health and substance use problems related to trauma and violence are invited to attend *SFCR-PP* sessions.

SFCR clinical facilitators also require training and experience in assessing and treating a wide range of mental health disorders within the context of the family. Clinical facilitators should have prior training and supervision in providing a variety of treatment approaches to children, adults, and families, individually and in groups, including family systems, parent-child interaction, cognitive-behavioral, and play therapies. Finally, clinical facilitators should have experience in the provision of trauma-focused treatment with children or adults.

SFCR provides a wonderful training opportunity for students from a variety of disciplines. Students who serve as part of an SFCR MFG facilitator team have the opportunity to observe clinical facilitators working with a diversity of families in multiple clinical modalities (multi-family, family, and small group) and also participate in leading various group activities under close supervision.

FAQ: What is the Minimum Number of Facilitators Required or is There a Recommended Ratio?

The minimum number of clinical facilitators required is based on several factors: the version of SFCR used, the total number and size of families enrolled, and the number and size of age-based breakout groups.

For the trauma treatment and SFCR-FTT models, a minimum of one trained clinical facilitator is needed for each family. At least one clinician per family must be present to facilitate co-constructing a family narrative. For these family narrative sessions, it is important that each facilitator is skilled and comfortable in conducting trauma-focused family therapy. If meeting this requirement is a challenge due to staff restrictions, there are some possible ways to alter the MFG schedule to accommodate fewer experienced clinical facilitators. Such modifications are addressed on a site-by-site basis.

In the MFG models, at least one facilitator must be present to cover each age-based breakout group. Possible groups outlined in the session guidelines include: caregivers, adolescents, latency-aged children, preschoolers, and babies and toddlers. However, there are several considerations that may alter the number of facilitators required. First, not all MFGs will have children to fill each age-based breakout group. For example, there may not be any adolescents enrolled so a facilitator is not required to staff this group. Second, some sites recruit families with children of specific ages to limit the number of breakout groups (either due to space or staff limitations). For example, sites may not recruit families with babies or toddlers because they are unable to staff this breakout group.

Finally, some breakout groups may need more than one facilitator to manage the group appropriately. This may be due to the age of the children, the number of children included in the group, and/or behavior concerns. Traditionally, breakout groups benefit from additional staff if there are several babies, toddlers, or young children, or if there is a child who has difficulty managing his or her behavior and may be disruptive to the other members of the group.

For the workshop model, approximately two to three facilitators are required given a group size of four to five families.

SFCR-PP is typically delivered by two trained peer leaders with clinical support available.

Other staff can include caseworkers, educators, direct care workers, trainees, family advocates, and legacy family members. Any additional facilitators can be members of the organization or community in which the group is taking place and bring an understanding of that community's culture and value system. See the section in Chapter 6 on Consumers as Facilitators.

Covering the Cost of SFCR

Determining a sustainable source of funding early in the process is important to full implementation over the long-term. SFCR is typically delivered as a clinical or family support service. Payers of mental health and social services reimburse for SFCR either through grants/contracts or fee-for-service billing.

Billing is dependent on a number of factors: the model chosen, the type of organization, and local/state/federal regulations. Relevant billing services include multi-family group, family therapy, and group (30 minutes) for age-related breakouts. Since the MFG formats are longer and more intense than most outpatient services, programs should explore whether billing under such service types as Intensive Outpatient Programs (IOP) are permissible.

INSTALLATION OR PREPARATION PHASE

Once an organization decides that SFCR is an intervention that will enhance the services they offer, the installation or preparation phase begins. Deliberateness is not only an important concept conveyed to families participating in SFCR; it is also critical for putting SFCR into practice.

During the installation or preparation phase, providers are encouraged to consider such questions as:

- SFCR requires training for all staff who will serve as facilitators. How will you support your staff in receiving this training?
- A team approach is important for delivering SFCR. What kind of team building will you implement?
- In terms of logistics, how will you manage the space requirements, provision of the meal, and purchasing and preparation of materials and supplies?
- What problems will you need to solve in order to utilize this model in your setting?

Training

Training is necessary for all facilitators of SFCR. Training consists of formal didactics covering constructive family coping, traumatic stress, and intervention content delivered as a two-day workshop. All intervention methods and materials are presented in detail, including review of videotaped sessions and rehearsal through role-plays. Facilitators also receive training on handling difficult situations that arise, specifically how to assist any participant dealing with difficult emotions and how to provide support and make appropriate referrals for caregivers who request additional services for themselves, their children, or their family.

For clinical facilitators, recommendations for supervised experience with the new intervention include implementation of specific skill-building activities during the course of family therapy with two to four families. This allows them to try out materials and activities designed to improve understanding of, and increase use of, constructive coping and to monitor the success of these intervention techniques.

An additional half-day advanced training is recommended for teams who will be conducting the trauma treatment model. This advanced training

FAQ: What is the Cost of Training and Ongoing Consultation?

Costs vary depending on the version of SFCR being used and the number of teams being trained. Training costs include a pre-planning phase, face-to-face training, and ongoing consultation.

focuses on conducting Module III, the family narrative sessions.

Team Building

Due to the intensity of SFCR, facilitator teams are encouraged. A team approach is required for the MFG versions. Much like a family, facilitator teams function best when roles are well defined, when team members all contribute to the success of each session, when communication between team members is open and direct, and when the teams are collaborative and cohesive. The training experience along with ongoing consultation, regular debriefing, and planning meetings emphasize these qualities.

Deliberate attention to team building at the organizational level can be critical to the success of SFCR. Establishment of guidelines for team functioning is essential as the team is forming. Open discussion of team functioning as an agenda item at each team meeting helps create and support positive team dynamics. Finally, in keeping with the foundations of SFCR, team-building rituals can significantly increase positive working relations.

The Logistics of Conducting SFCR

Planning for SFCR requires consideration of multiple logistics prior to initial implementation.

FAQ: What Time of Day is Best for Running SFCR MFG?

The time of day chosen is determined by staff availability, space availability, and when families are most likely to attend. SFCR groups have previously been conducted in the morning, afterschool, and early evening hours. Most commonly at mental health or trauma clinics, the trauma treatment MFGs are held in the early evening and a family dinner is served. The workshop version tends to be most flexible in terms of scheduling, and often lends itself to being run at various times during the day. Morning and early afternoon sessions have primarily been used with the workshop model.

This is especially relevant for organizations that have decided to use the MFG format. They must decide when to conduct SFCR sessions, find appropriate space, determine how to provide the family meals, and purchase and organize all materials.

Space Requirements

When considering where to deliver SFCR, convenience, safety, and familiarity are important factors. Families will be easier to engage if SFCR is being offered in a space that they know and feel comfortable traveling to/from and spending time in. Specific space requirements vary according to the version of SFCR.

To implement SFCR MFGs, a large group room is required that can accommodate all of the families who are members of the group, the facilitators, and space for serving a family meal. In addition, several smaller rooms are required for the age-based and family breakouts. The number of breakout rooms required depends on the number of age-based breakout groups and/or the total number of families enrolled within each MFG. A typical therapy office is usually large enough to accommodate the breakouts, although it depends on the number of participants.

For the age-based breakouts, each small group requires its own space to complete the activities. The maximum number of breakout groups is five: caregivers, adolescents, latency-aged children, preschoolers, and babies and toddlers. Most groups do not breakout into all five age groups, however.

For the family-based breakouts, each family requires their own space to complete their activities. The number of rooms required depends on the number of families recruited and enrolled.

It is important to note that at many sites, the space requirements are strongly considered when recruiting for the MFG. If space limitations are present, facilitators only recruit and enroll the number and size of families they are able to accommodate with the space they have available. Additionally, if needed, several sites have limited their recruitment to families with children in specific age ranges to limit the number of breakout groups.

SFCR-FTT sessions are typically held in large therapy offices able to accommodate entire families. SFCR -PP requires a group room spacious enough for the peer leaders and participants to gather comfortably in a circle for discussion and sharing.

Providing a Family Meal in the MFG Models

The meal component in the MFGs usually consists of a dinner, which can be served and consumed within the 30-minute time frame allotted. Dinners typically include kid-friendly meals that change from week to week. Menus have included spaghetti, chicken fingers and French fries, grilled cheese and soup, hamburgers, pizza, etc. Meals may either be served family style, in which there is a portion large enough for the entire family placed on each family's table, or as a buffet.

Sometimes breakfast or an afternoon snack is served instead of dinner. The type of meal is influenced by the time of day during which you will be running the group and, at times, the MFG version being used.

The type of the meal you are able to serve and the cost will likely be determined by the options available to your organization. For example, some clinics have an arrangement with a local restaurant for a set cost per person, provided that meals are selected from a limited menu. Some organizations include residential services and use the on-site food service to provide the meals. Many sites look for meal donations from local businesses.

The extent of mealtime preparations depends on what type of meal your site is able to provide, how the delivery of the food is arranged, and how you plan to serve the food. Weekly tasks may include ordering the food, picking up the food or arranging to meet a delivery person, setting up the room for mealtime (i.e., setting up the buffet, setting the tables), and cleaning up after the meal.

Materials

SFCR sessions are rapidly paced and each session includes multiple activities. The families are stimulated and active during sessions, interacting with each other around varied tasks. Materials used in SFCR include psychoeducational books, toys, games, props, and a variety of craft supplies. A complete supply list, including cost estimates, is included on the SFCR website (sfcr.umaryland.edu).

FAQ: What is the Cost of Materials?

For the trauma treatment MFG version, the cost for supplies is currently around $1,800. These supplies are predominantly reusable, and this will be a one-time cost.

For the high-risk version and SFCR-FTT, some supplies used in the trauma treatment MFG model are not needed. These are indicated on the supply list with an asterisk and decrease the cost accordingly.

SFCR-PP requires minimal supplies, primarily handouts and worksheets that can be copied.

Ongoing costs for SFCR depend on the version being run, the size of the groups, and the type of meal provided.

INITIAL IMPLEMENTATION

Once deliberate planning for SFCR has been completed, the initial implementation phase begins. The first time a new intervention is implemented always presents special challenges, and important supports, such as ongoing consultation and on-site supervision, are necessary. During the initial implementation phase, providers are encouraged to consider such questions as:

- Following SFCR training, staff are encouraged to begin using the intervention quickly and to concentrate on putting it into practice with fidelity. How will you support your staff in implementing SFCR with fidelity?
- On-site planning and debriefing sessions are also important. How will you support your staff's time for these activities? Who within your organization will provide oversight and administrative support?

- Weekly preparation for SFCR sessions is necessary. How will your team make the time to deliberately practice SFCR?
- How will your program identify clients and engage them to participate?
- What problems will you need to solve in order to utilize this model in your setting?

Consultation

Following training, facilitators are encouraged to start practicing SFCR quickly. During their initial practice of SFCR, ongoing consultation is necessary to ensure fidelity. Ongoing consultation consists of weekly calls with the facilitator team until they have completed each session at least once and bi-weekly calls through the second round. Consultation covers logistics, clinical issues, including family engagement, team functioning, and planning for upcoming sessions. Teams review any significant deviations from the manual and problem-solve how to get back on track.

Team Meetings

Facilitator teams practicing SFCR are strongly encouraged to meet weekly for debriefing and problem-solving any difficulties that were not handled in session, reviewing cases, and planning. Typically, teams meet for 30–60 minutes. The agenda for these meetings often includes a review of the last session, noting logistical problems and clinical issues. Specific attention should be given to the level of engagement shown by each family, with discussion of ideas for supporting continued participation. Clinical issues that require follow-up with the family, communication with other service providers or supports, or adaptations of SFCR strategies are raised. A discussion of team strengths, needs, and process is helpful for maintaining open communication and resolving problems.

Reviewing the objectives and content for the next session, as well as assigning specific roles for the MFG models, allows facilitators to be well prepared for the next session. Plans for handling any clinical issues (i.e., how the team will handle a disruptive child) are also discussed.

Establishing some team rituals including celebrating successes reinforces facilitators for the hard work that is required to implement SFCR. The team also gets to experience firsthand the benefits of carrying out rituals.

Monitoring Competence and Adherence to SFCR

To promote facilitator competence and adherence, facilitator roles are carefully outlined in SFCR session guidelines. The session guidelines also include notes for how facilitators can support the families as they take advantage of "here and now" opportunities to practice new ways of interacting. In MFG sessions, each facilitator assumes a specific role to help the activities run smoothly and assure active participation from all team members.

Competence and Adherence Measures

To encourage facilitators to maintain fidelity to the model, they are asked to complete competence and adherence measures following each session. These are self-report checklists that assist each facilitator to think about his or her role in carrying out the session as planned and as stipulated in the manual.

The Facilitator Competence measure is a 14-item instrument measuring how well a facilitator is carrying out the intervention. Items are presented in a five-point Likert scale format to assess the qualitative dimensions essential for implementation including cultural competence.

The Facilitator Adherence measure uses a yes/no question format to assess the technical aspects of implementation. The measure includes 16 items indicating both actions and procedures, as specified in the treatment manual, which a facilitator should and should not be doing during each session.

Weekly Preparation for SFCR Sessions

Deliberate planning and careful preparation are necessary for SFCR sessions to run smoothly and to provide experiences of predictability. When facilitators have everything set and ready to go well before the session, management of each activity improves. Ensuring that all the materials are on hand and well organized allows facilitators to concentrate their attention fully on the families. One of the skills emphasized to the families is anticipatory planning, and SFCR facilitators make use of this skill weekly by anticipating issues that might arise and problem-solving how each issue might be handled. Weekly preparation is critical to the success of SFCR.

Recruiting, Selecting, and Engaging Families

Families are recruited for enrollment, assessed for appropriateness, and, if appropriate, invited to take part in SFCR. Facilitators and staff who are knowledgeable about, and believers in, SFCR are the most effective recruiters. Successful recruitment efforts for a family trauma intervention must make the case that the systemic effects of exposure require the whole family to participate in treatment to achieve the best and most long-lasting outcomes.

In the MFG versions of SFCR, forming a community is an important component of the intervention. For this reason, five to six families

Strengthening Family Coping Resources: Facilitator Competence Measure

Name: _____

Organization: _____

Session Number: _____

How much did the facilitator demonstrate the following attributes/attitudes/competencies during the session?

Please use the following scale:

1	2	3	4	5
Rarely	**Seldom**	**Sometimes**	**Often**	**Most of the time**

1. I demonstrated a positive attitude.	1	2	3	4	5
2. I encouraged family members to interact together.	1	2	3	4	5
3. I encouraged the families to interact with each other.	1	2	3	4	5
4. I carried out activities in an organized fashion.	1	2	3	4	5
5. I demonstrated sensitivity to trauma-related issues.	1	2	3	4	5
6. I helped participants regulate expressions of distress.	1	2	3	4	5
7. I aided participants in resolving conflicts.	1	2	3	4	5
8. I helped participants make smooth transitions between activities.	1	2	3	4	5
9. I offered frequent encouragement and praise.	1	2	3	4	5
10. I empowered caregivers to maintain control of their children.	1	2	3	4	5
11. I offered suggestions for managing difficult situations.	1	2	3	4	5
12. I maintained a high degree of structure.	1	2	3	4	5
13. I facilitated the group's practice of rituals.	1	2	3	4	5
14. I assisted participants in reaching closure and leaving the session.	1	2	3	4	5

Strengthening Family Coping Resources: Facilitator Adherence Measure

Name: _____

Organization: _____

Session Number: _____

Did the facilitator (or team) complete the following activities during the session?

Please indicate Yes, No, or Not Applicable	Yes	No	NA
1. Introduced and explained the session's activities and schedule.			
2. Checked on the status of each family.			
3. Checked on homework due.			
4. Used handouts and discussion guides as indicated in manual.			
5. Covered the session's content as indicated in manual.			
6. Psychoeducation to teach ritual, routine, general trauma, safety.			
7. Skill building around structure and predictability.			
8. Skill building to increase safety.			
9. Taught or reinforced stress-reduction techniques (e.g., deep breathing, PMR).			
10. Taught problem-solving and decision-making strategies.			
11. Skill building around family narratives.			
12. Skill building around deliberate planning and follow-through.			
13. Skill building around strategies that improve limit setting and/or help create a positive family environment.			
14. Encouraged positive family interaction and fun.			
15. Assigned and explained homework due for next session.			
16. Ended the group on time.			

FAQ: How Much Non-Direct Time Does it Typically Take to Prepare for Sessions?

Preparation for SFCR involves two tasks: initial arrangements prior to session 1 and organizing for each session on a week-to-week basis. The initial prep, especially if it is the first time a site is implementing SFCR, can be fairly time-intensive. The preparation includes ordering or shopping for all materials, recruiting families, preparing the weekly materials, organizing the facilitator team, and other logistics (such as space, food, etc.). However, these tasks can be divided among several individuals and are started four to eight weeks prior to the start date, decreasing the burden on one person's schedule. Many SFCR teams prepare SFCR materials in bulk, arrange them by session, and have them available for use at all times.

Week-to-week preparation for sessions also includes three main tasks: meeting as a team for supervision and planning purposes (discussed earlier), prepping the materials for the upcoming session, and setup before each session. Material preparations are typically assigned to one or two individuals. These tasks include printing/copying all handouts (if not already organized and available) and gathering materials for each of the planned activities. The amount of time to complete these tasks varies based on the individual's experience with the materials and the nature of the activities planned for that session. Typically, these tasks can take anywhere from 10 to 30 minutes.

Setup for the MFG sessions involves arranging and setting the tables, hanging the posters, setting out the food, and arranging all of the materials so that they are easily accessible and organized. The time required for these tasks is dependent on the facility but usually takes less than 30 minutes.

should be recruited and ready to start at the same time. Recruitment can take some time (four to eight weeks) and should begin well before the first session is scheduled.

Specific recruitment strategies vary according to site. For example, some sites rely on referrals from therapists while other sites offer monthly or quarterly family nights and draw from the families who attend these events. Colorful recruitment flyers provide information to prospective families about the intervention and encourage participation.

Appropriate families are identified through an initial assessment process. Families are evaluated using standardized measures of exposure, symptoms, and family functioning. See Chapter 7 for a complete description of the assessment process.

Issues of family engagement and retention are critical to intervention effectiveness for the targeted population for two reasons: (1) previous trauma treatment research with children and their families demonstrate that the symptoms of stressor-related disorders (isolation, mistrust) may impede the establishment of therapeutic alliances (Chemtob, Novaco, Hamada, & Gross, 1997); and (2) families living in traumatic contexts may have cultural, logistical, and financial issues that impede engagement. Because of inherent difficulties engaging this population in interventions, significant efforts are made to identify and minimize any barriers to recruitment and to encourage attendance and participation.

Specific engagement strategies often mentioned in the intervention literature include provision of

→ **FIGURE 5.1** SFCR Recruitment Flyer

incentives and conveniences, such as a fun activity scheduled during each session, a dinner provided with each session, a door prize given to at least one family at each session, and transportation (Alvidrez, Azocar, & Miranda, 1996; Hall, 2001; Liontos, 1991; Miranda, Azocar, Organista, Munoz, & Lieberman, 1996; Thompson, Neighbors, Munday, & Jackson, 1996; State of Iowa, Department of Education, 1997). Child care is also recommended for parenting interventions, but is not necessary in SFCR as *all* family members are encouraged to attend. Refer to Chapter 6 on Clinical Considerations for additional information about recruitment, selection, engagement, and group cohesion.

FULL IMPLEMENTATION

Full implementation means that SFCR becomes a standard service or treatment option. During the full implementation phase, providers are encouraged to consider such questions as:

• How will your organization support ongoing implementation of SFCR?

- How will you handle turnover of staff trained in SFCR?
- How will you know when your organization has reached full implementation?

Once facilitators have completed training and initial implementation with consultation, they can turn their attention to full implementation. After completion of each case or group, facilitators are encouraged to review their experience, making note of both successes and challenges. With practice, facilitators gain comfort and expertise. They gain a better awareness of which families are most likely to participate fully and benefit. They master the content and timing of the therapeutic approaches used. They are able to anticipate and efficiently address problems or difficult situations that arise during sessions.

As facilitators gain experience, they may discover ways that SFCR might be adapted to better meet the needs of the families served. SFCR is a model with enough flexibility to allow such accommodations. A good rule of thumb is to make changes that do not alter objectives and still impart critical content. Consideration of broader adaptations should be discussed with the developer.

Once an organization has an SFCR team that has successfully completed initial implementation and has a fully implemented SFCR practice, staff turnover is a natural concern. To address the needs of organizations with experienced SFCR facilitator teams, a one-day training is available for new facilitators who are joining already established teams.

The following are indicators that SFCR has become institutionalized:

- All staff are aware of and knowledgeable about the model.
- An SFCR champion has emerged who loves SFCR, believes in its effectiveness, and is committed to keeping it alive within the organization.
- An experienced team of SFCR facilitators is established.
- Families are aware that SFCR is a standard treatment option and know how to access it. For example, SFCR is listed in brochures describing the organization's practice.
- Recruitment strategies are incorporated in everyday practice. When clients initiate treatment or services, treatment teams regularly review cases for appropriateness for SFCR.
- SFCR is offered consistently.
- The principles and even some of the activities used in SFCR are borrowed and used at the organizational level to foster resilience and a positive culture.

SUSTAINABILITY OF SFCR

The final stage in the implementation process, although organizations should be considering it from the beginning, is sustaining the practice. During the sustainability phase, providers are encouraged to consider such questions as:

- What are the key elements of sustainability?
- What are the main challenges that providers of SFCR have faced when trying to sustain its practice?

The sustainability stage involves continued monitoring of how the organization will support the practice over the long-term, including continued funding, staffing, and administrative support. One of the key strategies for sustaining a practice is keeping it vibrant through quality improvement (QI) opportunities (Fixen et al., 2005). A QI process provides a feedback loop between the SFCR team and administration regarding how well the intervention is working (methods for evaluating outcomes) with ideas about how to make it more effective or more tolerable. This process helps assure SFCR's ongoing ability to meet organizational and client needs.

Another key element of sustainable practice is celebrating success. Of course, organizations that implement SFCR recognize the importance of deliberate rituals that recognize and celebrate accomplishments. They establish such rituals early in the implementation process.

In practice, the major challenge to sustainability of SFCR has been staff turnover at the administrative level. As organizational leadership shifts, new priorities arise. Programs that require significant time and resources, such as SFCR, may be targeted for discontinuation at such times. Having an SFCR champion in place and solid evidence of effectiveness are important tools for contesting this challenge.

REFERENCES

Alvidrez, J., Azocar, F., & Miranda, J. (1996). Demystifying the concept of ethnicity for psychotherapy research. *Journal of Consulting and Clinical Psychology, 64,* 903–908.

Chemtob, C. M., Novaco, R. W., Hamada, R. S., & Gross, D. M. (1997). Cognitive-behavioral treatment for severe anger in posttraumatic stress disorder. *Journal of Consulting and Clinical Psychology, 65,* 184–189.

Fixsen, D. L., Naoom, S. F., Blase, K. A., Friedman, R. M., & Wallace, F. (2005). *Implementation research: A synthesis of the literature.* Tampa, FL: University of South Florida, Louis de la Parte Florida Mental Health Institute, The National Implementation Research Network (FMHI Publication #231).

Hall, G. C. N. (2001) Psychotherapy research with ethnic minorities: Empirical, ethical, and conceptual issues. *Journal of Consulting and Clinical Psychology, 69,* 502–510.

Liontos, L. B. (1991). *Involving at-risk families in their children's education.* Eugene, OR: ERIC Clearinghouse on Educational Management.

Miranda, J., Azocar, F., Organista, K. C., Munoz, R. F., & Lieberman, A. (1996). Recruiting and retaining low-income Latinos in psychotherapy research. *Journal of Consulting and Clinical Psychology, 64,* 868–874.

State of Iowa, Department of Education. (1997). *Parent involvement in education: A resource for parents, educators, and communities.* Eric Digest.

Thompson, E. E., Neighbors, H. W., Munday, C., & Jackson, J. S. (1996). Recruitment and retention of African American patients for clinical research: An exploration of response rates in an urban psychiatric hospital. *Journal of Consulting and Clinical Psychology, 64,* 861–867.

CHAPTER 6
CLINICAL CONSIDERATIONS AND STRATEGIES

As a trauma-focused family intervention, the clinical strategies and practice elements that comprise SFCR were selected to meet its two primary goals—to address or prevent traumatic distress exhibited by individual family members and the family as a whole, and to build coping resources to increase family protection and resilience. Regardless of the version of SFCR being implemented, it is an active intervention, and to be implemented effectively and with fidelity, facilitators must:

1. be familiar with core practice elements in SFCR for meeting its primary goals, including the trauma treatment practice elements embedded in the model and the strategies used to improve family coping;

2. appreciate the therapeutic mechanisms used in SFCR to support family members at all different ages and stages of development;

3. recognize the value of MFGs and consider the conditions necessary for conducting MFGs;

4. understand what it means to be an SFCR facilitator;

5. review ways in which SFCR can be adapted for specific populations and settings;

6. value the general clinical principals that are critical to SFCR; and

7. become knowledgeable about the variety of clinical strategies and techniques that are incorporated in SFCR.

FOUNDATIONS IN CORE ELEMENTS OF TRAUMA TREATMENT: REDUCING SYMPTOMS OF CHRONIC EXPOSURE

In studies of effective interventions, it has been demonstrated that many of them share common treatment elements and strategies (Chorpita, Delieden, & Weisz, 2005). This is certainly the case with trauma-focused treatments. Trauma-specific cognitive behavioral therapies (CBT) for PTSD have become first-line treatments and have broad empirical support. Detailed descriptions of CBT approaches with children and adults exist (Cohen, Berliner, & Mannarino, 2000; Cohen, Mannarino, & Staron, 2006b; March, Amaya-Jackson, Murray, & Schulte, 1998; Resick & Schnicke, 1992). Several manualized interventions are available (Cohen, Mannarino, & Deblinger, 2006a; March et al., 1998; Resick & Schnicke, 1992). Numerous randomized control trials support CBT's efficacy and multiple published studies support its effectiveness (Cohen, Mannarino, & Knudsen, 2005; Cohen, Deblinger, Mannarino, & Steer, 2004; Cohen et al., 2006b; Huey & Polo, 2008; Nishith, Resick, & Griffin, 2002; Resick, Nishith, Weaver, Astin, & Feuer, 2002). This research also generally affirms that effective CBT approaches typically include elements of cognitive therapy, exposure therapy, and anxiety management training (psychoeducation, coping skill development), direct exploration of the traumatic experience coupled with exposure/contingency reinforcement programs, evaluation and reframing of cognitions regarding the event, and support.

SFCR draws heavily on components of effective trauma treatment delivered within the framework of a family skill-building intervention.

Although not as well researched, core elements of treatment for complex trauma have also been identified (Cook et al., 2007). These treatment components target the key symptoms and areas of dysfunction. They include safety, self-regulation, self-reflective information processing, traumatic experiences integration, relational enhancement, and positive affect enhancement.

To further understand the common elements in child trauma treatment, the National Child Traumatic Stress Network's (NCTSN) National Center for Social Work Trauma Education and Workforce Development (NCSWTEWD) developed a manual of core child trauma treatment intervention objectives and practice elements (Strand, Hansen, & Courtney, 2013). Using this manual, 26 trauma treatments were coded in a manner similar to the process described by Chorpita et al. (2005) for the presence of these core intervention objectives and practice elements. Of the interventions reviewed, SFCR was one of eight interventions rated as representing all domains included in the coding manual (Strand, Hansen, & Layne, 2012). Use of a family format to deliver these core components was a somewhat unique feature of SFCR as compared with the other manuals reviewed.

In SFCR, trauma treatment practice elements are delivered in a format that successfully engages all family members in the healing process and simultaneously addresses the pathology that often co-exists in multiple family members. SFCR focuses on physiological, cognitive, behavioral, affective, and social mechanisms that influence the critical symptoms of trauma-related disorder (see Table 6.1).

Conducting a Phased Intervention

The structure of SFCR and the order of the sessions are central to good therapeutic outcomes. As in many trauma-focused interventions, skills presented early are used over and over again; some are important building blocks for later activities. For this reason, it is recommended that families attend regularly and many strategies to encourage weekly attendance and active participation are integrated in the treatment. Additionally, facilitators should be sensitive to following the prescribed order of the sessions and moving methodically through the intervention. However, clinical judgment is always relevant in making decisions about how to conduct SFCR.

FOUNDATIONS IN FAMILY TREATMENT: STRENGTHENING THE FAMILY'S PROTECTIVE FUNCTION

SFCR teaches constructive coping resources to strengthen a family's protective function potentially vulnerable to chronic exposure to chronic stress and trauma (Allen & Bloom, 1994; Davies & Flannery, 1998; Miller & Slive, 2004; Temple, 1997). SFCR accomplishes this using a family behavioral and skill-building framework. Supported by positive results from many well-designed studies, family behavioral and skill-building interventions demonstrate success at creating systemic or contextual change (Dishion & Andrews, 1995; Taylor & Biglan, 1998). In addition, consistent positive effects are shown when interventions combine family psychoeducation with a focus on parental/familial coping and/or behavioral strategies. The family framework in SFCR includes consideration of development across the lifespan, maintaining healthy family roles and boundaries, and working with families to develop a comfort zone within which they interact during sessions and, hopefully, at home.

→ TABLE 6.1 SFCR's Treatment Components and Links to Trauma EBPs

Focus	Components	Goals	Links to EBPs
Physiological	Enhancing safety	Identify points of potential danger for the family and develop safety plans for specific threats	Cognitive therapy, exposure therapy, anxiety management training, kinesthetic activity
	Stress inoculation skills	Enable use of specific skills to reduce physiologic manifestations of fear, anxiety, and stress	
	Exposure with responsive prevention	Reduce the intensity of overwhelming negative emotions such as fear, anxiety, helplessness, guilt, and shame	
	Mastery	Gain the physical sensation of being relaxed and in charge of accomplishing one's goals	
Cognitive	Psychoeducation	Normalize responses to the trauma and reinforce accurate cognitions about the event(s)	Cognitive therapy, anxiety management training, evaluation/reframing of cognitions, symbolic learning, reflectivity
	Cognitive processing	Teach methods for reaching shared, accurate thoughts related to trauma(s)	
	Cognitive coping	Focus on planning, problem-solving, follow-through with a particular emphasis on preventive coping	
	Narrative	Reach a shared meaning about the trauma(s)	
Behavioral	Behavioral regulation (limits)	Use executive functioning skills to execute painful behavior	Anxiety management training
	Parenting skills	Increase use of positive, effective, and safe strategies for managing children's behaviors	
Affective	Affective regulation	Increase use of healthy forms of emotional expression and attunement among family members; increase positive affect	Affect identification, emotion regulation coaching, anxiety management training, direct exploration of the traumatic experience, laughter
	Narrative	Identify and share affect related to traumatic experiences	
Social	Attachment	Building representations or working models of trusting relationships	Support, anxiety management training
	Narrative	Promote positive, healthy communication between family members about the traumatic events	

Developmental Issues to Consider

Families taking part in SFCR (except SFCR-PP) attend with members of all ages. To address the needs of each family member, facilitators must consider both the ways that development influences an individual's trauma response and the ways that the experience of trauma may alter the individual's course of development. Understanding the reactions of individuals to trauma necessitates a clear grasp of their developmental competencies around the time of the trauma and the potential for trauma to interfere with their expected developmental trajectory.

Facilitators must bear in mind that development plays a role in the varied reactions of family members. Individual members of a family, representing multiple developmental levels across the life span, will demonstrate different reactions to accumulated stressors and traumas. At various ages and stages, development alters an individual's ability to appraise a traumatic exposure and to mobilize coping resources. "An individual's developmental level both contributes to the resources that are available for coping and limits the types of coping responses the individual can enact" (Compas, Connor-Smith, Saltzman, Thomsen, & Wadsworth, 2001, p. 89).

Although considering age and stage are necessary across the life span, the fast pace of development during childhood adds significant complexity when working with families inclusive of children, especially families with young children. Childhood trauma victims experience a complex set of physiological, emotional, cognitive, and behavioral reactions that occur both during and after the traumatic event(s) and because development is occurring rapidly across all of these domains, viewing trauma within a developmental context is no easy task. A child's emerging capacities influence everything from their subjective experience of the traumatic event to their ability to make use of specific therapeutic techniques to aid recovery.

SFCR applies extensive knowledge of the emerging capacities related to child trauma responses to the recommendations for age-appropriate relaxation practices, the techniques used in narrative sessions, and the design of skill-building activities carried out in MFG breakout activities. SFCR facilitators are asked to coach caregivers and other adult family members on how to scaffold the skills needed for family activities so that family members of all ages are able to participate.

Age-Specific Breakout Groups

In the MFG sessions, developmental issues are handled in part through age-specific breakout groups. These are designed specifically for babies/ toddlers, preschoolers, latency-age children, teens, and adults. Each breakout group presents skill-building activities planned specifically for that age group and is introduced using materials and supplies that are developmentally appropriate. Content and materials to support these breakout sessions have been reviewed by developmental experts and tested with each age group.

Facilitators participate as leaders of specific age group breakout sessions. The same facilitator/ age group should remain consistent throughout the sessions to allow the age groups to develop a sense of cohesion and continuity. Planning for age-specific breakout groups requires matching the most developmentally appropriate activities to the skill level of the children attending (e.g., using the activity designed for the toddlers with the latency-age children if those attending are somewhat delayed).

Honoring the Rule that Caregivers are in Charge of Their Families

One of the primary aims of SFCR is to enhance the ability of caregivers to provide protection, nurturance, and positive experiences for their families. In SFCR sessions, this translates into a basic guiding principle that caregivers are in charge of their families. Caregivers are approached as experts and as decision-makers. Whenever possible, facilitators seek the input from, and permission of, caregivers before initiating interactions with their children.

Facilitators honor the rule that caregivers are in charge of their families by carefully observing how caregivers interact with their children to learn about the caregivers' parenting strengths. When facilitators see an opportunity to increase caregivers' skills, they use approaches that leave the caregivers in charge. They first try "in the ear" coaching, providing caregivers with subtle cues and suggestions for how they might handle an issue. As caregivers try new approaches to interacting with their children, facilitators scaffold the caregivers' skills by suggesting small steps of change. If caregivers are not successful, facilitators may model new ways of interacting along with encouragement for the caregiver to keep trying.

Family Approach to Emotional and Behavioral Regulation Coaching

Regulatory problems are associated with exposure to multiple traumas, especially for those exposed in childhood; problems involving difficulties regulating affect (including problems identifying and expressing emotions and persistent negativity), cognition (including difficulties with attention, threat detection, and executive functioning), and behavior (including difficulties with impulse control and behavioral inhibition) are common (Cook et al.,

2005; Courtois & Ford, 2009; Evans & English, 2002; Lengua, 2002; Raver, 2004). To counteract the dysregulation often experienced in the family, successful sessions in SFCR include multiple experiences of well-modulated family interaction.

Regulation is most often considered as individual or dyadic processes, but, in fact, is interdependent on all family members (Cummings, Goeke-Morey, & Papp, 2003; Fiese & Sameroff, 1999; Lunkenheimer, Shields, & Cortina, 2007; McHale, Kuersten, & Lauretti, 1996). For example, related to emotion regulation, Morris, Silk, Steinberg, Myers, and Robinson (2007) and Zeman, Cassano, Perry-Parrish, and Stegall (2006) have considered processes by which caregivers/families influence their children's emotional competence and have reached fairly similar conclusions. Their models include observation and modeling of affect expression and coping, the emotional climate or environment within the family, and parenting practices. Facilitators take advantage of the multiple opportunities during SFCR sessions to assist families in using these constructs to build co-regulation skills.

Observation and Modeling

Families provide a stage on which members can observe the way others act in different situations. Caregivers usually take the lead in modeling the behaviors and emotions that are acceptable in the family as there appears to be a hierarchy in how responses spread throughout the family system (Larson & Almeida, 1999; Morris et al., 2007). Children observe the way their caregiver responds to any given situation and model their own responses accordingly. Also of note, negativity is more contagious than positivity (i.e., negative affect is more often transmitted to others than positive affect) (Larson & Almeida, 1999).

Facilitators watch how this process unfolds within the family. They provide coaching to teach caregivers new skills at observation and modeling. They help caregivers remain in the lead role and model responses that are safe and predictable.

Climate within the Family

Facilitators structure SFCR sessions to provide a climate or environment that feels safe for all participants. They provide cues to help families recognize the characteristics of the environment that promote security and regulation.

During the multiple opportunities for family activity, families discover their own comfort zone guidelines. Facilitators support the family in their practice of maintaining interaction within this comfort zone. They may also assist this process by pointing out times when family interactions seem to be getting outside this zone. For example, a facilitator who observes a child starting to be inattentive and increasingly disruptive to the family interaction might point this out to the child's caregiver. The facilitator might work with the caregiver to try a down-regulation strategy and then re-engage the child in the family activity. Finally, facilitators make suggestions for helping the family generalize how to structure a co-regulated home environment.

Parenting Practices

Caregivers use a variety of parenting practices to teach their children about regulation. Effective use of parental coaching strategies differs depending on the age, developmental stage, and gender of the child.

In terms of emotion regulation, parenting practices are typically labeled either as emotion-coaching or emotion-dismissing (Gottman, Katz, & Hooven, 1997). Caregivers who use emotion-coaching strategies view emotional displays as opportunities for teaching and intimacy. They are receptive to their children's emotional expressions, label them, empathize with them, and encourage problem-solving. On the other hand, caregivers who use emotion-dismissing strategies are often uncomfortable with and disapproving of their children's emotional expressions.

Research provides support for the benefit of emotion coaching, suggesting a significant association with better emotion regulation, whereas emotion dismissing is linked to emotional and behavioral dysregulations (Eisenberg, Fabes, & Murphy, 1996; Lunkenheimer et al., 2007; McDowell, Kim, O'Neil, & Parke, 2002).

Facilitators observe the coaching strategies that caregivers use over several sessions to determine whether they employ predominantly emotion-coaching or emotion-dismissing strategies. They provide psychoeducation about, and reinforcement for, emotion coaching. They also provide guidance when they observe emotion dismissing. For example, if a facilitator observes a child crying and the caregiver telling them to "stop it right now," they might intervene by asking the caregiver to comfort the child, label the emotions they are experiencing, and problem-solve with the child to find solutions.

Another chance to provide some emotion-regulation coaching might come during a trauma narrative session. The facilitator might notice that the caregiver has become quiet and tearful while her children are talking about their father's incarceration. The facilitator might point out this change in affect to the family and help them label what the caregiver is feeling. The family can talk together about what is happening and how other family members feel when their caregiver is upset.

In SFCR, including the MFG versions, it is sometimes necessary to help caregivers introduce behavior reinforcement plans for family members whose behavioral dysregulation is interrupting sessions. Facilitators work with caregivers to identify the behaviors to target and to decide on appropriate reinforcers. Facilitators often have to model the use of the plan for the caregivers as it is first initiated. Caregivers should quickly learn how to monitor their children's behavior and to praise them when they are maintaining good control.

MULTI-FAMILY GROUPS (MFGS)

Knowledge of the background and strengths of MFGs is useful in understanding how the SFCR MFG versions function. Additionally, running MFGs requires consideration of group dynamics and how to follow a manualized protocol when all of the families are progressing at their own pace.

Background of MFGs

Treating multiple families simultaneously is an intervention strategy combining elements of group and family therapies (Asen, 2002). Pioneers in the field include Laqueur, and later McFarlane, who worked with families dealing with severe mental illness (Laqueur, La Burt, & Morong, 1964; McFarlane, 2002); McKay and colleagues, whose MFG targeted increasing access for urban families (McKay, Harrison, Gonzales, Kim, & Quintana, 2004); and Kumpfer and colleagues' prevention program for high-risk families (Kumpfer, DeMarsh, & Child, 1989).

Conceptually, MFGs are thought to work through improving social connections, enhancing communication skills, and encouraging direct and indirect learning among the families. McFarlane believed that "families might learn by seeing parts of themselves in others—including their own 'dysfunction'" (Asen, 2002, p. 5).

Treating multiple families at the same time is also considered to be an effective strategy for reducing stigma and improving engagement and participation (Asen, 2002; McFarlane, 2002; Weine et al., 2008). MFGs have shown consistent results at engaging families in treatment and improving participation (Brody, Murry, & Gerrard, et al., 2004; McKay, Gonzales, Quintana, Kim, & Abdul-Adil, 1999; McKay, Gonzales, Stone, Ryland, & Kohner, 1995). MFGs provide opportunities for families who may feel isolated to meet other families with similar experiences and concerns. By sharing their stories, families feel less alone.

Considering Elements of Group Therapy

As families are being selected, it is important to consider group composition. Obviously, various characteristics of families and family members affect group cohesion. Clinical experience doing the group provides some guidelines for selecting families who will likely form a cohesive group. For example, families come into the group with preferences and prejudices that, unfortunately, must be taken into account if the group is going to be cohesive and families are going to find the group supportive.

Further, families will only come to the group if they find it a safe experience, so facilitators work to create a group milieu that is inviting and contained. Individual family members with severe dysregulatory disorders (e.g., impulse control disorders, personality disorders) may prove too disruptive for inclusion in the MFG versions.

In the MFG versions, sessions include segments involving the whole family, segments focused on parental skill building, segments focused on child

Example of Group Composition Chart

Family ID	Brief Description	Caregivers	Children (age, gender)	Child Breakout Group Assignment			
				1	2	3	4
116	Single mother, two children from different fathers. History of domestic violence, physical abuse, and witnessing community violence.	Mother	Alex (10, M)			x	
			Michelle (13, F)				x

FAQ: How Do You Ensure/Create Group Cohesion among Families in SFCR?

An important part of engaging families in SFCR MFGs is the formation of a community. In the first session, families work together to determine group rules and the opening and closing rituals providing them ownership over their group. Over the course of SFCR, families are asked to share stories and other activities with the group (although they are never asked to share any information about their traumas with the group). These group activities allow relationships among families to grow.

Breakout groups divided by age also help with group cohesion. The caregiver breakout group is often critical to the families' engagement in the treatment process. Caregivers often form a close bond with each other, which seems to be an important factor in their level of participation. Additionally, the youth are given a chance to spend time with other kids their age and form friendships. Looking forward to seeing their friends can provide motivation for attending each week.

Activities supporting participation, such as reminder calls/postcards from facilitators, text messages encouraging participation, and network building, are integrated. In session 6, a family buddy system or phone tree is established so families can contact one another outside of sessions. This serves to both support participation in the group and cohesion among families.

skill building, and segments focused on network building with the entire multi-family group. Thus, it is sometimes necessary to choose families based on space or facilitator availability. For instance, if there are only three facilitators on the team, then breakout groups will be limited to one caregiver group and two youth age groups. Families who have children similar in age will need to be selected for the group.

The group composition chart is helpful for considering who will take part in the MFG, providing an overview of the families' histories and exposures, and determining who will participate in which breakout groups. See the example chart for one family.

Considering Elements of Family Therapy

Engagement and Participation

Family engagement and regular participation are important to cohesion and thus the success of each SFCR MFG. Thus, it is critical to establish rapport and a good working relationship with each family. This requires an investment in engaging each family in the treatment process.

For the 15-week trauma treatment MFG version, engagement is defined as occurring over the first three sessions. If a family is unable to begin the group or misses the first session or two, they should be encouraged to start coming as soon as possible. After the third session, families should not be added to the group. For the 10-week high-risk MFG, engagement is defined as occurring over the first two sessions and new families should not be added after the second session.

It is often helpful for facilitators to be paired with families early in the group. For example, the same facilitator would meet the same family for each family breakout. The same facilitator/family pairing should remain consistent throughout to allow the pair to develop a sense of trust and continuity.

Missed Sessions During the MFG

Over a 10- or 15-week period of an MFG, families will inevitably miss a session or two. Families who miss a session should be contacted within a day or so after the scheduled appointment. This lets the family know that they were missed and reinforces the importance of regular attendance. This is also an opportunity for facilitators to help families practice deliberate planning by discussing what might get in the way of making the next session.

Certain sessions can be missed without creating serious therapeutic issues, but some sessions are critical to the success of the treatment as they introduce skills that will be used later or are core components of the intervention. Table 6.2 lists the sessions and how a missed session should be handled.

Make-up sessions should be scheduled individually with the family and should be held as soon as possible after the missed MFG session. The content and activities from an MFG session can be covered comfortably in a 45-minute individual family session (mealtime is omitted).

FACILITATOR COMPETENCIES AND RESPONSIBILITIES

Being an SFCR facilitator requires certain competencies to carry out the intervention effectively. Specific competencies and responsibilities for consumers or legacy caregivers, who can fill important roles as facilitators on MFG teams, are also discussed. Finally, depending on his or her role on the team and the version of SFCR being implemented, an SFCR facilitator assumes multiple

➡ **TABLE 6.2** Handling Missed Sessions in the MFG

Session Number	Session Name	Action for Missed Session
1	Telling Family Stories	Hand out session materials for review
2	Ritual Family Tree	Hand out session materials for review
3	Family Diary	Hand out session materials for review
4	Feeling Safe I	*Make-up session needed*
5	Feeling Safe II	*Make-up session needed*
6	People Resources	Hand out session materials for review
7	Life Choices	Hand out session materials for review
8	Spirituality and Values	Hand out session materials for review
9	Things Get in the Way	*Make-up session needed*
HR10	Celebration!	Hand out session materials for review
10	Telling About What Happened	*Make-up session needed*
11	When Bad Things Happen I	*Make-up session needed*
12	When Bad Things Happen II	*Make-up session needed*
13	Marking the Trauma	*Make-up session needed*
14	Good Things Happen Too!	Hand out session materials for review
15	Celebration!	Hand out session materials for review

responsibilities to help families advocate and navigate to get their needs met.

Clinical Competencies

Facilitator competencies are closely tied to the primary aims of SFCR. Related to the aim of providing trauma treatment, facilitators are sensitive to the needs of trauma victims. They are aware of the physiological and emotional reactions that are triggered by reminders of traumatic events. They work closely with the family and with individual family members to identify these triggers and help participants regulate their expressions of distress. If a child in the family is being triggered, the facilitator helps his or her caregiver notice what is upsetting to the child and provides support as the caregiver tries to aid the child's attempts to modulate.

Facilitators are also keenly aware of the contagious nature of traumatic distress so pay careful attention to family, group, and team processes. Additionally, facilitators realize that trauma treatment is difficult and that they are not immune to the impact of vicarious trauma. They make consistent efforts to work through their own reactions to any trauma pain that is experienced during sessions.

SFCR facilitators, regardless of which version they are implementing, maintain a focus on specific issues related to constructive family coping. They attend each session with a positive attitude and high expectations. They make the children, the caregivers, and the families feel that their time in SFCR sessions is special. They establish structure and maintain a climate that is calm and feels safe, both physically and emotionally. When events happen to threaten the continuity or cohesion of any session, facilitators model flexible problem-solving skills and conflict resolution, yet manage to ensure that the session proceeds and the goals for the session are accomplished. They encourage a high level of participation from each family member attending regardless of their age, stage of development, or abilities. During the MFG sessions, they encourage each group to form a network and make positive use of all of the people resources available during each session. Finally, they have fun in their role and inspire the family/families to have fun.

Consumers as Facilitators[1]

Consumers make great additions to the SFCR MFG facilitator team. Importantly, this can be beneficial to everyone involved. The facilitator team gains an additional member who can share in the work and the fun of the group. The families participating in the MFG have the opportunity of getting to know people like themselves who are doing well. And consumers who have facilitated SFCR acknowledge that their experience positively impacted their own journey as a trauma survivor.

Choosing the right consumers to be peer facilitators requires a deliberate process. It is important to understand their motivation for being a facilitator and to know something about their previous treatment experiences. Consumer facilitators need to have lots of energy and to be dependable. They must be able to make a commitment to being present in sessions every week for the duration. They need to be self-aware and able to separate their own emotions and experiences from others. They need to acknowledge their own trauma history and have a plan for how to handle their own emotional responses if triggered. Consumer facilitators need to have a knowledge base about trauma and training in SFCR. Of course, this would involve training in confidentiality.

When deciding whether a consumer is a good fit, they should be given sufficient information about the intervention, about the kinds of families who participate, about expectations for facilitators, about the potential to be triggered, and about the risks and rewards of being a facilitator. Similar to an informed consent process, consumers should be given a chance to review all of this information and to ask questions before making a decision.

When consumers do join the team, it is important to clearly determine what role they will assume. This may evolve over the weeks as they become more comfortable with the group structure. For example, consumers may be most comfortable as observers early on and be leading activities by the end of the 10- or 15-week MFG. Having an opportunity to take part in the many roles of a facilitator, from organizing supplies and ordering the food to leading activities during group, helps facilitators make choices about their involvement that fit their personalities and their circumstances. Including consumer facilitators in team meetings and clinical supervision is valuable.

The lead facilitator may need to play a special role with consumer facilitators. They need to be available to provide support when needed and to check in with the consumers on a regular basis about how they are experiencing the group.

Facilitators' Role in Supporting Family Treatment

Integrating SFCR within a Plan of Care

In practice, SFCR has been used in combination with a variety of other treatments and services. Families have participated in SFCR at the beginning of a course of treatment or after family members have completed other treatments, including trauma-specific treatments. Because the data demonstrating best practice are not yet available, these decisions should be made on a case-by-case basis.

Thus, one of the roles of SFCR facilitators involves helping families determine whether this intervention is right for them at this particular time. Including SFCR in a family's plan of care should be considered in light of any other services that the family is already receiving and the other services that the family will likely need. Developing a comprehensive plan with the family involves considering what treatments and services are necessary, deciding who in the family will participate in what services, and determining the best sequence of services.

Case Management

Families who participate in SFCR often have complex needs and are involved with multiple service providers. Although SFCR facilitators do not take on a formal case management role with each family, in an attempt to provide a safe and beneficial experience for families they may serve some of the functions. SFCR facilitators stay in close contact with the families while they are participating. Weekly calls are normal. These calls serve to keep the family connected, to review any concerns from the previous session, to remind the family of how they can practice what they worked on during the session, to problem-solve any barriers to full participation, and to just simply let the family know that someone cares.

Often during SFCR additional treatment or service, needs are identified and facilitators may be involved in linking families with new services. Facilitators can assist by identifying appropriate resources, making referrals, and initiating contacts. Follow-up with encouragement is typically necessary to make sure that the linkage is successful.

SFCR facilitators also serve an important case management role by communicating with other treatment and service providers. With appropriate releases for exchange of information, coordination of care is best accomplished when all professionals and other supports are sharing information regularly. Communication of issues that come up in session is often beneficial to the family.

SFCR AND DIVERSITY

Since family practices, such as coping skills, rituals, routines, mealtimes, and storytelling, are very heterogeneous, SFCR acknowledges and preserves this heterogeneity. To be acceptable to a wide variety of families, SFCR presents skills, processes, and structure while being content-neutral. Specific coping practices that work within one family do not necessarily work for another family. Facilitators work with each family to remember, rediscover, plan, and implement coping skills, routines, rituals, and traditions that are comfortable, satisfying, and meaningful to all family members.

The intervention methods, activities, and materials included in SFCR are culturally sensitive, presented at the understanding/reading level of the participants, supportive of many different family forms, and valuing of the strengths within each family. Facilitators utilize a wide variety of teaching methods, activities, and formats to provide appropriate learning experiences for diverse participants.

Although a manualized intervention, there is flexibility for adaptations necessary to meet the needs of specific settings and populations. SFCR has been implemented in multiple treatment and service settings. SFCR has also been utilized with specific populations, such as families who have experienced domestic violence, homelessness, and urban or rural poverty. In each case, small adaptations have been made to meet the realities of the setting. For some populations or settings, more substantial adaptations are necessary. Several such adaptations are described along with the process used.

Adapting SFCR for Latino Families[2]

The MFG versions of SFCR have been adapted for use with Latino families who are either bilingual or speak Spanish exclusively. Working closely with the intervention developer, a group of clinical facilitators with Latino heritages who were interested in implementing SFCR with this population took the lead in adapting the manual and materials and in translating all of the session materials, handouts, and homework into Spanish (Samuels, Schudrich, & Altschul, 2009).[3] In addition to reviewing the manual and materials, this stakeholder workgroup also reviewed and recommended changes to the assessment process and to the family

engagement strategies used. Additionally, the workgroup generated practical guidelines for the use of translators, recruitment of bilingual, bicultural staff, involvement of former consumers, establishment of vocabulary norms (e.g., glossary for communication between families and facilitators), and the role of lead facilitator using a bilingual clinician.

The workgroup's first task was to identify priority needs and assess for potential areas of SFCR content that needed modifications. Each session was reviewed for specific adaptations required, including replacement of psychoeducational materials with culturally relevant and language-appropriate books and movie clips, and for translation needs. New resources were selected in the hope that the equivalent symbolic meaning would carry through, even if they were not exact translations of the original items. Second, they gathered and used feedback from Latino families and SFCR facilitators. Materials, including facilitator scripts in the session guidelines, handouts, and homework, were translated by Spanish-speaking facilitators and clinicians. Translated materials were reviewed by a committee that included bilingual speakers. The adapted versions and all of the materials were then used during five MFGs to determine feasibility and acceptability.

Several examples of modifications illustrate this process.

Based on the concept of *respeto*, psycho-education and support for all family members (including children) to express emotions in respectful manner became an important issue. Facilitator notes were added regarding the importance of paying respect, within cultural norms, in order to establish rapport and ensure engagement with key family members. Given that this is a trauma-focused treatment, facilitators are encouraged to delicately balance *respeto* with considerations for the importance of creating space and validation of children (or other persons lower in the hierarchy) to express their own experiences of the traumas.

In session 5, facilitators teach relaxation techniques and culturally congruent relaxation techniques (i.e., praying, visiting a *sobador*) are included to highlight tools the Latino families may already be familiar with and use, and therefore can be seen as strengths.

Facilitators working with Latinos are encouraged to explore how faith impacts perception of the trauma and of seeking help. Using the concept of "God's Will" that many Latinos ascribe to, not only as a way to explain why something happened to them, but also as a reason for which this therapeutic intervention has entered their path, provides an opportunity to heal rather than a burden they must carry.

Adapting SFCR for Individual Family Treatment[4]

SFCR-FTT was created to meet the needs of settings unable to implement the MFG versions and for families who are unwilling or unsuitable to participate in an MFG format. SFCR-FTT is a family trauma treatment created by combining the core principles of SFCR with the beginning framework of child and family traumatic stress intervention (CFTSI) (Berkowitz, Stover, & Marans, 2010). SFCR-FTT provides more flexibility to tailor the intervention to the needs of a specific family.

SFCR-FTT is a manualized family therapy delivered in weekly one-hour sessions. The first module comprises six sessions focused on assessment, information exchange about trauma and its impact, building motivation for creating systemic change, setting goals related to the coping strategies needed by the family, and introducing some basic skills.

The second module includes six skill-building sessions. Based on the assessment of family distress and current coping strategies, sessions are chosen to enhance specific adaptive and protective family coping skills. Sessions can target safety, deliberateness, structure, problem-solving, family relations, communication, sources of support, regulation, and positive affect/memories. The number of sessions can be modified based on how quickly the family masters skills or their need for additional coping resources.

As in the trauma treatment MFG, the third module involves co-construction of a family trauma narrative. Sessions allow the family to use their coping skills to tell their trauma story safely and to move to meaning making and resolution at their own pace. A final session celebrates the family's accomplishments.

Adapting SFCR for Peer-to-Peer Recovery Groups[5]

In peer-to-peer recovery programs, women frequently talk of the many ways in which stressful relationships pose threats to their continued recovery. Of particular concern to these women is the intergenerational toll of trauma, violence, substance abuse, and mental health problems. Substance abuse, mental disorders, violence, and trauma can each disrupt relationships with parents, siblings, children, and grandchildren. Women in recovery are acutely aware of the difficult relationships they had with their own parents and families and how they are recreating these relationships in the next generation. Women express grave concerns about their relationships with their children and their families. The content and strategies that comprise SFCR seemed to provide an excellent method for helping women (and potentially men) deal with these concerns.

The adaptation process for the peer-to-peer model was undertaken in partnership with women in recovery. These women, who were already serving as peer leaders, participated in a training based on SFCR objectives and strategies. Following the training, a small group of peer leaders worked with the developer to adapt SFCR concepts and activities for one-hour peer-mentored group sessions. Materials were also modified for use with this format. There are 20 groups included in SFCR-PP arranged under five conceptual headings: Family, Traditions, Routine, Safety, and Connections.

Peer mentors piloted all SFCR-PP materials in one-to-one and group peer mentoring sessions with mothers in the context of a peer recovery community. Sessions and materials were modified based on feedback from these initial trials. Given success with the training and use of SFCR in peer-led groups, a formal training protocol and family peer-mentoring guide have been completed.

In the new adapted format, SFCR-PP provides an exceptional opportunity for helping individuals place structure and process around their own family practices, beliefs, values, and cultural contexts and improve their protective function. As individuals learn new coping skills, they are encouraged to promote positive change in their family's daily life and home environment. They are encouraged to believe that they have the ability to use their new skills to create chain reactions that positively impact future generations.

GUIDELINES FOR SFCR PRACTICE

Confidentiality

Explaining the concept of confidentiality to each family and, in the MFG models, with the group as a whole is necessary. Families should be made aware of the fact that there is an expectation in SFCR MFGs that experiences shared by other families are private and should be never be talked about outside of group.

Additionally, in the MFG models, as facilitators talk with families about whether SFCR is a treatment option for them, they should be informed that they will *never* be expected to talk in front of the other families about their traumatic exposures. They may choose to share some of their experiences, but will not be asked to do so.

Families should always be informed that facilitators are mandatory reporters and are obligated by law to report any suspected abuse of vulnerable family members or serious threats of harm to self or others.

Managing Crises

Families who participate in SFCR are often crisis-oriented. This is, in part, because they are continually exposed to high-stress situations, including new traumas, and, in part, because their coping resources have been depleted. Dealing with frequent crises can derail treatment. SFCR facilitators are encouraged to use strategies to help families deal with crisis situations without interrupting the flow of sessions.

Early in SFCR, if a family is frequently in crisis, they should be coached on effective crisis management strategies. Such strategies might include accurately appraising the crisis, looking for adaptive strategies to manage the situation safely, asking for and accepting resources from supports, and problem-solving to determine best possible solutions. If families continue to struggle with crises, they can be encouraged to revisit these strategies. If possible, much of this work should be done outside of regularly scheduled SFCR MFG sessions.

An entire session in SFCR-FFT is devoted to helping the family learn how to evaluate crisis situations and manage them safely. This session format and materials can also be used with families participating in the MFG to assist them in dealing with crises.

Sometimes a crisis or a new trauma occurs that prevents a family from participating in SFCR. Facilitators should help the family determine whether they can continue or whether it would be best to take a break and return to SFCR once they are more stable.

At the start of each session, SFCR facilitators "check in" with the family about what might get in the way of their full participation in the activities planned. These brief moments allow families to let facilitators know about any crisis they are dealing with while at the same time committing to put whatever the problem is aside and be fully present with their family during the session.

Session Routines

Given SFCR's foundation in ritual and routine theory, an established routine is followed for each session, including a beginning and ending practice, a set schedule of activities, use of the same space each week, and each session starting and ending on time.

Each SFCR session starts in the same way and each session ends the same way. The opening and closing segments are quite deliberate and help to establish consistency and predictability. This is important for establishing the safety and certainty needed by families who have experienced chronic trauma.

In the MFG versions, an important part of the opening and closing are the ritual activities adopted by the families. These rituals help establish a unique identify for each MFG. Each group varies in the ritual they choose but all groups become invested in making sure that the rituals occur in much the same manner each week.

CLINICAL STRATEGIES IN SFCR

SFCR includes a wide variety of clinical strategies and practice elements. Each session includes multiple activities and moves at a fairly rapid pace in order to keep all family members engaged. Some background about and explanation of some of the specific techniques will enhance the ability of facilitators to carry them out with fidelity.

Building Family Routines

Helping families establish and practice functional routines is fundamental to SFCR. Families design routines related to daily structure, stress management, safety, and values. Early in the intervention, facilitators provide some psychoeducation defining routines, describing why routines are important, and talking about the best ways to develop routines that work (see inset).

Family members are asked to use a structured approach to designing a new routine or improving a daily routine that is not achieving its intended goal. This approach involves listing each step and then stipulating the who, what, when, and where of each step. Families are asked to put their new or improved routines in practice during the next week.

Development of routines is coupled with preventive problem-solving to ensure that nothing gets in the way. Each time a family develops a routine, they are asked to think about what could go wrong that might prevent them from carrying it out. They discuss what they would do in the event that things did go wrong, so that they could successfully follow through on their routine. This two-part exercise is repeated in multiple activities as families

Some things to think about when developing a routine are:

- How many steps are involved?
- Is there an order or sequence for the steps?
- How much time is needed to do all the steps?
- Is there an organizing action or cue that starts the routine off?
- Is someone in charge of making sure that the activity gets done?

develop other routines, such as their relaxation routine or their safety routine.

Problem-Solving

Planning and problem-solving are good skills for families to have and are especially important for families who have experienced chronic adversity:

> Deliberate planning and follow through, which often requires effective problem-solving, focuses attention on the here and now (rather than the traumatic past and may also provide an anecdote to feelings of futurelessness), creates a sense of efficacy, and provides opportunities for success (Folkman & Moskowitz, 2000; Kiser, 2007).
>
> (Figley & Kiser, 2013, p. 105)

In SFCR, families learn a variety of methods for both individual and collaborative problem-solving, including preventive problem-solving, negotiation, consensus seeking, and brainstorming.

Preventive problem-solving, which involves anticipating what might go wrong and identifying ways to handle situations in the event that things do go wrong, is an important coping skill for families

who deal with unpredictable and uncontrollable circumstances. Preventive problem-solving helps families take some control over the situation by being prepared and ready to take action, instead of reaction. Multiple therapeutic activities, such as the process for developing routines just described, help families develop preventive problem-solving skills.

Regulation Skills

Studies show clear evidence linking early adversity with alterations in both structure and function of major biological stress management systems, alterations that are apparent in childhood and persist over the life course (Loman & Gunnar, 2010; Seeman, Epel, Gruenwald, Karlamangla, & McEwen, 2010; Shonkoff, Boyce, & McEwen, 2009). Since everyone in the family is vulnerable to such dysregulations, in SFCR, regulation skills are taught to the whole family.

Families are asked to try out a variety of regulation activities during SFCR sessions and to develop a relaxation or regulation practice at home. Facilitators introduce families to safety, affect attunement, relaxation (deep breathing, progressive muscle relaxation), imagery, and mindfulness activities. They pick techniques for each family based on their interests, age of family members (appropriate for even the youngest family member), and trauma history. Facilitators are mindful of the fact that some techniques may be triggering for certain families based on their exposures. Resources providing creative, developmentally appropriate practices are readily available and easily accessible.

Once the families have learned several techniques, they design a relaxation practice routine for home. Families quickly develop a favorite and this becomes their "go-to" practice when any family member or the whole family becomes dysregulated.

Paired Breathing

Paired breathing practices help promote attunement and co-regulation. In paired breathing activities, family members pay close attention to and try to match each other's rate of inhalation and exhalation. Family members can start in dyads or as a whole family and sit facing each other. Facilitators start this activity by counting for several cycles of inhalations and exhalations so that everyone in the family synchronizes their breathing.

Families might then put a hand on each other's bellies to match breaths. In dyads, family members can also sit back to back, paying attention to the other's breathing and trying to synchronize.

Safety

Families who live in circumstances permeated with threat and danger have difficulty feeling safe. Even when no threat exists, families may be anticipating danger and feel they must be prepared for action. This is their status quo. Their physiological and psychological systems for recognizing and appreciating a sense of safety and protection are not well developed and difficult to access.

Safety Mapping

One powerful therapeutic activity in SFCR involves families constructing a map showing their living environment and labeling places where they feel safe or threatened. This concept is borrowed from geomapping and used in a novel way with individual families to provide them with ideas about how to identify, label, and communicate with each other about their safety concerns (Aronson, Wallis, O'Campo, & Schafer, 2007).

Safety mapping is a three-part activity. First, the family draws and illustrates their map. Facilitator instructions for this activity might be:

Let's use this large piece of paper to draw a map of your neighborhood. First, draw your street and then place your house on it. Fill in the street with other houses and stores and traffic signals and street signs. Let's draw the roads you walk or drive to get to school, church, etc.

Next, the family labels the places listed on their map according to how safe they feel while at this place. Each family member might have a different perspective on his or her sense of safety and would label that place accordingly. The family can spend time discussing what happens at each place that makes them feel safe or unsafe.

Safety mapping can be difficult for some families, especially if they are drawing places where traumas have occurred. Facilitators should be aware of the potential for triggered reactions and be prepared to help families regulate.

Caregivers may also be distressed during this activity if they learn about places where, and times when, their children do not feel safe. For some of the families who have participated in SFCR, caregivers have been disheartened to discover that there is no place that their children experience a sense of safety.

Finally, after completing the mapping and labeling activity, the family chooses a place that feels unsafe and devises a routine to increase their sense of safety. Many times, the new routine involves family members watching out for each other or working together to protect themselves. The safety maps can be revisited later in treatment with differences over time in the labeling of places as safe or unsafe indicating changes in sense of safety.

A clinical example illustrates how one family established a safety routine. The 6- and 8-year-old children in the Banks family looked over their map and labeled the walk to the bus stop and waiting at the bus stop as a place and time when they did not feel safe. They told their mother about some older kids who hung around, bullied them, and tried to get them to do things that were not safe. They told her about having their lunches or money stolen on a regular basis. Their mother had not heard about these problems before. As she asked them more questions about their concerns, the children were able to say that they only felt scared in the mornings.

The family decided to develop a safety routine around going to school. In the short-term, Ms. Banks agreed to walk the children to the bus stop and wait with them until the bus arrived. She also thought that she would talk to some other caregivers to see whether they could work out a way for one other adult to be around every morning to help supervise.

Another example illustrates the power of this activity. A young boy, Sam, had been working with a school guidance counselor for over a year due to witnessing domestic violence between his parents.

Following a successful course of treatment and a break, Sam came back when the courts granted his dad weekend visitation. Although Sam wanted to see his dad, he was throwing up and having nightmares in anticipation of going to his home. His father lived in a dangerous neighborhood and Sam did not feel safe visiting. If he tried to share his fears with his father, he would say, "You don't have to fear anything when I am around," so he would shut down. He was unwilling for anyone to talk with his dad about these fears because he would just get mad.

After several individual sessions, Sam was able to use some skills to soothe himself, but suddenly one day he came in grinning and announced to his therapist, "I don't have to stay at my dad's anymore. I go to my cousin's house and my dad either goes home or stays there, too." Sam showed his therapist the safety map that he made with his dad during SFCR. He explained that it was during this activity that he was able to tell his dad he felt safe everywhere but in and around his home. Together, they developed a safety routine that meant he would not have to go to his house and they were following through on it.

Building Strong Supports

Difficulties with interpersonal relations and altered social schemas make it difficult for many families who have experienced accumulated traumatic circumstances to build strong support networks, to ask for help during stressful times, to receive help when offered, and to come to the aid of others. Several techniques, in addition to the MFG format, are used to assist families in exploring the social supports available to them and to gain an understanding of how they can access these resources when faced with stressful situations.

Sociograms

Sociograms are charts or tools for exploring social space (Moreno, 1951). They are common to many therapies as a tool for helping individuals or families identify their social support systems (Mattaini, 1995). Sociograms are concentric circles labeled by categories of supports. In SFCR, the information gathered from the sociograms is used in the family sculpture activity.

In the MFG models, sociograms are used in breakout sessions to help family members identify who provides support for them during times of stress. The individual is in the center of the circles, the immediate family (or the "family" as defined by its members) is the next circle. Extended family supports are listed in the next concentric circle followed by friends and neighborhood or community supports. The individual is asked whom in each category they "turn to in times of need."

In SFCR-FTT, the family completes a sociogram together. As the family fills in the sociogram, facilitators are looking for agreement among family members about who to include in each circle. Facilitators are also observing whether there are family members who seem especially disengaged from family social supports.

Family Sculpture

In Module II of SFCR, a family sculpture exercise is introduced. A family sculpture was chosen for inclusion in SFCR to help families gain an understanding of the people resources that are available to the family during periods of stress.

Family sculpture, as a therapeutic technique, has its origins in experiential family therapy. Important names in the history of family sculpture include Constantine, Duhl, David Kantor, Virginia Satir, and Peggy Papp (Hernandez, 1998).

There are numerous versions of family sculptures, all of which focus on providing the family with a visual/spatial/symbolic representation of their family around a specific family dynamic. Family members are positioned in "physical space to represent relationships and roles within the family system" (Bischof & Helmeke, 2005, p. 257). This therapeutic technique can be a powerful tool for helping families "develop awareness and insight into their personal participation in ongoing interactional patterns" (Bischof & Helmeke, 2005, p. 260). It can evoke powerful emotions and meanings (Nøvik & Solem, 2003). It can also be a vehicle for change within the family.

Sculpting in a group setting with family members present involves three basic steps:

1. *Establishing the sculpture.* This step involves introducing the exercise along with defining the space and context to be used. The focus is defined by the family and the facilitator to depict a specific time, event, or issue in the family's life. The introduction to the family is meant to reduce any anxiety that they may have about participating by outlining the benefits. At this step, the sculptor is identified. In SFCR, the family sculpture is introduced by using the story of *Anansi, The Spider* (McDermott, 2009). This myth illustrates the use of people resources to save Anansi (or Ananse).

2. *Sculpting.* This step involves placing people in the sculpture and positioning them until they feel 'right' from the sculptor's vantage point. It is important for the sculptor to pick who will play each family member. As players are being added to the sculpture, the sculptor and the facilitator pay attention to the position, posture, facial expression, gesture, and actions of the people taking part. Taking a systemic view of the sculpturing exercise is important. During this step, the sculptor adds himself/herself to the sculpture. Players should be placed in the sculpture in relationship not only to the sculptor but to everyone being depicted. In addition to family members, the sculptor adds people who form the family's support system. Because sculptures often contain movable actors, this step can include putting the sculpture in motion.

3. *Processing or debriefing the sculpture.* This step involves the family working to make meaning out of their sculpture, incorporating differing perspectives from multiple family members, thinking about the impact of the activity, and the implications for their family moving forward. Observations from those watching the sculpture may also be elicited. Allowing all of the sculpture participants to exit their roles

is important and can be facilitated by having a deliberate ending to the sculpture activity (i.e., thanking all participants and having them return to their seats).

Timelines

Timelines are used for multiple purposes in mental health treatment and are a common therapeutic activity in trauma treatments. Timelines are used to help clients organize events sequentially to provide an overview of their history. In SFCR, two different applications of timelines are used.

Family Timeline

Families are asked to create a timeline, listing key events in the family's life cycle. Families are encouraged to include positive events rather than focusing their attention on just the bad things that have happened to them. Coming up with positive events is often challenging for families who are stuck with traumas as their dominant family storyline. The timeline provides perspective on the families' past and families are asked to leave space on their timelines to imagine and deliberately plan for a different, more hopeful future. Families come back to their timeline later in session and add some goals that they have set for themselves.

A clinical example helps to illustrate how the timeline provides perspective for families regarding their past, present, and future. A family participating in SFCR included three siblings and their paternal grandmother. These children had been multiply traumatized by physical abuse, domestic violence, and unstable residences while in their mother's care. At the beginning of treatment, each child resented their grandmother "for taking them away from their mom," and wanted very much to return home. A particularly notable session for this family was the family timeline session. Each family

member had a slightly different path to their arrival at the current day, but each child's future included growing up at grandma's house and visiting mom when "she got better." This new family unit had worked very hard on developing routines and family rituals and the children had learned that grandma's home was a safe and predictable place to live.

Trauma Timeline

At the beginning of the trauma narrative process, families make a list of the traumatic events that they have experienced. This trauma timeline includes events that were experienced by the whole family, as well as events that happened to individual family members. Once the family has generated their list, they decide on which events to include on their family trauma timeline and these events are ordered chronologically. Families use this trauma timeline to catalogue their exposure to catastrophic events and to make decisions about which events were most impactful by rating each event from least to most stressful. They use this timeline to decide how to focus their co-constructed trauma narrative.

Humor and Laughter

Humor and laughter are powerful strategies for coping with stress. Use of humor and laughter increases the expression of positive emotions and often relieves constant feelings of fear, worry, or sadness that accompany traumatic distress. Humor and laughter are encouraged in every session of SFCR. A goal of each session is that families share some positive moments and become comfortable expressing and modulating positive feelings while engaged in joint activity. Facilitators serve as role models for using humor and laughter in healthy ways and intervene when families or individual family members are using them in ways that cause hurt feelings or misunderstandings.

One SFCR session is entirely devoted to encouraging families to share fun times full of humor and laughter. During this session, families identify things that they do or could do to feel good, have fun, and share laughs. Families also concentrate on finding regular opportunities to celebrate the good things that happen.

Family Storytelling and Narrative

An entire chapter is devoted to the use of storytelling and narrative in SFCR (see Chapter 4).

Homework

Many of the skills taught in SFCR require practice. Practice during session is important, but practice at home is necessary for the skills to become incorporated in daily family functioning. Except in the workshop versions, homework is assigned to families at the end of most sessions. Homework in SFCR meets one of two purposes. It either makes use of skills taught or introduces concepts applied in the next session.

Facilitators are encouraged to follow some basic guidelines for encouraging families to follow through with their homework. When introducing the homework activity, they provide a clear rationale and instructions. They ask the families to make a commitment to carrying it out by asking some specific questions about how they will complete it. They reinforce the idea that the homework is important to healing but is also designed to encourage shared family activity and fun. Finally, facilitators make deliberate efforts to recognize families who complete their homework as it is reviewed or referred to in the next session.

NOTES

1. Special thanks to Christina Adams and Rachel Wax for their thoughtful feedback on serving as consumer facilitators.
2. Section based on Pasillas, Kiser, Gentry, Hernandez, and Bautista (2010).
3. Acknowledgments for the Latino adaptation go to Rebecca Pasillas who led the effort and to DePelchin Children's Center's staff; Blanca Hernandez, Judy Gentry, Vanessa Austin, Bianca Walker, Margaret Green; University of California San Francisco staff Élida Bautista and Joyce Dorado; House of Ruth, Baltimore staff Cecilia Suarez. Translations were done by Cecilia Suarez and Marilyn Camacho, House of Ruth, Baltimore, MD; Ana Torres-Thornton, DePelchin Children's Center, Houston, TX; and the Spring Branch Committee, DePelchin Children's Center, Houston, TX.
4. Acknowledgments for the SFCR-PP adaptation go to Steven Berkowitz, MD who co-authored the first three sessions of this new version.
5. Acknowledgements for the SFCR-PP adaptation go to Charlene Cotton, Regia Acheampong, and Khalisha Faunteroy; and to Community Connections, especially to Maxine Harris, Renee Robertson, Christina Buswell, Corinne Meijer, and Rebecca Wolfson Berley, for having the vision to use SFCR in this way and for collaborating to make this adaptation a reality. This adaptation of SFCR was supported in part by funding from the Center for Substance Abuse Treatment (Substance Abuse and Mental Health Services Administration) under the Recovery Community Support Program.

REFERENCES

Allen, S. N., & Bloom, S. L. (1994). Group and family treatment of post-traumatic stress disorder. *Psychiatric Clinics of North America, 17*, 425–437.

Aronson, R., Wallis, A., O'Campo, P., & Schafer, P. (2007). Neighborhood mapping and evaluation: A methodology for participatory community health initiatives. *Maternal and Child Health Journal, 1*, 373–383.

Asen, E. (2002). Multiple family therapy: an overview. *Journal of Family Therapy, 24,* 3–16.

Berkowitz, S., Stover, C., & Marans, S. (2010). The child and family traumatic stress intervention: Secondary prevention for youth at risk of developing PTSD. *Journal of Child Psychology and Psychiatry, 52,* 676–685. doi:10.1111/j.1469-7610.2010.02321.x.

Bischof, G. H., & Helmeke, K. B. (2005). Family sculpture procedures. In M. Cierpka, V. Thomas & D. Sprenkle (Eds.), *Family assessment: Integrating multiple clinical perspectives* (pp. 257–281). Cambridge, MA: Hogrefe Publishers.

Brody, G. H., Murry, V. M., Gerrard, M., Gibbons, F. X., Molgaard, V., McNair, L., Brown, A. C., Wills, T. A., Spoth, R. L., Luo, Z., Chen, Y., & Neubaum-Carlan, E. (2004). The strong African American families program: Translating research into prevention programming. *Child Development, 75,* 900–917.

Chorpita, B. F., Daleiden, E., & Weisz, J. R. (2005). Modularity in the design and application of therapeutic interventions. *Applied and Preventive Psychology, 11,* 141–156.

Cohen, J. A., Berliner, L., & Mannarino, A. P. (2000). Treating traumatized children: A research review and synthesis. *Trauma, Violence, & Abuse, 1,* 29–46.

Cohen, J. A., Mannarino, A. P., & Knudsen, K. (2005). Treating sexually abused children: One year follow-up of a randomized controlled trial. *Child Abuse & Neglect, 29,* 135–145.

Cohen, J. A., Mannarino, A. P., & Deblinger, E. (2006a). *Treating trauma and traumatic grief in children and adolescents.* New York: Guilford Press.

Cohen, J. A., Mannarino, A. P., & Staron V. (2006b). Modified cognitive behavioral therapy for childhood traumatic grief (CBT-CTG): A pilot study. *Journal of the American Academy of Child & Adolescent Psychiatry, 45,* 1465–1473.

Cohen, J. A., Deblinger, E., Mannarino, A. P., & Steer, R. A. (2004). A multisite, randomized controlled trial for children with sexual abuse-related PTSD symptoms. *Journal of the American Academy of Child & Adolescent Psychiatry, 43,* 393–402.

Compas, B. E., Connor-Smith, J. K., Saltzman, H., Thomsen, A. H., & Wadsworth, M. E. (2001). Coping with stress during childhood and adolescence: Problems, progress, and potential in theory and research. *Psychological Bulletin, 127,* 87–127.

Cook, A., Spinazzola, J., Ford, J., Lanktree, C., Blaustein, M., Cloitre, M., DeRosa, R., Hubbard, R., Kagan, R., Liautaud, J., Mallah, K., Olafson, E., & van der Kolk, B. (2005). Complex trauma in children and adolescents. *Psychiatric Annals, 35,* 390–398.

Cook, A., Spinazzola, J., Ford, J., Lanktree, C., Blaustein, M., Sprague, C. Cloitre, M. DeRosa, R., Hubbard, R., Kagan, R., Liautaud, J., Mallah, K., Olafson, E., & van der Kolk, B. (2007). Complex trauma in children and adolescents. *Focal Point, 21,* 4–8.

Courtois, C. A., & Ford, Julian D. (Eds.). (2009). Treating complex traumatic stress disorders: An evidence-based guide. New York: Guilford Press.

Cummings, E. M., Goeke-Morey, M. C., & Papp, L. M. (2003). A family-wide model for the role of emotion in family functioning. *Marriage and Family Review, 34,* 13–34.

Davies, W. H., & Flannery, D. J. (1998). Post-traumatic stress disorder in children and adolescents exposed to violence. *Pediatric Clinics of North America, 2,* 341–353.

Dishion, T. J., & Andrews, D. W. (1995). Preventing escalation in problem behaviors with high-risk young adolescents: Immediate and 1-year outcomes. *Journal of Consulting and Clinical Psychology, 63,* 538–548.

Eisenberg, N., Fabes, R. A., & Murphy, B. C. (1996). Parents' reactions to children's negative emotions: Relations to children's social competence and comforting behavior. *Child Development, 67,* 2227–2247.

Evans, G. W., & English, K. (2002). The environment of poverty: Multiple stressor exposure, psychophysiological stress, and socioemotional adjustment. *Child Development, 73,* 1238–1248. doi:10.1111/1467-8624.00469.

Fiese, B. H., & Sameroff, A. J. (1999). The stories that families tell: Narrative coherence, narrative interaction, and relationship beliefs. *Monographs of the Society for Research in Child Development, 64,* 1–36.

Figley, C., & Kiser, L. J. (2013) *Helping traumatized families* (2nd ed.). New York: Routledge.

Folkman, S., & Moskowitz, J. T. (2000). Positive affect and the other side of coping. *American Psychologist, 55*, 647–654.

Gottman, J. M., Katz, L. F., & Hooven, C. (1997). *Meta-emotion*. Mahwah, NJ: Lawrence Erlbaum.

Hernandez, S. L. (1998). The emotional thermometer: Using family sculpting for emotional assessment. *Family Therapy: The Journal of the California Graduate School of Family Psychology, 25*, 121–128.

Huey, S. J., & Polo, A. J. (2008). Evidence-based psychosocial treatments for ethnic minority youth. *Journal of Clinical Child & Adolescent Psychology, 37*, 262–301. doi:10.1080/15374410701820174.

Kiser, L. J. (2007). Protecting children from the dangers of urban poverty. *Clinical Psychology Review, 27*, 211–225.

Kumpfer, K. L., DeMarsh, J. P., & Child, W. (1989). Strengthening families program: Children's skills training curriculum manual, parent training manual, children's skill training manual, and family skills training manual (prevention services to children of substance-abusing parents). Social Research Institute, Graduate School of Social Work, University of Utah.

Laqueur, H. P., La Burt, H. A., & Morong, E. (1964). Multiple family therapy: Further developments. *International Journal of Social Psychiatry, 10*, 69–80.

Larson, R. W., & Almeida, D. M. (1999). Emotional transmission in the daily lives of families: A new paradigm for studying family process. *Journal of Marriage and the Family, 61*, 5–20.

Lengua, L. J. (2002). The contribution of emotionality and self-regulation to the understanding of children's response to multiple risk. *Child Development, 73*, 144–161.

Loman, M. M., & Gunnar, M. R. (2010). Early experience and the development of stress reactivity and regulation in children. *Neuroscience & Biobehavioral Review, 34*, 867–876. doi:10.1016/j.neubiorev.2009.05.007.

Lunkenheimer, E. S., Shields, A. M., & Cortina, K. S. (2007). Parental emotion coaching and dismissing in family interaction. *Social Development, 16*, 232–248.

McDermott, G. (2009). *Anansi the spider: A tale from the Ashanti*. New York: Harcourt School Publishers.

McDowell, D. J., Kim, M., O'Neil, R., & Parke, R. D. (2002). Children's emotional regulation and social competence in middle childhood: The role of maternal and paternal interactive style. *Marriage & Family Review, 34*, 345–364.

McFarlane, W. (2002). *Multi-family groups in the treatment of severe psychiatric disorders*. New York: Guilford Press.

McHale, J. P., Kuersten, R., & Lauretti, A. (1996). New directions in the study of family-level dynamics during infancy and early childhood. In J. P. McHale & P. A. Cowan (Eds.), *Understanding how family-level dynamics affect children's development: Studies of two-parent families* (pp. 5–26). San Francisco, CA: Jossey-Bass.

McKay, M. M., Gonzales, J. J., Stone, S., Ryland, D., & Kohner, K. (1995). Multiple family therapy groups: A responsive intervention model for inner city families. *Social Work with Groups, 18*, 41–56.

McKay, M. M., Gonzales, J., Quintana, E., Kim, L., & Abdul-Adil, J. (1999). Multiple family groups: An alternative for reducing disruptive behavioral difficulties of urban children. *Research on Social Work Practice, 9*, 593–607.

McKay, M. M, Harrison, M., Gonzales, J., Kim, L., & Quintana, E. (2002). Multiple-family groups for urban children with conduct difficulties and their families. *Psychiatric Service, 53*, 1467–1468.

March, J. S., Amaya-Jackson, L., Murray, M. C., & Schulte, A. (1998). Cognitive-behavioral psychotherapy for children and adolescents with posttraumatic stress disorder after single incident stressor. *Journal of the American Academy of Child & Adolescent Psychiatry, 37*, 585–593.

Mattaini, M. A. (1995). Visualizing practice with children and families. *Early Child Development and Care, 106*, 59–74.

Miller, J. K., & Slive, A. (2004). Breaking down the barriers to clinical service delivery: Walk-in family therapy. *Journal of Marital & Family Therapy, 30*, 95–103.

Moreno, J. L. (1951). *Sociometry, experimental method, and the science of society: An approach to a new political orientation*. Boston, MA: Beacon House.

Morris, A. S., Silk, J. S., Steinberg, L., Myers, S. S., & Robinson, L. R. (2007). The role of the family context in the development of emotion regulation. *Social Development, 16*, 361–388.

Nishith, P., Resick, P. A., & Griffin, M. G. (2002). Pattern of change in prolonged exposure and cognitive-processing therapy for female rape victims with post-traumatic stress disorder. *Journal of Consulting and Clinical Psychology, 70*, 880–886.

Nøvik, T. S., & Solem, M. (2003). Family distance matters. *Clinical Child Psychology and Psychiatry, 8*, 261–271.

Pasillas, R., Kiser, L. J., Gentry, J., Hernandez, B. N., & Bautista, E. M. (2010) Adapting a multi-family trauma group treatment: Strengthening family coping resources, for use with Latino families. Symposium presented at the National Latino Psychological Association Annual Meeting, San Antonio, TX.

Raver, C. C. (2004). Placing emotional self-regulation in sociocultural and socioeconomic contexts. *Child Development, 75*, 346–353. doi:10.1111/j.1467-8624.2004.00676.x.

Resick, P. A., & Schnicke, M. K. (1992). Cognitive processing therapy for sexual assault victims. *Journal of Consulting and Clinical Psychology, 60*, 748–756.

Resick, P. A., Nishith, P., Weaver, T. L., Astin, M. C., & Feuer, C. A. (2002). A comparison of cognitive-processing therapy with prolonged exposure and a waiting condition for the treatment of chronic posttraumatic stress disorder in female rape victims. *Journal of Consulting and Clinical Psychology, 70*, 867–879.

Samuels, J., Schudrich, W., & Altschul, D. (2009). *Toolkit for modifying evidence-based practice to increase cultural competence*. Orangeburg, NY: Research Foundation for Mental Health.

Seeman, T., Epel, E., Gruenewald, T., Karlamangla, A., & McEwen, B. S. (2010). Socio-economic differentials in peripheral biology: Cumulative allostatic load. *Annals of the New York Academy of Sciences, 1186*, 223–239. doi:10.1111/j.1749-6632.2009.05341.x.

Shonkoff, J. P., Boyce, W. T., & McEwen, B. S. (2009). Neuroscience, molecular biology, and the childhood roots of health disparities: Building a new framework for health promotion and disease prevention. *Journal of the American Medical Association, 301*, 2252–2259.

Strand, V., Hansen, S., & Layne, C. (2012). Report on results of coding project to identify common intervention objectives and practice elements across 26 trauma-focused intervention manuals. Unpublished Report.

Strand, V., Hansen, S., & Courtney, D. (2013). Common elements across evidence-based trauma treatment: Discovery and implications. *Advances in Social Work, 14*, 334–354.

Taylor, T., & Biglan, A. (1998). Behavioral family interventions for improving child-rearing: A review of the literature for clinicians and policy makers. *Clinical Child and Family Psychology Review, 1*, 41–60.

Temple, S. (1997). Treating inner-city families of homicide victims: A contextually oriented approach. *Family Process, 36*, 133–149.

Weine, S., Kulauzovic, Y., Klebic, A., Besic, S., Mujagic, A., Muzurovic, J., Muzurovic, J., Spahovic, D., Sclove, S., & Pavkovic, I. (2008). Evaluating a multiple-family group access intervention for refugees with PTSD. *Journal of Marital and Family Therapy, 34*, 149–164.

Zeman, J., Cassano, M., Perry-Parrish, C., & Stegall, S. (2006). Emotion regulation in children and adolescents. *Developmental and Behavioral Pediatrics, 27*, 155–168.

Chapter 7

Measuring Change in Trauma Symptoms and Constructive Coping

In this era of accountability and emphasis on using interventions that have proven effectiveness, it is important to demonstrate both under controlled conditions and in real-world settings that SFCR works for the families who participate. The evidence supporting SFCR, which is summarized in this chapter, indicates that it is a possibly efficacious intervention.

Those providing SFCR in community settings serving a wide variety of families are critical to demonstrating its effectiveness. To successfully carry out their important role as evaluators of the model, facilitators must:

1. appreciate the importance of the assessment process used to determine eligibility for SFCR and to measure change after the group has ended;

2. realize the current evidence regarding whether SFCR works based upon the data collected by the developer along with the data they have submitted to date; and

3. gain perspective on how the future research agenda might inform clinical practice.

MEASURING PRE-POST CHANGE

Assessment Strategies

The primary goals of SFCR are to decrease the impact of chronic trauma on identified family members and to increase protective family coping resources. To understand whether SFCR is accomplishing these objectives, measurement of both traumatic distress and family coping is incorporated as an integral part of this manualized intervention.

This assessment, using standardized instruments, is conducted prior to a family starting the intervention and repeated shortly after they have finished.

All providers of SFCR are trained to use a standardized assessment protocol and provided with technical assistance regarding the collection of reliable and valid data.

Measurement Protocol

Assessing Impact of Trauma

To measure the first goal, family members are assessed to determine their level of exposure to trauma and also their level of trauma-related distress.

Measures Used to Assess Children

(Optional) Traumatic Events Screening Inventory for Children—(TESI-C-Brief) and Parent Report (TESI-PR) (Ford et al., 2000) is a measure of experiencing and witnessing of a variety of traumatic events for children 3–18 years of age. There are two forms, the TESI-C-Brief for use directly with a child (age 4 and older) and the TESI-PRR for use with parents. TESI-C-Brief covers 16 events arranged hierarchically. Follow-up questions provide some detail regarding age of onset, intensity, and chronicity. The inventory can be used in interview format or as self-report. The authors recommend scoring each potential event using DSM criterion A (American Psychiatric Association, 2000). The TESI-C-Brief and TESI-PR have adequate test-retest reliability (Ribbe, 1996; Stover & Berkowitz, 2005).

UCLA PTSD Reaction Index for DSM-5 (UCLA RI 5) (Pynoos & Steinberg, 2013) is a self-report instrument keyed to DSM PTSD symptoms for school age youth who report traumatic stress experiences. Participants are presented with a list of 14 traumas, state whether they experienced the trauma (yes/no), and then identify the trauma they consider most bothersome. A five-point scale from 0 (none of the time) to 4 (most all the time) is used to rate 27 PTSD symptoms falling into four symptom categories: re-experiencing, avoidance, negative cognitions and mood, and arousal. In addition, the measure includes four dissociative symptoms designed to identify dissociative subtype. A parent report version also exists. An Overall PTSD Severity Score is calculated by summing the scores for each question that corresponds to a DSM symptom and a PTSD Severity Subscore is calculated for criterion symptoms. A partial or full diagnosis can be made by determining whether an individual meets DSM-5 symptom criteria in each cluster (American Psychiatric Association, 2013). Earlier versions of this measure demonstrated good internal consistency and test-retest reliability data (Steinberg, Brymer, Decker, & Pynoos, 2004; Steinberg et al., 2013).

Trauma Symptom Checklist for Young Children (TSCYC) (Briere, 2005) is a 90-item caregiver-report measure of post-traumatic symptoms, including those related to complex trauma. TSCYC comprises two validity scales and nine clinical subscales (Posttraumatic Stress-Intrusion (PTS-I), Posttraumatic Stress-Avoidance (PTS-AV), Posttraumatic Stress-Arousal (PTS-AR), Posttraumatic Stress-Total (PTS-TOT), Sexual Concerns (SC), Anxiety (ANX), Depression (DEP), Dissociation (DIS), and Anger/Aggression (ANG)). SFCR uses the TSCYC for young children who cannot complete the UCLA RI. The TSCYC has demonstrated good reliability and validity (Briere et al., 2001; Gilbert, 2004).

Child Behavior Checklist (CBCL) (Achenbach & Edelbrock, 1991; Achenbach & Rescorla, 2001) requires a parent to rate, on a three-point scale, each of 118 problems as they are perceived to reflect the child's behavior over the past six months. The instrument measures eight to nine subscales that can be collapsed into Internalizing, Externalizing, and a Total Score. Statistical data on reliability and validity have been well established and are reported elsewhere. The clinical cut-off score for the CBCL is a T score of 63 or greater with 60–63 considered in the borderline range of psychopathology. However, studies with samples of low-income children demonstrate higher mean scores (Kendall, Marrs-Garcia, Nath, & Sheldrick, 1999).

Measures Used to Assess Caregivers

PTSD Checklist—Civilian for DSM5 (PCL-5) (Weathers et al., 2013) is designed to assess self-reported levels of the 20 DSM-5 symptoms of PTSD. The respondent is asked to rate how much the problem described in each statement has bothered him or her over the past month. Total symptom severity scores range from 0 to 80. Strong psychometric properties have been shown for internal consistency and test retest reliability of the PCL-C DSM-IV version (Blanchard, Jones-Alexander, Buckley, & Forneris, 1996).

Brief Symptom Inventory-18 item (BSI) (Derogatis, 2000) is an 18-item self-report inventory of adult (18 years and older) psychological symptoms. The BSI yields a Global Severity Index and three subscales, including Somatization, Depression, and Anxiety. Based on empirical findings, it is recommended as a clinically meaningful instrument to measure symptom severity in adults with affective disorders (Prinz et al., 2013).

Assessing the Family

To measure the second goal, family members are assessed to determine how their family is functioning and coping.

Measures Used to Assess Parenting

The Parenting Stress Index-Short Form (PSI-SF) (Abidin, 1995) is a 36-item scale measuring caregiver stress and inappropriate parenting. It is appropriate for parents of children ages 1 month to 12 years. Each statement is rated using a five-point Likert scale indicating how much that item disturbed the caregiver in the past week and yields scores for Parental Distress (contributing parental factors), Difficult Child (contributing child factors related to parenting stress and dysfunction), and Parent-Child Dysfunction Interaction. The PSI-SF has a clinical cut-off, of which 90 is indicative of significant parenting stress. Evidence shows strong psychometric properties with internal consistency and six-month test-retest reliability.

Measures Used to Assess Family Functioning and Constructive Coping

The McMaster Family Assessment Device (FAD) or the General Functioning Subscale (FAD-GF) (Epstein, Baldwin, & Bishop, 1983; Miller, Epstein, Bishop, & Keitner, 1985) is a Likert scale instrument designed to measure family functioning based upon the McMaster Model. The FAD scores reflect a family member's perception of his or her family functioning. These instruments can be completed by family members over the age of 12 years. The FAD is a 60-item measure and the FAD-GF includes 12 items. Items are scored on a four-point scale from 1 ("healthy") to 4 ("unhealthy"). The FAD provides scores for seven scales, including problem-solving, communication, roles, affective responsiveness, affective involvement, behavior control, and overall functioning. The FAD-GF comprises only the scale measuring overall functioning. Clinical cut-off scores indicating healthy versus unhealthy functioning have been established with sensitivity and specificity (Miller et al., 1985).

Adequate test-retest reliability and concurrent validity have been reported (Byles, Byrne, Boyle, & Offord, 1988; Ridenour, Daley, & Reich, 1999).

Family Crisis Oriented Personal Evaluation Scales (F-COPES) (McCubbin, Olson, & Larsen, 1996) is a 30-item measure designed to assess family-level coping and completed by adolescents and adults. Dimensions derive from the Family Resiliency model. They include acquiring social support, reframing, seeking spiritual support, mobilizing family to acquire/accept help, and passive appraisal. Items are scored on a five-point Likert scale from always to never. Subscale scores and a total score are calculated. Total possible scores range from 30 to 150, with higher scores indicating higher levels of coping and problem-solving ability. Subscale scores and a total score are calculated. The F-COPES has evidence of reliability and validity.

Assessing Family Engagement and Participation

Facilitators maintain participation logs indicating sessions attended, including consecutive sessions attended, contact hours, and sessions attended by all members. Take-home assignments completed and returned are also tracked.

Family feedback is obtained after each session to gather information about family commitment, progress toward goals, and buy-in. Families are asked to provide candid input about what they like and do not like about each session. Families also provide ratings of their satisfaction with the intervention when they finish.

Qualitative Measures

Additionally, several qualitative techniques for understanding traumatic distress and constructive family coping are used in multiple sessions.

Safety Maps

During SFCR, families construct a map showing their living environment. They rate places where they feel safe and places where they feel threatened. Families can refer to their maps later in treatment and provide updated ratings, with differences in these ratings over time providing an indication of change in perceptions of safety.

Co-Constructed Family Narratives

Following multiple opportunities for family storytelling, each family in the treatment versions engages in family narrative. Assessment of the family's narrative processes over the course of the intervention can provide markers for improvements in coping resources.

Family Photos

Over the course of SFCR, facilitators compile a collection of family photos taken both during and between sessions. By conducting photo analysis, these pictures provide a source of qualitative data regarding change in family relations and dynamics (Higgins & Highley, 1986; Weiser, 1993).

Family Diaries

Parents and other family members can be asked to complete diaries of their daily routine. Changes in the way families carry out their daily routine may be recorded using this method.

Family Mealtime Observations (Research Groups Only)

Each multi-family session begins with a family meal. Three times over the course of the intervention, each family's meals are videotaped for further review using the Family Mealtime Q-Sort (Kiser, Medoff, Black, Nurse, & Fiese, 2010). Mealtimes are evaluated to determine whether the family is making positive changes in their mealtime routine interactions.

EVIDENCE BASE FOR SFCR

SFCR is a possibly efficacious treatment. Results from the two studies demonstrating positive results are presented. A future research agenda provides facilitators with some understanding of the many questions that remain unanswered regarding SFCR.

Study 1: Open Trials

Development of SFCR followed a multi-step process (National Institute on Drug Abuse's (NIDA) Stage Model of Behavioral Therapies Research) (Rousaville, Carroll, & Onken, 1999). Step two of that process involved testing of the new manualized intervention to determine feasibility and preliminary measurement of outcomes.

Open trials of SFCR used a pre-post design to allow for close monitoring of the intervention structure and content (Kiser, Donohue, Hodgkinson, Medoff, & Black, 2010). The outcomes of interest were the process measures collected to monitor participation, cultural sensitivity and acceptability, clinician competence, intervention integrity, and child outcomes.

The sample included children, ages 1–12 years old, recruited from urban outpatient clinics. Eligible children had been exposed to multiple traumas that met DSM IV Criterion A and also met partial or full criteria for PTSD (American Psychiatric Association, 2000). Families participated in either a 14- or 15-week MFG version of SFCR. Eight groups were conducted over 36 months with an average of 4.25 families initially enrolled in each group.

Each session was videotaped and 10 percent were randomly chosen and monitored for clinician competence and adherence. Facilitators demonstrated clinical competence in conducting the groups (average rating 4.3 out of 5 or "most of the time"). Trained facilitators were 92 percent compliant at maintaining the structure of the groups and introducing the content as stipulated in the manual.

Families actively engaged and participated in SFCR as evidenced by 53 percent completion rates, average attendance at 85 percent of scheduled sessions for families who completed the group, and over 50 percent completion of homework. Families reported high satisfaction with the intervention, with all items rated 3.89 or higher on a five-point scale.

Pre-post data on 19 children were analyzed. Change was assessed using t-tests for dependent samples and effect sizes were calculated using Cohen's D. Significant reductions in overall PTSD symptoms, including re-experiencing and arousal symptoms, were found. On the CBCL, caregivers reported significant reductions in internalizing symptoms, including anxiety and depression, social problems, aggressive behaviors, and attention problems.

Major limitations of this preliminary study included the small sample size and lack of a comparison group. However, the results suggested that SFCR demonstrates feasibility, tolerability, and positive effects on children's symptoms. These promising results supported the need for further research on SFCR.

Study 2: Implementation Research

Since publication of the feasibility trial, two SFCR MFG versions are being implemented nationally with pre-post data submitted to the developer (Kiser, Backer, Winkles, & Medoff, in press). A total of 14 sites contributed data to evaluate the impact of SFCR on the children and families participating. The sample used for this study included 185 families who participated in SFCR groups conducted by these providers. Twenty-seven families participated in high-risk groups and 158 families participated in the trauma treatment groups. Pre-post data were submitted on 103 children.

The identified child in this sample had a mean age of 10.7 (2.8 SD) years. Fifty-seven percent of the children were female. The children experienced a wide variety of trauma types and all of them had experienced multiple traumas. Race and ethnicity was reported by the primary caregiver and the sample was primarily African American (66 percent) and non-Hispanic (76 percent). Over half of the families (61 percent) reported having a family income of under $20,000. Most of the caregivers were female (89 percent). There were no differences on demographic or outcome variables at pre-assessment between the sample with follow-up (N = 103) and those without follow-up (N = 82).

A linear mixed model was used to assess change over time. The model included time (baseline, post-intervention), and a random intercept to account for the non-independence of the repeated measures and a random effect to account for clustering of individuals in MFGs (Proc Mixed).

Results of these analyses demonstrate that child PTSD symptoms are significantly reduced post-SFCR by both caregiver and child report. Children report significant reductions in overall symptoms and re-experiencing symptoms. By parent report, child total, avoidance, and arousal symptoms decrease significantly on pre-post assessments.

Caregivers also report significant reductions in their child's behavior problems. Parents report significant reductions in their child's anxious/depressed, social, attention, rule-breaking, and aggressive behaviors, as well as on the summary scales of internalizing, externalizing, and total problems. In addition, parents report significant reductions on the CBCL Dysregulation Profile.

Caregivers report significantly healthier family functioning as measured by the Family Assessment Device-12. They also report decreased parenting stress on the Parenting Stress Index-Short-Form.

Effect sizes were calculated using Cohen's D. They were generally in the medium range.

Moderation by gender of child, or age (< 10 years versus > 10 years) was assessed by adding age group and gender, as well as the interaction of each, with time to the models. Results of these analyses indicate no differences in treatment effects based on gender or age.

The results presented go beyond those previously published to document significant improvements in family functioning and coping in addition to significant positive effects on children's symptoms of trauma-related distress. Although further research is essential, SFCR meets its primary intervention goals when delivered in multiple real-world settings.

Collection of data from community settings presents some challenges that reduce the reliability and generalizability of the results. One of the biggest limitations is the number of participants with complete pre-post data. Although there were no differences found between those with or without post assessments, bias is always a concern when large amounts of missing data are involved. Other limitations of the practice-based evidence presented include the lack of a control group and reliance on caregiver report of child behavior problems, parenting stress, and family functioning. The strength of the data collected from multiple provider sites is that it reflects on the changes one might expect when SFCR is provided in real-world settings.

SFCR Research Agenda

Many research questions remain regarding SFCR including matters related to feasibility, tolerability, efficacy, effectiveness, and mechanisms of change. Various issues in each area are presented and explored briefly.

Feasibility

Multiple versions of SFCR have been created in order to increase flexibility of implementation and address issues related to feasibility. Results of Study 2 indicate that the MFG versions of SFCR are feasible in multiple types of provider and community settings. Feedback from these sites, however, suggests that staffing the treatment version can be challenging in some settings. The high-risk group mitigates that challenge somewhat but does not offer the same intensity of treatment. Research comparing the two versions would provide guidance to providers about when each MFG should be used with which families.

Tolerability

In terms of tolerability, although attendance rates are promising, additional research is needed to define treatment completion or the number of sessions needed to support positive outcomes and to identify families who are most likely to receive the dose of SFCR that maximizes benefit. This information would allow facilitators to target families for participation who have the greatest likelihood of receiving a therapeutic dose. Research on tolerability would also illuminate the reasons for dropout or barriers to full participation. Use of this knowledge could inform improvements to family engagement strategies and use of family supports to bolster regular attendance.

Efficacy

Examining the effects of SFCR using a randomized controlled study design, preferably with an active trauma-specific treatment as a control condition, is a crucial next step. This would provide evidence of SFCR's efficacy under conditions of high internal validity. Significant and positive results from several randomized controlled trials are necessary to meet the standards for an evidence-based practice.

Effectiveness

Continued efforts to collect practice-based evidence from the multiple providers offering SFCR remains part of the future research agenda. Efforts to simplify and further standardize data collection procedures have been undertaken. Additional steps are being taken to answer important questions about the model.

The current assessment protocol focuses on one identified child in the family, although there are frequently other family members, including the caregivers, vulnerable to or suffering from stressor-related symptoms and disorders. Determining whether SFCR is helpful in reducing symptoms and distress in multiple family members would clarify the benefits of using this family treatment approach. Measures of caregiver exposure and symptoms are being added as an option for community providers. Measurement of change at additional time points, such as six months or one year following completion of SFCR, would be important for determining longer-term benefits.

Research designed to elucidate the mechanisms of change is also being considered. Several hypothesized mechanisms of change are candidates for study. Increased social support may be an important mechanism of change for families who participate in the MFGs. Or, the development of and deliberate follow-through with family rituals and routines may be a significant contributor to positive outcomes. Or, participation in SFCR may improve family and individual regulatory processes leading to reductions in symptoms of distress.

REFERENCES

Abidin, R. R. (1995). *Parenting stress index* (3rd ed.). Odessa, FL: Psychological Assessment.

Achenbach, T. M., & Edelbrock, C. (1991). *Manual for the Child Behavior Checklist.* Burlington, VT: University of Vermont Department of Psychiatry.

Achenbach, T. M., & Rescorla, L. A. (2001). *Manual for the ASEBA School-Age Forms & Profiles.* Burlington, VT: University of Vermont, Research Center for Children, Youth, & Families.

American Psychiatric Association. (2000). *Diagnostic and statistical manual of mental disorders* (4th ed.). Washington, DC: American Psychiatric Association.

American Psychiatric Association. (2013). *Diagnostic and statistical manual of mental disorders* (5th ed.). Washington, DC: American Psychiatric Association.

Blanchard, E. B., Jones-Alexander J., Buckley, T. C., & Forneris, C. A. (1996). Psychometric properties of the PTSD Checklist (PCL). *Behaviour Research and Therapy, 34,* 669–673.

Briere, J. (2005). *Trauma Symptom Checklist for Young Children (TSCYC): Professional manual.* Odessa, FL: Psychological Assessment Resources.

Briere, J., Johnson, K., Bissada, A., Damon, L., Crouch, J., Gil, E., Hanson, R., & Ernst, V. (2001). The Trauma Symptom Checklist for Young Children (TSCYC): Reliability and association with abuse exposure in a multi-site study. *Child Abuse Neglect, 25,* 1001–1014.

Byles, J., Byrne, C., Boyle, M. H., & Offord, D. R. (1988). Ontario Child Health Study: Reliability and validity of the General Functioning subscale of the McMaster Family Assessment Device. *Family Process, 27,* 97–104.

Derogatis, L. R. (2000). *BSI-18: Administration, Scoring and Procedures Manual.* Minneapolis, MN: National Computer Systems.

Epstein, N. B., Baldwin, L. M., & Bishop, D. S. (1983). The McMaster Family Assessment Device. *Journal of Marital & Family Therapy, 9*, 171–180.

Ford, J. D., Racusin, R., Ellis, C. G., Daviss, W. B., Reiser, J., Fleischer, A., & Thomas, J. (2000). Child maltreatment, other trauma exposure, and posttraumatic symptomatology among children with oppositional defiant and attention deficit hyperactivity disorders. *Child Maltreatment, 5*, 205–217.

Gilbert, A. M. (2004). Psychometric properties of the Trauma Symptom Checklist for Young Children (TSCYC). *Dissertation Abstracts International*, 65.

Higgins, S., & Highley, B. (1986). The camera as a study tool: Photo interview of mothers and infants with congestive heart failure. *Children's Health Care, 15*, 119–122.

Kendall P. C., Marrs-Garcia A, Nath, S. R., & Sheldrick R. C. (1999). Normative comparisons for the evaluation of clinical significance. *Journal of Consulting and Clinical Psychology, 67*(3), 285–299.

Kiser, L. J., Backer, P., Winkles, J., & Medoff, D. (in press). Strengthening family coping resources (SCFR): Practice-based evidence for a promising trauma intervention. *Journal of Couple and Family Psychology*.

Kiser, L. J., Donohue, A., Hodgkinson, S., Medoff, D., & Black, M. M. (2010). Strengthening family coping resources: The feasibility of a multi-family group intervention for families exposed to trauma. *Journal of Traumatic Stress, 23*, 802–806. doi:10.1002/jts.20587.

Kiser, L. J., Medoff, D., Black, M. M., Nurse, & Fiese, B. H. (2010). Family ritual mealtime Q-sort: A measure of ritual and routine mealtime functioning. *Journal of Family Psychology, 24*, 92–96.

McCubbin, H. I., Olson, D., & Larsen, A. (1996). Family-crisis oriented personal scales (F-COPES). In H. I. McCubbin, A. I. Thompson, & M. A. McCubbin (Eds.), *Family assessment: Resiliency, coping and adaptation—Inventories for Research and Practice* (pp. 455–507). Madison, WI: University of Wisconsin System.

Miller, I., Epstein, N., Bishop, D., & Keitner, G. (1985). The McMaster Family Assessment Device: Reliability and validity. *Journal of Marital and Family Therapy, 11*, 345–356.

Prinz, U., Nutzinger, D. O., Schulz, H., Petermann, F., Braukhaus, C., & Andreas, S. (2013). Comparative psychometric analyses of the SCL-90-R and its short versions in patients with affective disorders. *BMC Psychiatry, 13*, 1–9.

Pynoos, R., & Steinberg, A. (2013). UCLA PTSD Index for DSM-5.

Ribbe, D. (1996). Psychometric review of traumatic event screening instrument for children (TESI-C). In: B. H. Stamm (Ed.), Measurement of stress, trauma, and adaptation (pp. 386–387). Lutherville, MD: Sidran Press.

Ridenour, T. A., Daley, J. G., & Reich, W. (1999). Factor analyses of the Family Assessment Device. *Family Process, 38*, 497–510.

Rousaville, B., Carroll, K., & Onken, L. (1999). *NIDA's stage model of behavioral therapies research: Getting started and moving on from stage 1*. Treatment Research Branch, National Institute on Drug Abuse.

Steinberg, A. M., Brymer, M., Decker, K., & Pynoos, R. S. (2004). The UCLA PTSD Reaction Index. *Current Psychiatry Reports, 6*, 96–100.

Steinberg, A. M., Brymer, M., Ghosh Ippen, C., Kim, S., Ostrowski, S. A., Gully, K. J. & Pynoos, R. S. (2013). Psychometric properties of the UCLA PTSD Reaction Index. *Journal of Traumatic Stress, 26*, 1–9.

Stover, C. S., & Berkowitz, S. J. (2005). Assessing violence exposure and trauma symptoms in young children: A critical review of measures. *Journal of Traumatic Stress, 18*, 707–717.

Weathers, F. W., Litz, B. T., Keane, T. M., Palmieri, P. A., Marx, B. P., & Schnurr, P. P. (2013). The PTSD Checklist for DSM-5 (PCL-5). Available at www.ptsd.va.gov (accessed September 10, 2014).

Weiser, J. (1993) *Phototherapy techniques: Exploring the secrets of personal snapshots and family albums*. San Francisco, CA: Jossey-Bass.

PART III

SESSION GUIDELINES

USING THE MFG SESSION GUIDELINES AND SUPPORTING MATERIALS

The manual and supporting materials provide a comprehensive description of SFCR, the modules, and each individual session.

The description of each module indicates the purpose with a description of its theoretical underpinnings. A listing of the sessions included within each module is also provided.

Each session is outlined in detail. Session guidelines include:

 An overview summarizing the goals of the session.

 A section, labeled Threads, outlining the *protective family coping resources* that are developed during the session, along with suggested links to home behavior and processes that can be presented during the session.

 Description of the preparation needed.

 A schedule of activities.

 Homework due and to be assigned.

A list of all supplies and supporting materials needed for the session.

 Listing of materials needed.

 Listing of handouts needed.

 Listing of posters needed.

 Listing of books needed.

The session schedule provides detailed instructions about each activity within a session. This schedule includes:

 Specific objectives for the activity.

 Name of the activity and time frame.

 Listing of materials needed for the activity.

 Listing of handouts needed for the activity.

 Listing of posters needed for the activity.

 Listing of books needed for the activity.

 Scripted instructions for leading the session. The instructions indicate which facilitator is taking the lead, and give examples of what the facilitator might say to the group (italicized statements) and instructions for the facilitators to follow (plain text).

Notes provide helpful suggestions about roles for the other facilitators. The intention for these detailed instructions is to give the facilitators/ clinicians a solid understanding of how each activity is supposed to be introduced and structured. It is important that these instructions are followed closely; however, it is not the intention that the scripts be read verbatim. In fact, the groups run more smoothly when the facilitators/clinicians are very familiar with the instructions and scripts and only need to refer to them occasionally during the session.

 ## Homework Due

Supporting materials include all of the handouts, homework assignments, and posters needed for the group, along with recommendations for preparing them. All supporting materials are available on the SFCR website (sfcr.umaryland.edu). A list of supplies needed to conduct SFCR is also included.

SFCR Trauma Treatment Overview

Module I: Rituals and Routine

Pre-Session	Evaluating Trauma and Family Functioning
1	Telling Family Stories
2	Ritual Family Tree
3	Family Diary

Module II: Protective Coping Resources

4	Feeling Safe I
5	Feeling Safe II
6	People Resources
7	Life Choices
8	Spirituality and Values
9	Things Get in the Way
HR10	Celebration!

Module III: Trauma Resolution and Consolidation

10	Telling About What Happened
11	When Bad Things Happen I
12	When Bad Things Happen II
13	Marking the Trauma
14	Good Things Happen Too!
15	Celebration!
Post	Re-Evaluating Trauma and Family Functioning

Module I
Rituals and Routine

This module provides families with an understanding of how ritual and routine can provide the foundation for supporting basic family processes . . .

Ritualization indicates the extent to which a family enjoys a dynamic ritual life that is continuous over time. It includes various features of family rituals: breadth across ritual activities (based upon having at least a modicum of rituals), elaboration of rituals, continuity over time in carrying out rituals, and positive feeling about ritual observation by family members.

Daily routines include a range of activities typically practiced by families. They range from "bigger" routines (that can also become rituals in some families), such as dinner times, to more "mundane" routines, such as observing regular bedtimes for children, developing leisure time hobbies, and a wide range of likely activities that characterize the day-to-day life of most families with children.

Role clarity suggests the extent to which family members have well understood and acceptable role distribution when it comes to carrying out the duties that need to be done in the family on a regular basis or during special occasions. In some families, this might mean that one member may be carrying most of the responsibility for these activities while in other families everyone shares the responsibility. Two facets of role clarity include leadership and shared responsibilities.

MODULE OVERVIEW

Session Number

Pre-Session	Evaluating Trauma and Family Functioning
1	Telling Family Stories
2	Ritual Family Tree
3	Family Diary

Module I PRE-SESSION Evaluating Trauma and Family Functioning

 ## Objectives

- To assess history of trauma exposure and current symptoms of distress.
- To have a conversation with each family about their history of traditions, routines, and rituals.

 ## Threads

- Evaluation helps provide both the family and the team with important information for supporting treatment and for strengthening the family's coping abilities across all of the *protective family coping resources.*

 ## Preparation

- Schedule a convenient time to meet with the family for about three hours.
- Prepare all materials.
- Prepare research folder with copies of standardized measures labeled with subject number, informant code, and date of administration.
- Copy consent form (research group only).

 ## Session Overview

| Activity 1 | Joining | 20 minutes |
| Activity 2 | Assessing Trauma Symptoms and Measuring Family Functioning | 120 minutes |

 ## Materials

- Pens/pencils
- Paper
- Assessment measures, including initial satisfaction form
- Research folder

 ## Handouts

- Consent forms (research group only)
- Assent Forms (research group only)
- SFCR Group Calendar   M1.Pre.Group.Calendar

Module I PRE-SESSION Evaluating Trauma and Family Functioning

ACTIVITY 1: JOINING

 20 MINUTES

 Goals

- To explain about the treatment and the assessment process.

 Materials

- Consent form (research group only)
- Assent form (research group only)
- Consent for audio/videotaping (research groups)
- Assent for audio/videotaping (research groups)

 Instructions

Interviewer: *Thanks for agreeing to meet with me today. We are about to start a program that looks at family traditions and helping families use their traditions to strengthen their family life and to cope with bad things that happen. Before we start that program, we like to talk with each family to get to know them and to learn about how trauma has affected their lives.*

Explain about the program and the research process. (Research group only: Complete the consent process. Read the consent forms and have caregiver(s) sign. Meet with the child or children and explain the assent forms and the child or children sign.)

Module I PRE-SESSION *Evaluating Trauma and Family Functioning*

ACTIVITY 2: ASSESSING TRAUMA SYMPTOMS AND MEASURING FAMILY FUNCTIONING

 120 MINUTES

 Goals

- To assess the impact of trauma on individual family members and the family.

 Materials

- Research folder with pre-labeled instruments
- Pens/pencils/crayons
- Paper

 Handouts

- SFCR group calendar

 Instructions

Administer the instruments from the folder.

Offer to read each instrument to them, if they would like.

Collect all of the completed instruments and return them to the research folder.

Check to make sure that all of the questions are answered.

Note any concerns you have about the validity of the answers.

Give the family the SFCR group calendar.

Interviewer: *Here is a calendar that will tell you about all of the group sessions. You can use it to keep track of when the group will meet and what you can expect at each session.*

Help the family to fill it in, noting the month, day, and time that the group will meet.

Interviewer: *Thanks for taking time to meet with me today. I hope that you will enjoy the program about family traditions.*

Module I

Telling Family Stories

Objectives

- To reinforce the sense of identity and belonging to the family by telling family stories.
- To encourage sharing about the family between parents and children.
- To introduce the families to the concepts of traditions, routines, and rituals.

Threads

- Connectedness and positive memories—strengths and family resilience factors can be stressed as families connect to make positive memories of shared family time.
- Deliberateness—rituals and routines are established during this first session. The link between planning and follow through can be made explicit for families and generalized from group to examples from home.
- Co-Regulation—families begin to explore and practice establishing and maintaining a comfort zone for interaction.
- Resource Seeking—this session sets the foundation for community building and using social networks for support.

Preparation

- Type in the names and print the **Name.Cards** (half-fold cards or cardstock folded).
- Type in the names and print the **Family.Name.Labels** (Avery 5163).
- Print and cut the **SFCR Reminder Postcards** (postcards).
- Print the **Group.Schedules** (business cards; Avery 5371).
- Send out postcards to remind families of first group.
- Food and facilities planning and preparation.
- Decide on facilitators' roles.
- Update on the status of each family in the group.
- Anticipate any problems that might arise during the session.

Session Overview

Activity 1	Family Meal	30 Minutes
Activity 2	What is a Family Tradition?	30 Minutes
Activity 3	Telling Family Stories	35 Minutes
Activity 4	Establishing Group Rituals	15 Minutes
Activity 5	Closing	10 Minutes

Homework to be Assigned

- Complete album page
- Relative interview

Module I SESSION 1 *Telling Family Stories*

Materials

- Tables (one for each family)
- Centerpieces
- Nameplates and session schedules (one for each family)
- Nametags
- Place settings/napkins
- Nutritious meal/drinks
- Video camera, remote microphones, and tapes (research groups only)
- Tape recorders and tapes (one for each family)
- Materials for family albums (cardboard or cardstock for covers, paper, hole punch, yarn or string, decorating materials, glue) (one for each family)
- Toy dinnerware and food
- Pens/pencils/markers/crayons/scissors/ruler/paper
- Folders (one for each family)
- Flipchart/blackboard

Handouts

- Introduction to Family Traditions and Routines   M1.S1.Intro
  M1.S1.Kids.Game1
  M1.S1.Kids.Game2
- Family Rituals and Routines Charts   M1.S1.Adoles.Game1
  M1.S1.Adoles.Game2
- *A Story, A Story* (condensed version)   M1.S1.Story
- Relative Interview   M1.S1.Interview
- Family Rating Form   M1.S1.Feedback
- Participant Log   M1.S1.Log
- Clinician Rating Form   Clinician.Measures

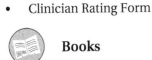

Books

- *A Story, A Story*
- *Feast for 10*
- *The Kissing Hand*
- *Mother Goose Nursery Rhymes*

Posters

- Rules Poster   Group.Rules.Poster
- Group Rituals Poster   Group.Rituals.Poster
- Brainstorming Poser   Brain.Rules.Poster

Module I

ACTIVITY 1: FAMILY MEAL

 30 MINUTES

 Goals

- To facilitate an intimate family interaction.
- To increase awareness of the importance of routine within each family.

 Materials

- Nametags
- Tables (one for each family)
- Centerpieces
- Nameplates and session schedules (one for each family)
- Place settings/napkins
- Nutritious meal/drinks
- Video camera, remote microphones, and tapes (research groups only)

 Posters

- Rules Poster

 Instructions

Facilitators prepare room by setting tables (one for each family). A simple centerpiece for each table is a nice touch. A nameplate and schedule for the session's activities are also placed on each table. Hang the Rules Poster in a prominent place where all can see it.

Food should be pre-cooked and ready to serve. Food can be served buffet or family style.

Parent(s) gather their children around a table and share a meal together. Before serving the food:

Lead Facilitator: *We are so happy to have you, and your family, join us tonight. The first thing we will do is introduce everyone.*

Proceed with introductions starting with the families and then the facilitators. Start with one parent and have the parent introduce him or herself first and then each of the other members of the family.

Module I

SESSION 1 *Telling Family Stories*

We will be spending the next 15 weeks together sharing about family traditions. We will talk about the ways that families spend time together, celebrate the good things that happen to them, and help each other get through the bad times. We will talk about big family events and things that happen every day in families. We will make things, play games, and share things about our families and ourselves.

At the start of every group, we will share a meal. First, let's thank (name of cooks) for fixing this wonderful meal. Please help yourselves to some food. Parents, why don't you serve your children first and then make a plate for yourself?

Start the opening routine after the families have finished eating and cleaning up (20–25 minutes).

Since this is a group time, we really want everyone to take part in all of the activities. To help that go smoothly, we have a couple of rules and these are posted on the wall. Let's go over them now.

Refer to poster of rules and review. Have the group add additional rules, if they want. One important rule is confidentiality. Explain confidentiality to the families.

Another way we can help the group go well is to check with each family to find out how they are doing and if there is anything going on in their lives that will make it difficult for them to take part today. Ask each family the following question:

So, is there anything going on right now that might get in the way of your family taking part in today's group?

It is now time to begin our activities for tonight focusing on your family's traditions and routines. If you will look at the schedule now, I will tell you a little bit about tonight's group.

Introduce each activity briefly.

Note 1: Facilitators who are not talking should spread around the room, monitoring families' reactions and level of participation. This is an opportunity to observe the families' mealtime interactions.

Note 2: One facilitator should take on the role of process monitor, making sure that the session runs smoothly and proceeds in a timely fashion. The process facilitator should encourage families to start finishing their dinner and cleaning up their tables after about 20 minutes to make sure that this activity is finished within 30 minutes and the group is ready to begin the next activity on time.

Module I

SESSION 1 *Telling Family Stories*

ACTIVITY 2: WHAT IS A FAMILY TRADITION?

 30 MINUTES

 Goals

- To increase adult and child understanding of family traditions, routine, and rituals.

 Materials

- Toy dinnerware and food
- Unbreakable mirrors
- Materials for scrapbook pages (paper, hole punch, glue)
- Decorating materials

 Handouts

- Introduction to Family Traditions and Routines
- Family Ritual and Routine Charts

 Books

- *The Kissing Hand*
- *Feast for 10*

 Instructions

Lead Facilitator: *It is now time to break into smaller groups. We will do this almost every group, so let's spend a minute talking about how we will do it. Each facilitator will take a different group, one for the adults, one for the teenagers, one for the older children, one for the younger children, and one for the babies. Tonight, because it is our first group and we are still getting to know each other, we will split into just three groups. The parents will go with (facilitator's name), the youth will go with (facilitator's name), and our youngest members will go with (facilitator's name).*

Facilitators gather their groups together. When the groups are formed and quiet, facilitators move one group at a time to their designated areas.

Module I

Telling Family Stories

Let the families know that if information that is concerning is shared in the small groups, facilitators may talk with parents/guardians after the group about what the child said or did.

Lead Facilitator (Adult Group): Hand out "Introduction to Family Traditions and Routines." Ask parents to reminisce about the way things were done in their families when they were growing up.

Think for a minute about being 5 years old. Think about what is was like to be a part of your family when you were little. Think about what it meant to be part of your family as you were growing up.

Encourage them to share memories about special events, birthdays, holidays, bedtime, etc. Use these descriptions to teach about the important characteristics of ritual and routine. Refer to the facilitator's discussion guide for this activity. The most important points to be covered are highlighted. Some group members may have difficulty with this activity if they grew up under stressful, abusive, or unhappy circumstances. Do not push anyone to share more than they are comfortable sharing. Acknowledge that sometimes, family memories can be painful. Facilitator should begin to wrap up this activity in about 25 minutes.

Co-Facilitators (All Youth Group): Introduce the concept of family traditions by asking youth to discuss how their family marks and celebrates certain holidays, special events, and birthdays, as well as day-to-day routines such as bedtime, dinnertime, and going off to school. Show charts. Encourage each participant to share one of their family's routines or traditions. Once everyone has had a chance to share, facilitators will distribute the scrapbook pages, one per youth, asking them to draw or write about their favorite routine or tradition within their family. Explain that these pages will become part of a family memory book that the youth can share with their parents/caregivers upon rejoining the larger group. Youth may be prompted to share their scrapbook page with the group.

Co-Facilitator (Young Child and Baby Group): Separation issues may arise when these very young children are asked to leave their mothers/caregivers. Facilitators need to be sensitive to this issue and use strategies to help with separations. Some ideas include having the baby take something of the mother's to the breakout group, having the mothers hug the baby, tell them where they will be, and how long they will be apart, using the book *The Kissing Hand*. Facilitator reads *Feast for 10* and shows everyone the pictures. The children play at having their own feast with toy plastic food provided. Facilitator plays with the babies using peek-a-boo and mirror play.

Note 1: Facilitators for each group should start wrapping up the discussions or games after 25 minutes to allow three to four minutes to transition back to the family meeting room.

Module I   SESSION 1   Telling Family Stories

ACTIVITY 3: TELLING FAMILY STORIES

 35 MINUTES

 Goals

- To reinforce family storytelling.
- To help families create a shared history.

 Materials

- Tape recorders (one for each family)
- Materials for family scrapbooks (cardboard for covers, paper, hole punch, yarn or string, glue) (one for each family)
- Decorating materials

 Handouts

- *A Story, A Story* (condensed version)

 Books

- *A Story, A Story*

 Instructions

Lead Facilitator: *As we get started with the next activity, I have a book to share with you.*
Read/summarize *A Story, A Story*. Using the handout with the condensed version makes the story easier to get through in the amount of time allotted.

Co-Facilitator: *I am willing to bet that each and every family here has some great stories to tell. Tonight, we are going to get a chance to hear some of those stories. Please gather your families around and get comfortable. Now spend a few minutes thinking about something good that the whole family experienced together in the past few years. Once you have decided on something good that happened to your family, discuss this event. Just pretend that you were sitting around and someone brought it up.*

Facilitators should turn on the tape recorder for each family. Allow about 10–15 minutes for storytelling.

Module I SESSION 1 Telling Family Stories

Co-Facilitator: About 10 minutes into this activity, start handing out the materials for making a family scrapbook.

We want you to be able to remember this group, but more importantly, we want you to build family memories. Telling family stories is one way to do that, making a scrapbook is another way. Tonight, we want you to make a scrapbook page about your family story for a new family album. These will be yours to keep. Work together as a family for about 15 minutes to start your page.

Lead Facilitator: *We know that you aren't finished yet; you can take some materials home and finish there. It will be a nice chance for your family to do something together during the week.*

Module I [SESSION 1] Telling Family Stories

ACTIVITY 4: ESTABLISHING GROUP RITUALS

 15 MINUTES

 Goals

- To set appropriate limits for the group.
- To increase ownership of the group by the families.
- To practice planning and implementation of rituals and routine.

 Materials

- Markers
- Flipchart

 Posters

- Brainstorming Rule Poster
- Rituals Poster

 Instructions

Co-Facilitator: *We have one more activity for tonight. Rituals and routines are not just part of families; other groups share rituals and routines as a way of structuring their time together. When you come to these groups every week, we will have a schedule that will be pretty much the same each week. We can also share some traditions; for example, a way that you might like to begin or end the group each week or something special that you would like to include as part of the family meal each week. Let's plan those now by "brainstorming." Brainstorming is a problem-solving technique that many groups use. Brainstorming has only a few simple rules. Refer to the poster and review the rules. In the next 8–10 minutes, I will write down as many ideas as you can think of.*

Let the group generate ideas for about 8–10 minutes and record them on the flipchart.

Now, let's decide which of these we would like to try each week. Will someone come and write these on our Group Rituals Poster? Thanks.

Help the group decide on some group rituals.

That worked well and we came up with great ideas! Brainstorming is something that you can do with your family when you are trying to plan or solve problems. It is a good way to make sure that everyone in the family has a "voice."

Module I SESSION 1 *Telling Family Stories*

ACTIVITY 5: CLOSING

 10 MINUTES

 Goals

- To increase sense of group cohesion.
- To practice planning and implementation of rituals and routine.
- To assure continuity from one session to the next.

 Handouts

- "Relative" Interview
- Family Rating Form
- Participant Log
- Clinician Rating Form

 Instructions

Lead Facilitator: *We want to thank everyone for taking part in tonight's group. It is now time to finish this session and at the end of every group, we will do a few things to end the group and to get ready for the next group. So let's spend a minute talking about how we will do it. First, we will make sure that all of tonight's activities are finished. Then, we will talk about what will happen next week and tell you what you can do to get ready.*

Before we leave, we will check that everyone knows what jobs they have to help clean up. Finally, we will close with the ending ritual that you decided on during tonight's group.

Co-Facilitator: *Is there anything that we still need to do to finish tonight's activities?*

I want to let each family know what a good job they did.

Tell each family or a family member one thing that they did especially well.

Co-Facilitator: Introduce and review the topic for next week.

Next week, we will talk about your family's heritage. To get ready for the activities next week, we have a simple project for you to do. Pick someone or several people to talk with who can tell you about your family's history. Call or visit that person and find out about what traditions have been important to your family over the years.

Module I

Telling Family Stories

Hand out the "Relative Interview."

There are instructions on this handout and some questions that you might want to ask whomever you call. Before you go tonight, please give us an idea of whom you might like to talk with about your family. Just fill in the sheet on top and hand it to one of the leaders. Bring these back with you next week; you will need them for the activities planned. Also, during the week, please get your family all together at least once to finish your scrapbook pages. Bring them back next week so that we all can see.

Lead Facilitator: *We want to make sure that we stay in touch with you during the week, so a facilitator from the group will get your number and find out the best times to call you.*

Each facilitator obtains phone numbers and best times to call from two families. They make plans to call each family during the week to remind them of their homework and to attend the next session.

Now, let's end by (closing rituals).

Families share closing rituals, if desired. Cue families to acknowledge the end of group to other family members as well.

Before you leave every week, we have a short form for you to fill out to let us know how the group went. Please complete it now and hand it in. Thanks.

Facilitators complete participant log and clinician rating form.

 Homework to be Assigned

- Complete scrapbook page
- "Relative" Interview

Module I

Ritual Family Tree

 Objectives

- To help families discover the richness and uniqueness of their traditions from the past and present.
- To facilitate discussion of family heritage and identity between parent(s) and children.
- To illustrate a family's heritage and share it with others.
- To seek a commitment within each family to uphold and further develop this heritage.

 Threads

- Connectedness: The importance of a systemic view of the family is highlighted in this session, including issues of collaboration, a role for each family member, and celebration of the collective nature of the family; themes of nurturing and "taking care of" are introduced.
- Deliberateness: Deliberate practice of rituals across time encourages the family to plan, problem-solve, and follow through, no matter what gets in the way.
- Resource Seeking: Planting the community garden reinforces that the group is an excellent source of new supports.
- Positive Affect: Strengths and family resilience factors can be stressed as families connect with positive memories of their family of origin.

 Preparation

- Send out postcard to remind families of group.
- Prepare all materials, including purchasing plants.
- Food and facilities planning and preparation.
- Decide on facilitators' roles.
- Update on the status of each family in the group.
- Anticipate any problems that might arise during the session.

 Homework Due

- Relative Interview.

 Session Overview

Activity 1	Family Meal	30 Minutes
Activity 2	Growing Your Tree	45 Minutes
Activity 3	Sharing a Heritage	15 Minutes
Activity 4	Planting a Family Garden	20 Minutes
Activity 5	Closing	10 Minutes

Module I

Homework to be Assigned

- Diary

Materials

- Tables (one for each family)
- Centerpieces
- Nameplates and session schedules (one for each family)
- Place settings/napkins
- Nutritious meal/drinks
- Poster boards (one for each family)
- Pens/pencils/crayons/markers
- Glue/tape
- Construction paper
- Children's scissors
- Camera
- Old newspaper
- Potting soil
- Containers (pots, baskets) (one for each family and one for the group)
- Small plants or fragrant herbs (one for each person in each family, and one for each family and facilitators)
- Water

Handouts

- Relative Interview   M1.S2.Interview
- Ritual Family Tree Handout M1.S2.Tree.Handout
- Earth Prayer   M1.S2.Prayer
- Diary   M1.S2.Diary
- Family Rating Form   M1.S2.Feedback
- Participant Log   M1.S2.Log
- Clinician Rating Form   Clinician.Measures

Posters

- Rules Poster   Group.Rules.Poster

Module I
Ritual Family Tree

ACTIVITY 1: FAMILY MEAL

 30 MINUTES

 Goals

- To facilitate an intimate family interaction.
- To increase awareness of the importance of routine within each family.

 Materials

- Nametags
- Tables (one for each family)
- Centerpieces
- Nameplates and session schedules (one for each family)
- Place settings/napkins
- Nutritious meal/drinks
- Video camera, remote microphones, and tapes (research groups only)

 Posters

- Rules Poster

 Instructions

Facilitators prepare the room by setting tables (one for each family). A simple centerpiece for each table is a nice touch. A nameplate and schedule for the session's activities are also placed on each table. Hang the poster with group rules listed in a prominent place where all the families can see it.

Food should be pre-cooked and ready to serve. Food can be served buffet or family style. Parent(s) gather their children around a table and share a meal together.

Lead Facilitator: *We are so happy to have you back with us tonight. First, let's thank (names of the cooks) for fixing this wonderful meal. Please help yourselves to some food. Parents, why don't you serve your children first and then make a plate for yourself?*

After the families have eaten and cleaned up (20–25 minutes), proceed with the opening routine.

Module I

SESSION 2 *Ritual Family Tree*

Co-Facilitator: *We hope you enjoyed your dinner. You decided to start the group by (opening ritual) so let's begin that way.*

Proceed with ritual planned by the group.

Just like last week, since this is a group time, we really want everyone to take part in all of the activities. To help things go smoothly, we have a couple of rules and these are posted on the wall. Let's go over them again, now.

Refer to the poster of rules and review.

Another way we can help the group go well is to check with each family to find out how they are doing and if there is anything going on in their lives that will make it difficult for them to take part today.

Ask each family the following question: *So, is there anything going on right now that might get in the way of your family taking part in today's group?*

It is now time to begin our activities for tonight focusing on tracing your family's special heritage. If you will look at the schedule now, I will tell you a little bit about tonight's group.

Introduce each activity briefly.

Note 1: Facilitators who are not talking should spread around the room, monitoring families' reactions and level of participation. Facilitators encourage and model appropriate conversation, sharing, and supervision of children. A facilitator might stop at the table of a family and offer encouragement, praise, and suggestions for managing different situations (behavior management, cueing, discipline). Work with families on interactions/behaviors occurring "in the moment." Remember to be sensitive to and empowering of the parent(s).

Note 2: One facilitator should take on the role of process monitor, making sure that the session runs smoothly and proceeds in a timely fashion. The process facilitator should encourage families to start finishing their dinner and cleaning up their tables after about 20 minutes to make sure that this activity is finished within 30 minutes and the group is ready to begin the next activity on time.

Module I SESSION 2 Ritual Family Tree

ACTIVITY 2: GROWING YOUR TREE

 45 MINUTES

 Goals

- To help the family discover its roots based on information from the past and present.
- To encourage cooperation and active participation by all family members.
- To facilitate discussion about current rituals important to each family member.
- To encourage deliberate planning in each family.

 Materials

- Pencils/crayons/markers
- Glue/tape
- Poster board (one for each family)
- Construction paper
- Scissors

 Handouts

- Ritual Family Tree Handout

 Instructions

Co-Facilitator: *We asked you to call or meet with someone who knows your family during the week. You were going to ask them a bunch of questions about your family's heritage. If you have not already shared what you talked about with the whole family, please talk with your family now and tell them what you learned.*

Each family reviews and discusses important information from their "relative" interview(s).

Hand out "Ritual Family Tree Handout" to help families focus on their family's ritual heritage.

Give families about 5–10 minutes to complete this.

Co-Facilitator: *Now, we are going to make ritual family trees. Each family can come and get a piece of poster board and the other supplies that you need to make your tree. You have seen other family trees that list the people in each generation, well; we are going to make family ritual trees that trace the rituals, traditions, and routines that are special to your family.*

Module I

Ritual Family Tree

Family decides how they want to depict their family tree based on design, color, cut out leaves, flowers, fruits, etc. to depict areas of growth on their tree, routines that have died, etc. Young children are given specific tasks to keep them engaged; for instance, decorate poster board, drawing pictures of family members and pasting them on poster, etc.

Note 1: Facilitators can help families think about what they want to present about their family tree to the larger group in the next activity. Families may want to share their trees by identifying particular rituals, traditions that are special to them, discuss ways one tradition may have changed over time, identify any special discoveries in this exercise, and specify which traditions they wish to continue or renew.

ACTIVITY 3: SHARING A HERITAGE

 15 MINUTES

 Goals

- To share a family's heritage with the larger group.
- To heighten awareness of the diversity and richness of a family's history.
- To provide "ideas" to others about developing rituals.

 Materials

- Family Ritual Trees
- Camera

 Instructions

Lead Facilitator: *You put a lot of work into making your ritual family trees, so why don't we share them. Each family will have only a few minutes so let's give them our attention and respect by staying quiet and listening to them. What family would like to share first? OK, Please bring your family and your poster up here so that everyone will be able to see what you made.*

Let family present their tree. Take picture of family as they present their tree to the group.

Module I
Ritual Family Tree

ACTIVITY 4: PLANTING A FAMILY GARDEN

 20 MINUTES

 Goals

- To further develop the idea that family roots are important, that family members grow together and individually, and that the care is needed for each family to fully develop and flower.

 Materials

- Old newspaper
- Potting soil
- Containers (pots, baskets) (one for each family and one for the group)
- Small plants or fragrant herbs (one for each person in each family and community garden)
- Water

 Handouts

- Earth Prayer

 Instructions

Prepare materials for planting the family gardens. Cover each table with newspaper.

Lead Facilitator: *Now, we have a special activity to help us think about the way that families work. Each family is going to plant a family garden. You will get a planter and then one small plant for each person in your family. Plant all the small plants together in the one container. While the families are planting, read the Earth Prayer.*

If this prayer seems too long, it can be handed out or condensed. Make the connections between how the plants/roots will grow together and influence each other. Emphasize that, to grow, the plants need taking care of just like family members.

Co-Facilitator: *Now we will plant a group garden to illustrate the way we have become a community and are growing together.*

Module I

Each family chooses a plant and plants it in a multi-family garden basket. The Facilitator team can also add a plant. Each family takes home their garden, the multi-family garden remains at the facility for the group to tend.

Co-Facilitator: *Now let's clean up.*

> *Note 1*: Facilitators can work with each family to help them arrange and plant their family garden. During the activity, encourage parent(s) to have a discussion of individual strengths and how the family helps its members grow. For kincare/foster/adoptive families, expand discussion to how the new family is influenced by the child and the history/customs the child brings with him or her and vice versa.

ACTIVITY 5: CLOSING

10 MINUTES

Goals

- To increase sense of group cohesion.
- To practice planning and implementation of rituals and routine.
- To assure continuity from one session to the next.

Handouts

- Diary
- Family Rating Form
- Participant Log
- Clinician Rating Form

Module I

Ritual Family Tree

 Instructions

Lead Facilitator: *We want to thank everyone for taking part in tonight's group. It is now time to finish this session and at the end of every group, we do a few things to end the group and to get ready for the next group.*

Co-Facilitator: *Is there anything that we still need to do to finish tonight's activities? I want to let each family know what a good job they did.*

Tell each family, or a family member, one thing that they did especially well.

Introduce and review the topic for next week.

Co-Facilitator: *Next week, we will talk about family routines. To get ready for next week, we want you to keep a diary of your family's activities again. You don't have to write in your diary each day, but try to write in it about three times during the week. We just want you to think about how you start your day, what you do in the middle of the day, how you do your evening meal, and how you end the day. There are instructions on the diary, in case you forget.*

Lead Facilitator: *We want to make sure that we stay in touch during the week, so one of the facilitators will call you again. Now, let's end with our closing ritual.*

Families share closing rituals, if desired. Cue families to acknowledge the end of group to other family members as well.

Lead Facilitator: *Please complete your family rating form now and hand it in. Thanks.*

Facilitators complete participant log and clinician rating form.

 Homework to be Assigned

- Diary

Module I

 ## Objectives

- To review the importance of routines and structure in daily family life.
- To discuss aspects of routines that support healthy individual and family functioning.
- To identify family routines that are and are not working and modify ones that are not.

 ## Threads

- Deliberateness: This session is about deliberate practice of daily routines. It incorporates notions of planning, problem-solving, and follow-through. It stresses taking control of the things that a family can take control of in their family life.
- Structure: The skill of building successful routines is introduced and will be reinforced in later sessions as families build relaxation and safety routines. Sequencing, which is a skill used both for routines and narrative, is also practiced during this session.
- Connectedness: The Family Job Chart exercise highlights the fact that each member of the family needs a job/role and can contribute to the family's success. This is another important component of family functioning that extends beyond routine to storytelling and resilience.

 ## Preparation

- Send out postcard to remind families of group.
- Prepare all materials.
- Food and facilities planning and preparation.
- Decide on facilitators' roles.
- Update on the status of each family in the group.
- Anticipate any problems that might arise during the session.

 ## Homework Due

- Completed Diary

 ## Session Overview

Activity 1	Family Meal	30 Minutes
Activity 2	Sharing Diaries	30 Minutes
Activity 3	Developing Routines	30 Minutes
Activity 4	Family Job Chart	20 Minutes
Activity 5	Closing	10 Minutes

Module I

Family Diary

 Homework to be Assigned

- Complete Job Charts
- Observation

 Materials

- Tables (one for each family)
- Centerpieces
- Nameplates and session schedules (one for each family)
- Place settings/napkins
- Nutritious meal/drinks
- Stick-ums in five different colors
- Game timer
- Sequencing cards
- Star stickers (one pack for each family)
- Paper
- Pens/pencils/crayons/markers

 Handouts

Conversation Prompts	M1.S3.Prompts (Avery 5371)
Diary	M1.S3.Diary
Routine Category Cards	M1.S3.Routines.Cards (Avery 5371)
Daily Routines Worksheet	M1.S3.Daily.Routines.WS
Teen Routines Worksheet	M1.S3.Teen.Routines.WS
Family Job Chart	M1.S3.Family.Job.Chart
Your Child and Feeling Scared Observation	M1.S3.Scared.Observation
Family Rating Form	M1.S3.Feedback
Participant Log	M1.S3.Log
Clinician Rating Form	Clinician.Measures

 Posters

Rules Poster	Group.Rules.Poster
Daily Schedule	M1.S3.Daily.Schedule

Books

- *The Kissing Hand*

Module I

ACTIVITY 1: FAMILY MEAL

 30 MINUTES

 Goals

- To facilitate an intimate family interaction.
- To increase awareness of the importance of routine within each family.

 Materials

- Tables (one for each family)
- Centerpieces
- Nameplates and session schedules (one for each family)
- Place settings/napkins
- Nutritious meal/drinks
- Video camera, remote microphones, and tapes (research groups only)

 Handouts

- Conversation Prompts

 Posters

- Rules Poster

 Instructions

Facilitators prepare room by setting tables (one for each family). A simple centerpiece for each table is a nice touch. A nameplate and schedule for the session's activities are also placed on each table. Hang poster with group rules listed in a prominent place where all the families can see it.

Food should be pre-cooked and ready to serve. Food can be served buffet or family style.

Parent(s) gather their children around a table and share a meal together. Before serving the food:

Module I

Lead Facilitator: *We are so happy to have you back with us tonight. First, let's thank (names of cooks) for fixing this wonderful meal. Please help yourselves to some food. Parents, why don't you serve your children first and then make a plate for yourself.*

Co-Facilitator: *Eating a meal together is a good time to talk with family members and have a casual conversation. Sometimes, though, it is hard for families to know what to talk about. To help with that, you might want to ask each other the questions or talk about the ideas on these cards. Each family will get a set. Try them out; other families thought that they were a lot of fun.*

After the families have eaten and cleaned up (20–25 minutes), proceed with the opening routine.

Lead Facilitator: *We hope you enjoyed your dinner. You decided to start the group by (opening ritual), so let's begin that way.*

Proceed with planned ritual.

Refer to poster of rules and review.

Ask each family the following question: *So, is there anything going on right now that might get in the way of your family taking part in today's group?*

Lead Facilitator: *It is now time to begin our activities for tonight. This session focuses on daily routines. If you will look at that schedule now, I will tell you a little bit about tonight's group.*

Proceed with introducing each activity briefly.

Note 1: Facilitators encourage and model appropriate conversation, sharing, and supervision of children. Facilitators try several methods to stimulate conversation including joining the family and modeling or use of conversation prompts. A facilitator might stop at the table of a family and offer encouragement, praise, and suggestions for managing different situations (behavior management, cueing, discipline). Work with families on interactions/behaviors occurring "in the moment." Remember to be sensitive to and empowering of the parent(s).

Note 2: One facilitator should take on the role of process monitor, making sure that the session runs smoothly and proceeds in a timely fashion. The process facilitator should encourage families to start finishing their dinner and cleaning up their tables after about 20 minutes to make sure that this activity is finished within 30 minutes and the group is ready to begin the next activity on time.

Module I

ACTIVITY 2: SHARING DIARIES

 30 MINUTES

 Goals

- To identify the importance and role of routine in daily family life.
- To identify family routines that are and are not working.

 Materials

- Completed Diaries
- Stick-ums in different colors for each family

 Handouts

- Diary

 Posters

- Daily Schedule

 Instructions

Co-Facilitator: I want to start with an activity designed for families to share your diaries. We asked you to fill out diaries for several days during the past week and bring them back with you tonight.

Let each family that brought theirs back show the group by holding them up at their table for everyone to see. Hand out a set of stick-ums to each family. Each family should have a different color.

Co-Facilitator: *Please, look through your diaries and write some of your daily activities on stick-ums. If you start the day by having breakfast, then you would write that on one stick-um.*

Give the families about 10 minutes to complete this.

Co-Facilitator: *Now, we would like to complete the Daily Schedule poster. Let's start in the morning, how do you start your days? Which family would like to go first? Please, let's show our respect for each family, by*

Module I

listening to them. Come, put your stick-ums on the poster, and tell us how you start the day. How do you feel then? Does the morning go smoothly?

Try to point out routines. Look for times that went smoothly and/or areas with conflict and make connections about routine or lack thereof. Encourage each family to take a turn. Give lots of praise to each family as they share.

> *Note 1*: Facilitators who are not talking should spread around the room, monitoring families' reactions and level of participation. A facilitator might stop at the table of a family and offer encouragement, praise, and suggestions for managing different situations (behavior management, cueing, discipline). Work with families on interactions/behaviors occurring 'in the moment." Remember to be sensitive to and empowering of the parent(s).

ACTIVITY 3: DEVELOPING ROUTINES

 30 MINUTES

 Goals

- To discuss aspects of family routines that support healthy individual and family functioning.
- To identify and modify dysfunctional family routines.

 Materials

- Sequencing cards
- Game timer/stopwatch/clock

 Books

- *The Kissing Hand*

Module I

 Handouts

- Routine Category Cards
- Daily Routines
- Teen Routines

 Instructions

Lead Facilitator: *It is now time to break into smaller groups. Remember, each facilitator will take a different group, one for adults, one for teens, one for older children, one for younger children, and one for babies. Let's begin by forming those groups.*

Facilitators gather their groups together. When the groups are formed and quiet, facilitators move one group at a time to their designated areas.

Lead Facilitator (Adult Group): Hand out "Daily Routines" and lead a discussion for about 10 minutes. Then hand out the "Routine Change Worksheet" and have the adults complete it. Focusing on one or two problem areas (since there is literature supporting the regulatory effects of structured evening activity, developing routines related to getting ready for bed in the evening is a good choice), look at the number of tasks involved, consider the timing and ordering of the tasks, and look for an organizing action for establishing the routine. It might work best to talk through the worksheet and have the adults complete it as you talk. Another option is to pick one adult to work with and develop a workable routine. Facilitator should begin to wrap up this activity in about 25 minutes.

Co-Facilitator (Teen Group): Hand out "Teen Routines" and lead a discussion for about 10 minutes. Then hand out the "Routine Change Worksheet, Adolescent Version" and have the teens complete it. Focusing on one or two problem areas (getting ready in the mornings or getting ready for bed in the evening as examples), look at the number of tasks involved, consider the timing and ordering of the tasks, and look for an organizing action for establishing the routine. It might work best to talk through the worksheet and have the teens complete it as you talk. Facilitator should begin to wrap up this activity in about 25 minutes.

Co-Facilitator (Older Child Group): Have the children divide into two teams. Read a routine category. Have each team write down all of the activities that make up that routine. Use a game timer, a stopwatch, or a clock and give the teams about one minute for each. Count up all of the responses.

Co-Facilitator (Young Child Group): Introduce the sequencing cards and let the children each have a turn putting a set in order and telling about it. This will help the children look at the steps to building routine. Sometimes, kids that have been chronically traumatized have difficulties with this task. If this is the case, let them arrange the cards however they think they should go, and then have them tell the story of what

Module I

was happening. During the course of telling the story, sometimes they realize their mistake, and when this happens, tell them that they can rearrange the cards again if they want to, and encourage the other kids to help.

Co-Facilitator (Baby Group): Separation issues may arise when these very children are asked to leave their mothers/caregivers. Facilitators need to be sensitive to this issue and use strategies to help with separations. Some ideas include having the baby take something of the mother's to the breakout group, having the mothers hug the baby, tell them where they will be and how long they will be apart, using the book *The Kissing Hand.*

Lead the toddlers in a game of "Simon Says" or "Follow the Leader." Use songs/activities such as "So Early in the Morning" or "This Little Piggy" to engage babies.

Note 1: Facilitators for each group should start wrapping up the discussions or games after 25 minutes to allow three to four minutes to transition back to the family meeting room.

ACTIVITY 4: FAMILY JOB CHART

 20 MINUTES

 Goals

- To create a family culture where everyone takes part and everyone has a role in making sure that the family's daily life runs smoothly.
- To remind the family to pay attention when members follow through with their responsibilities.

 Materials

- Pens/pencils
- Star stickers (one pack for each family)

Module I

 SESSION 3 *Family Diary*

 Handouts

- Family Job Charts

 Instructions

Co-Facilitator: *Our last activity tonight is to help everyone in your family take part in making sure that the things that need to get done get done.*

Hand out the "Job Chart" and have families complete it. Everyone in the family should have a task. This task is best completed by everyone working together, but parents may need to assign some jobs. After 10–12 minutes, have families share their job charts with the group. Hand out a package of star stickers to each family to use during the week as all of the chores get done as planned. Make copies of the job charts for distribution in later sessions.

> *Note 1:* Facilitators can add comments and feedback about cooperation, making everyone feel useful, having realistic expectations of small children, etc.

ACTIVITY 5: CLOSING

 10 MINUTES

 Goals

- To increase sense of group cohesion.
- To practice planning and implementation of rituals and routine.
- To assure continuity from one session to the next.

Module I

 Handouts

- Your Child and Feeling Scared Observation
- Family Rating Form
- Participant Log
- Clinician Rating Form

 Instructions

Lead Facilitator: *We want to thank everyone for taking part in tonight's group. It is now time to finish this session and at the end of every group, we do a few things to end the group and to get ready for the next group.*

Co-Facilitator: *Is there anything that we still need to do to finish tonight's activities?*

Co-Facilitator: *I want to let each family know what a good job they did.*

Tell each family, or a family member, one thing that they did especially well.

Introduce and review the topic for next week.

Co-Facilitator: *Next week, we will start talking about safety and how to make families feel safer. Take some time this week to observe ways that you express feeling scared.*

Hand out "Observations."

Co-Facilitator: *Remember to bring back your job charts covered with stickers so that we can see how everyone worked together!*

Lead Facilitator: *We want to make sure that we stay in touch during the week, so one of the facilitators will call you again. Now, let's end by closing rituals.*

Families share closing rituals, if desired. Cue families to acknowledge the end of group to other family members as well.

Lead Facilitator: *Please complete your family rating form now and hand it in. Thanks.*

Facilitators complete participant log and clinician rating form.

 Homework to be Assigned

- Complete Job Charts
- Observation

Module II
Protective Coping Resources

This module builds six protective family coping resources:

Deliberateness strategies in SFCR support effective coping as a problem-focused coping mechanism. Deliberate planning and follow-through help, family members focus attention on getting things done and create positive feelings about successfully carrying out routines and rituals.

Structure and Safety entails insulation from danger, rapid stabilization of family functioning, and establishing regularity in daily family life. Skill-building activities teach families to effectively use daily routines that help family members understand what to expect and by establishing rules and limits for day-to-day life. Rituals and routines can aid families in feeling and being safer.

Connectedness involves close, stable relationships and commitment to building a sense of belonging. Connectedness involves healthy attachments, confidence in protection, positive emotional bonds, healthy communication, and shared beliefs and values.

Resource Seeking strategies are directed at helping the family identify who they can rely on and increasing the availability of resources they can access when encountering threats. SFCR encourages families to involve others in their family life, especially in times of stress, accept assistance when needed, and also give to others when the opportunity arises.

Co-Regulation and Crisis Management involve joint family activities that provide multiple opportunities for families to define their comfort zone and to contain emotional expression within a safe range. Families are coached to build and use a variety of skills/resources to improve the chances that they will have sufficient resources to cope with new or ongoing threats without moving into crisis responding.

Positive Affect, Memories, and Meaning refers to the creation of understanding regarding what is important to the family and to the explanations used by the family to justify both positive and negative events that affect the family. It includes helping families make memories of shared experience filled with expressions of laughter and positive affect. It encompasses the symbolic meaning of rituals to the family.

MODULE OVERVIEW

Session Number

4   Feeling Safe I

5   Feeling Safe II

6   People Resources

7   Life Choices

8   Spirituality and Values

9   Things Get in the Way

HR 10   Celebration!

Module II

Feeling Safe 1

Objectives

- To increase each individual family member's sense of safety.
- To improve the parents' ability to help their children feel safe and the children's ability to look to parents for protection.

Threads

- *Structure and Safety*: This session begins to build family stress inoculation skills. It also focuses on establishing a relationship between setting firm limits and safety. This provides a good opportunity to introduce the issue of parental/caregiver guilt over the children's exposure to trauma and how this guilt can undermine setting and enforcing appropriate limits.
- *Co-Regulation*: Families are encouraged to learn and practice stress inoculation skills together at home. There are also multiple opportunities during the remaining sessions that these skills are taught or practiced. These skills are important for the family's ability to recognize and co-regulate the expression of intense emotions during the family trauma narrative.
- *Connectedness*: Attunement is introduced. The observation given as homework is used to help family members recognize others' distress cues.

Preparation

- Send out postcard to remind families of group.
- Prepare all materials.
- Food and facilities planning and preparation.
- Decide on facilitators' roles.
- Update on the status of each family in the group.
- Anticipate any problems that might arise during the session.

Homework Due

- Job Charts
- Observation

Session Overview

Activity 1	Family Meal	30 Minutes
Activity 2	Sit Back, Relax	40 Minutes
Activity 3	Telling Family Stories II	15 Minutes

Module II

Activity 4	Knowing the Limits	25 Minutes
Activity 5	Closing	10 Minutes

Homework to be Assigned

- Relaxation Practice

Materials

- Tables (one for each family)
- Centerpieces
- Nameplates and session schedules (one for each family)
- Place settings/napkins
- Nutritious meal/drinks
- Tape recorders and tapes (one for each family)
- Sets of toy fencing (one for each family)
- Plain business cards
- Sheet protectors
- Star stickers (one pack for each family)

Handouts

• Conversation Prompts	M1.S4.Prompts (Avery 5371)
• Setting Limits Handout	M1.S4.Setting.Limits.Handout
• Stress	M1.S4.Stress
• Relaxation	M1.S4.Relaxation
• Relaxation Routine Worksheet and Log	M1.S4. Relaxation.Routine.WS
• My Safe Place	M1.S4.Safe.Place
• Family Rating Form	M1.S4.Feedback
• Participant Log	M1.S4.Log
• Clinician Rating Form	Clinician.Measures

Posters

• Rules Poster	Group.Rules.Poster

Books

- *The Tales of Peter Rabbit*

Module II   SESSION 4 Feeling Safe 1

ACTIVITY 1: FAMILY MEAL

 30 MINUTES

 Goals

- To facilitate an intimate family interaction.
- To increase awareness of the importance of routine within each family.

 Materials

- Tables (one for each family)
- Centerpieces
- Nameplates and session schedules (one for each family)
- Place settings/napkins
- Nutritious meal/drinks
- Video camera, remote microphones, and tapes (research groups only)

 Handouts

- Conversation Prompts

 Posters

- Rules Poster

 Instructions

Facilitators prepare room by setting tables (one for each family). A simple centerpiece for each table is a nice touch. A nameplate and schedule for the session's activities are also placed on each table. Hang poster with group rules listed in a prominent place where all the families can see it.

Food should be pre-cooked and ready to serve. Food can be served buffet or family style.

Parent(s) gather their children around a table and share a meal together. Before serving the food:

Lead Facilitator: *We are so happy to have you back with us tonight. First let's thank (name of cooks) for fixing this wonderful meal. Please help yourselves to some food. Parents, why don't you serve your children first and then make a plate for yourself.*

Module II

Parent(s) should be encouraged to serve their children and then themselves.

Lead Facilitator: *To help your family have a good time during dinner, you might want to ask each other these questions or talk about the ideas on these cards.*

Hand out conversation prompts.

After the families have eaten and cleaned up (20–25 minutes), proceed with the opening routine.

Co-Facilitator: *We hope you enjoyed your dinner. You decided to start the meal by (opening ritual), so let's begin that way.*

Proceed with ritual planned by the group.

Co-Facilitator: *Just like last week, since this is a group time, we really want everyone to take part in all of the activities. To help that go smoothly, we have a couple of rules and these are posted on the wall. Let's go over them again, now.*

Ask each family the following question: *So, is there anything going on right now that might get in the way of your family taking part in today's group?*

Lead Facilitator: *It is now time to begin our activities for tonight. If you will look at the schedule now, I will tell you a little bit about tonight's group.*

Proceed with introducing each activity briefly.

Note 1: Facilitators encourage and model appropriate conversation, sharing, and supervision of children. Facilitators try several methods to stimulate conversation including joining the family and modeling or use of conversation prompts. A facilitator might stop at the table of a family and offer encouragement, praise, and suggestions for managing different situations (behavior management, cueing, discipline). Work with families on interactions/behaviors occurring "in the moment." Remember to be sensitive to and empowering of the parent(s).

Note 2: One facilitator should take on the role of process monitor, making sure that the session runs smoothly and proceeds in a timely fashion. The process facilitator should encourage families to start finishing their dinner and cleaning up their tables after about 20 minutes to make sure that this activity is finished within 30 minutes and the group is ready to begin the next activity on time.

Module **II**   SESSION 4 *Feeling Safe 1*

ACTIVITY 2: SIT BACK, RELAX

 40 MINUTES

 Goals

- To introduce relaxation skills for families.
- To increase the families' skills for coping with severe stress and trauma.
- To increase skills for coping with threat.
- To tie relaxation and sense of safety together.

 Materials

- Pens/Pencils

 Handouts

- Stress Handout
- Relaxation Handout
- My Safe Place
- Developing Relaxation Routines Worksheet and Log

 Instructions

Lead Facilitator: *Before we start the first activity tonight, I want to take time for families to share their job charts from last week. Also, how many parents observed your child? This session focuses on safety. So let's get started. It is now time to break into smaller groups. Remember, each facilitator will take a different group, only tonight each family is going to be a small group.*

Facilitators should join their assigned family at this time. Facilitators move one family at a time to their designated areas.

Family Facilitators: *Tonight, our small group activity is about relaxation. We are going to work together to learn about relaxation and to come up with a relaxation routine that you and your family can use.*

Pass out the "Stress" and "Relaxation Handout" and spend about five minutes reviewing the importance/benefits of relaxation with the family.

Module II

SESSION 4 *Feeling Safe 1*

Family Facilitators: *Now, let's learn how to do it.*

When the facilitator introduces the concept of stress, parent(s) are asked about times during the observation of their child for homework that they noticed an expression or behavior that indicated the child was upset, distressed, or scared. Note that these might be cues about when to use relaxation.

Family Facilitators: *Let's start with an exercise that we use with lots of our families. First, let's set the mood. Can everyone find a comfortable seat? I am going to turn off some of the lights.*

Introduce a simple deep breathing activity and have the family practice for 5–10 minutes. A good breathing activity for families with young children is "blowing out birthday candles." Now introduce a simple progressive relaxation activity and have the family practice for 5–10 minutes. A good relaxation activity for families with young children is "robot to rag doll."

Discuss with the family which type of relaxation activity they like the best.

Using "My Safe Place," briefly present the idea of guided imagery. Explain that this is another type of relaxation exercise. Then proceed with the "Safe Place" guided imagery activity. Have family members shut their eyes and imagine a place where they feel safe. Have them go to that place. Ask them to spend some time in that place. Have them look around. Have them identify the sights, sounds, smells, feel, etc. of their safe space. After a short time, ask them to leave their safe place and come back to the room. Discuss their experiences and have them share their safe places if they are willing.

Family Facilitators: *Now, let's talk about how you could do this at home.*

Work with the family to fill out the Relaxation Routine Development Worksheet.

Family Facilitators: *To help you keep track of when you practice, please complete the Relaxation Routine Log and bring it back with you. Just fill in the time that you practiced each day and rate how relaxed you felt when you were finished.*

Note 1: Facilitators for each family should start wrapping up the discussions after 35 minutes to allow three to four minutes to transition back to the family meeting room.

Module II

ACTIVITY 3: TELLING FAMILY STORIES II

 15 MINUTES

 Goals

- To reinforce family story telling.
- To help families create a shared history.
- To start families talking about mildly negative events.

 Materials

- Tape recorders and tapes (one for each family)

 Instructions

Co-Facilitator: *Tonight, we are going to get a chance to hear some more family stories. Please gather your families around and get comfortable. Now spend a few minutes thinking about a time that something a little bit scary or a little bit stressful happened to your family over the past two to three years. Once you have decided on something to talk about, just pretend that you were sitting around and someone brought it up.*

Facilitators should turn on the tape recorder for each family. Allow about 10–15 minutes for storytelling.

Note 1: Facilitators who are not talking should spread around the room, monitoring families' reactions and level of participation. A facilitator might stop at the table of a family and offer encouragement, praise, and suggestions for managing different situations (behavior management, cueing, discipline). Remember to be sensitive to and empowering of the parent(s). Facilitators should not become part of the family conversation, but might want to gently encourage families to elaborate, to get everyone's point of view, to talk about how they felt at the time, etc.

159

Module II

ACTIVITY 4: KNOWING THE LIMITS

 25 MINUTES

 Goals

- To increase awareness of the benefits of predictability and limits on sense of safety.
- To communicate family limits and rules publicly.

 Materials

- Toy fencing
- Plain business cards or other small sheets of paper
- Sheet protectors

 Handouts

- Setting Limits Handout

 Books

- *The Tales of Peter Rabbit*

 Instructions

Facilitator (Adult, Teen, and Older Child Group): Hand out "Setting Limits" and lead a discussion. Talk with the families for about five minutes on the importance of clear expectations and limits for family safety. Talk about predictability and knowing what to expect. Also talk about guilt and problems keeping high expectations when you are feeling bad about things that have happened.

Hand out Fences and Cards. Have each family build their fence. Explain that fences are for setting boundaries and so are limits. Have families brainstorm and write limits on the cards. From these cards, have each family decide on three most important limits for their family and put these inside their fence.

Then hand out the "Family Limits Worksheet" and have the families write their three limits inside the fence. On the other side of the worksheet, have the families list behaviors that fall outside the limit and the

Module II

SESSION 4 *Feeling Safe I*

consequences for those behaviors. It might work best to talk through the worksheet and have the adults complete it as you talk. Put these sheets inside sheet protectors or laminate to take home.

Facilitator should begin to wrap up this activity in about 25 minutes.

Co-Facilitator (Young Child and Baby Group): Have the young children and babies join with a facilitator in the corner of the meeting room to allow parents, teens, and older children the opportunity to openly discuss limits for their family. Depending on the age of the group:

Young children: *First, we will have a short story time. Please sit in a circle around me. I am going to read the story Peter Rabbit. How many of you have already heard this story?*

Read story about limits and discuss. This should take 10 minutes.

Young children: *Now we are going to play a game.*

Babies: Present the babies with a choice of two developmentally appropriate, safe toys to play with. The baby should pick one toy and play with it. When babies lose interest, they can pick another toy to play with.

ACTIVITY 5: CLOSING

 10 MINUTES

 Goals

- To increase sense of group cohesion.
- To practice planning and implementation of rituals and routine.
- To assure continuity from one session to the next.

 Materials

- Job Charts
- Star stickers (one pack for each family)

 Handouts

- Family Rating Form
- Participant Log
- Clinician Rating Form

Module II

Feeling Safe 1

 Instructions

Lead Facilitator: *We want to thank everyone for taking part in tonight's group. It is now time to finish this session and at the end of every group, we do a few things to end the group and to get ready for the next group.*

Co-Facilitator: *Is there anything that we still need to do to finish tonight's activities?*

Co-Facilitator: *I want to let each family know what a good job they did.*

Tell each family, or a family member, one thing that they did especially well.

Introduce and review the topic for next week.

Co-Facilitator: *Next week, we will talk some more about safety and how to make families feel safer. We know you all will be feeling relaxed after practicing all week. Here are extra copies of your job chart and more stickers so that you can keep on working together to get everything done.*

Lead Facilitator: *We want to make sure that we stay in touch during the week, so one of the facilitators will call you again. Now, let's end by (closing rituals).*

Families share closing rituals, if desired. Cue families to acknowledge the end of group to other family members as well.

Lead Facilitator: *Please complete your family rating form now and hand it in. Thanks.*

Facilitators complete participant log and clinician rating form.

 Homework to be Assigned

- Relaxation Practice

Module II

Objectives

- To increase each individual family members' sense of safety.
- To improve the parents' ability to help their children feel safe and the children's ability to look to parents for protection.
- To build safety routines.

Threads

- *Deliberateness*: This session continues the practice of deliberate practice of daily routines with a specific application involving safety. It again stresses taking control of the things that a family can take control of in their family life.
- *Structure and Safety*: Development and practice of safety routines provides the family with an opportunity to work together to increase structure related to family members' sense of safety.
- *Connectedness*: The safety mapping exercise gives each individual member of the family the opportunity to share their perspective. This is another important skill related to family collaboration and meaning making. Practicing safety routines means that family members are looking out for each other.

Preparation

- Send out postcard to remind families of group.
- Prepare all materials.
- Food and facilities planning and preparation.
- Decide on facilitators' roles.
- Update on the status of each family in the group.
- Anticipate any problems that might arise during the session.

Homework Due

- Relaxation Practice Log

Session Overview

Activity 1	Family Meal	30 Minutes
Activity 2	Confidence in Protection	30 Minutes
Activity 3	Mapping Safety	25 Minutes
Activity 4	Safety Routines	25 Minutes
Activity 5	Closing	10 Minutes

Module II

 ### Homework to be Assigned

- Implement Safety Routine
- Safety Resources Hunt

 ## Materials

- Tables (one for each family)
- Centerpieces
- Nameplates and session schedules (one for each family)
- Place settings/napkins
- Nutritious meal/drinks
- Assorted parent and baby toys
- Poster boards (one for each family)
- Rulers
- Pencils, markers, crayons
- Job charts and packages of star stickers (one for each family)

 ## Handouts

Conversation Prompts	M2.S5.Prompts
Your Child and Feeling Safe	M2.S5.Child.Feeling.Safe
Safety Mapping Labels	M2.S5.Safety.Map.Labels (print on Avery #5163)
My Safe Plan	M2.S5.Safe.Plan
Safety Routines Worksheet	M2.S5.Safety.Routines.WS
Family Rating Form	M2.S5.Feedback
Safety Resources Hunt	M2.S5.Safety.Res.Hunt
Safety Resources Hunt (for Baltimore groups)	M2.S5.Safety.Res.Hunt.Baltimore
Participant Log	M2.S5.Log
Clinician Rating Form	Clinican.Measures

 ## Posters

- Rules Poster   Group.Rules.Poster

 ## Books

- *Warm, Safe, and Snug (2)*
- *Go Away, Big Green Monster!*
- *The Kissing Hand*

Module *II*

ACTIVITY 1: FAMILY MEAL

 30 MINUTES

 Goals

- To facilitate an intimate family interaction.
- To increase awareness of the importance of routine within each family.

 Materials

- Nametags
- Tables (one for each family)
- Centerpieces
- Nameplates and session schedules (one for each family)
- Place settings/napkins
- Nutritious meal/drinks
- Video camera, remote microphones, and tapes (research groups only)

 Handouts

- Conversation Prompts

 Posters

- Rules Poster

 Instructions

Facilitators prepare room by setting tables (one for each family). A simple centerpiece for each table is a nice touch. A nameplate and schedule for the session's activities are also placed on each table. Hang poster with group rules listed in a prominent place where all the families can see it.

Food should be pre-cooked and ready to serve. Food can be served buffet or family style.

Parent(s) gather their children around a table and share a meal together. Before serving the food:

Lead Facilitator: *We are so happy to have you back with us tonight. First, let's thank (name of cooks) for fixing this wonderful meal. Please help yourselves to some food. Parents, why don't you serve your children first and*

Module II

SESSION 5 *Feeling Safe II*

then make a plate for yourself. To help your family have a good time during dinner, you might want to ask each other these questions or talk about the ideas on these cards.

Hand out conversation prompts.

After the families have eaten and cleaned up (20–25 minutes), proceed with the opening routine.

Co-Facilitator: *We hope you enjoyed your dinner. You decided to start the meal by (opening ritual), so let's begin that way.*

Proceed with planned ritual.

Refer to poster of rules and review.

Ask each family the following question: *So, is there anything going on right now that might get in the way of your family taking part in today's group?* Make link between checking in with family members to be sure each person can participate (problem-solving, helping with a task) or may be overburdened, staying attuned to the mood and needs of all family members during other family activities.

Co-Facilitator: *It is now time to begin our activities for tonight. If you will look at that schedule now, I will tell you a little bit about tonight's group.*

Proceed with introducing each activity briefly.

Co-Facilitator: *This session focuses on safety again. So, let's get started. Before we start the first activity tonight, I want to take time for families to share their completed Relaxation Logs from last week.*

> *Note 1:* Facilitators who are not talking should spread around the room, monitoring families' reactions and level of participation. Facilitators encourage and model appropriate conversation, sharing, and supervision of children. A facilitator might stop at the table of a family and offer encouragement, praise, and suggestions for managing different situations (behavior management, cueing, discipline). Work with families on interactions/behaviors occurring "in the moment." Remember to be sensitive to and empowering of the parent(s).

> *Note 2:* One facilitator should take on the role of process monitor, making sure that the session runs smoothly and proceeds in a timely fashion. The process facilitator should encourage families to start finishing their dinner and cleaning up their tables after about 20 minutes to make sure that this activity is finished within 30 minutes and the group is ready to begin the next activity on time.

Module II   SESSION 5 Feeling Safe II

ACTIVITY 2: CONFIDENCE IN PROTECTION

 30 MINUTES

 Goals

- To understand the universality of protection of our young and vulnerable.
- To discover ways that caregivers work to keep their young safe.
- To encourage attention to safety cues and the notion of finding safety in each other.

 Materials

- Assorted parent and baby toys

 Handouts

- Your Child and Feeling Safe
- My Safe Plan

 Books

- *Warm, Safe, and Snug (2)*
- *Go Away, Big Green Monster!*
- *The Kissing Hand*

 Instructions

Lead Facilitator: *It is now time to break into smaller groups. Remember, each facilitator will take a different group, one for adults, one for teens, one for older children, one for younger children, and one for babies. Let's begin by forming those groups.*

Facilitators gather their groups together. When the groups are formed and quiet, facilitators move one group at a time to their designated areas. Remind families that if information is shared in the small groups that is concerning, facilitators may talk with parents/guardians after the group about what the child said or did.

Lead Facilitator (Adult Group): Read *Warm, Safe, and Snug* and lead a discussion for about 10 minutes. Then hand out "Your Child and Feeling Safe" and have the adults complete it. Focusing on the things that

Module II

parents do now to help their children feel safe, have the parents share and discuss ways to keep their family safe. Facilitator should begin to wrap up this activity in about 25 minutes.

Co-Facilitator (Teen Group): Hand out "My Safe Plan" and have the children complete it. Lead a discussion for about 10 minutes focusing on the things that the children do now to feel safe. Facilitator should begin to wrap up this activity in about 25 minutes.

Co-Facilitators (Older Child Group): Hand out "My Safe Plan" and have the children complete it. Lead a discussion for about 10 minutes focusing on the things that the children do now to feel safe. Facilitator should begin to wrap up this activity in about 25 minutes.

Co-Facilitators (Young Child Group): Read *Go Away, Big Green Monster!* Discuss some things that children can to do when they are scared.

Co-Facilitators (Baby Group): Separation issues may arise when these very young children are asked to leave their mothers/caregivers. Facilitators need to be sensitive to this issue and help with separations. Some ideas include having the baby take something of the mother's to the group, having the mothers hug the baby, tell them where they will be and how long they will be apart, using *The Kissing Hand*. Read *Warm, Safe, and Snug*. Play with parent and baby toys. Focus on nurturing skills.

> *Note 1:* Facilitators for each group should start wrapping up the discussions or games after 25 minutes to allow three to four minutes to transition back to the family meeting room.

ACTIVITY 3: MAPPING SAFETY

 25 MINUTES

 Goals

- To increase awareness of safety concerns.
- To identify threats.

Module II

Feeling Safe II

 Materials

- Poster boards (one for each family)
- Rulers
- Pencils, markers, crayons

 Handouts

- Safety Mapping Labels

 Instructions

Co-Facilitator: *On your table you will find a poster board, a ruler, a pencil, and some stickers. Work together as a family to draw a map of your home and your neighborhood.*

Invite the family to draw a map of their neighborhood.

Identify houses, schools, stores, hospitals, churches, relative and friends' homes, etc. Include the place(s) where violence has occurred and places the child considers safe with its accompanying details.

Co-Facilitator: *Let's use this large piece of paper to draw a map of your neighborhood. First, draw your street and then place your house on it. Fill in the street with other houses and stores and traffic signals and street signs. Let's draw the roads you walk or drive to get to school, church, etc. Now let's work with your maps to figure out where you feel there is danger and where you feel safe. Pick out places that feel safe. Show the places that do not feel safe or that feel dangerous. If people in your family feel differently about some places, that's OK. Use the stickers to identify "Who is with you when you are in these places," "When you are there and how much time are you there," and "How you feel when you are at those places." Work on this map for about 25 minutes.*

Some places may be reminders of or triggers for the traumatic event(s) so facilitators should be monitoring for these reactions and providing support.

Note 1: Keep the families' safety maps for use later in the group.

Module II

ACTIVITY 4: SAFETY ROUTINES

 25 MINUTES

 Goals

- To increase the family's ability to stay safe.
- To diminish the risk of further exposure to trauma.
- To reinforce the use of routines.

 Materials

- Family Safety Maps

 Handouts

- Safety Routines Worksheet

 Instructions

Co-Facilitator: *Now, we are going to use your map as a tool. Please review your map and decide on one time or place that you would like to change the way you feel. Pick a time or place that you would like to feel safer. Let's use the "Safety Routine Worksheet" to figure out a way to make that happen. Remember the things we learned about routines. Work together as a family to develop a routine that would help you feel safer at the time or place that you chose.*

ACTIVITY 5: CLOSING

 10 MINUTES

 Goals

- To increase sense of group cohesion.
- To practice planning and implementation of rituals and routine.
- To assure continuity from one session to the next.

Module II

SESSION 5 *Feeling Safe II*

Materials

- Job charts and packages of star stickers (one for each family)

Handouts

- Family Rating Form
- Participant Log
- Clinician Rating Form

Instructions

Lead Facilitator: *We want to thank everyone for taking part in tonight's group. It is now time to finish this session and at the end of every group, we do a few things to end the group and to get ready for the next group.*

Co-Facilitator: *Is there anything that we still need to do to finish tonight's activities? I want to let each family know what a good job they did.*

Tell each family, or a family member, one thing that they did especially well.

Introduce and review the topic for next week.

Co-Facilitator: *Next week, we will talk about the people who are involved with your family and support you.*

Refer to Facilitator Instructions and hand out "Safety Resources Hunt."

Co-Facilitator: *Also remember to do your safety routine this week. Here are extra copies of your job chart and more stickers so that you can keep on working together to get everything done.*

Lead Facilitator: *We want to make sure that we stay in touch during the week, so one of the facilitators will call you again. Now, let's end by (closing rituals).*

Families share closing rituals, if desired. Cue families to acknowledge the end of group to other family members as well.

Lead Facilitator: *Please complete your family rating form now and hand it in. Thanks.*

Facilitators complete participant log and clinician rating form.

Homework to be Assigned

- Implement Safety Routine
- Safety Resources Hunt

Module II

 ## Objectives

- To help families realize that social networks constitute important coping resources.
- To help families become aware (on both cognitive and emotional levels) of their existing networks, including their strengths and weaknesses.
- To facilitate problem-solving and modeling via group participation in improving the quality of each family's social network through one of two main mechanisms: (1) improving existing supports; and (2) adding additional supports.
- To provide families with skills for identifying, accessing, and managing relationships, supports, and community links.

 ## Threads

- *Resource Seeking:* This session continues the theme of people resources as coping resources. The Family Sculpture exercise brings out many issues related to social support, coping, and safety for families to consider. At the end of the session, families plan a way to connect with each other during the week. An important message to all of the families is the importance of both receiving and giving support.

 ## Preparation

- Send out postcard to remind families of group.
- Prepare all materials.
- Food and facilities planning and preparation.
- Decide on facilitators' roles.
- Update on the status of each family in the group.
- Anticipate any problems that might arise during the session.

 ## Homework Due

- Implement Safety Routines
- Safety Resources Hunt

 ## Session Overview

Activity 1	Family Meal	30 Minutes
Activity 2	Identifying/Evaluating Resources	30 Minutes
Activity 3	Family Sculptures	50 Minutes
Activity 4	Closing	10 Minutes

Module II

Homework to be Assigned

- Seeking Support
- Contacting Each Other

Materials

- Tables (one for each family)
- Centerpieces
- Nameplates and session schedules (one for each family)
- Place settings/napkins
- Nutritious meal/drinks
- Play tunnel
- Pens/pencils/crayons/markers
- Camera
- Job charts and star stickers (one pack for each family)

Handouts

• Conversation Prompts	M2.S6.Prompts
• Sociograms	M2.S6.Sociograms
• People Help	M2.S6.People.Help
• Mrs. Katz and Tush (condensed version)	M2.S6.Katz.and.Tush Facilitators
• Instructions and Questions Handout	M2.S6. Instructions.Questions
• Family Sculpture Outline and Action Plan	M2.S6.Sculpture.Outline
• Phone Tree	M2.S6.Phone.Tree
• Family Rating Form	M2.S6.Feedback
• Contact Sheets	M2.S6.Contact.Sheets
• Participant Log	M2.S6.Log
• Clinician Rating Form	Clinician.Measures

Posters

• Rules Poster	Group.Rules.Poster

Books

- *Mrs. Katz and Tush*
- *So Much*
- *Anansi the Spider: A Tale from the Ashanti*

Module II

ACTIVITY 1: FAMILY MEAL

 30 MINUTES

 Goals

- To facilitate an intimate family interaction.
- To increase awareness of the importance of routine within each family.

 Materials

- Tables (one for each family)
- Centerpieces
- Nameplates and session schedules (one for each family)
- Place settings/napkins
- Nutritious meal/drinks
- Video camera, remote microphones, and tapes (research groups only)

 Handouts

- Conversation Prompts

 Posters

- Rules Poster

 Instructions

Facilitators prepare room by setting tables (one for each family). A simple centerpiece for each table is a nice touch. A nameplate and schedule for the session's activities are also placed on each table. Hang poster with group rules listed in a prominent place where all the families can see it.

Food should be pre-cooked and ready to serve. Food can be served buffet or family style.

Parent(s) gather their children around a table and share a meal together. Before serving the food:

Lead Facilitator: *We are so happy to have you back with us tonight. Let's begin. First let's thank (name of cooks) for fixing this wonderful meal. Please help yourselves to some food. Parents, why don't you serve your*

Module II

children first and then make a plate for yourself. To help your family have a good time during dinner, you might want to ask each other these questions or talk about the ideas on these cards.

Hand out conversation prompts.

After the families have eaten and cleaned up (20–25 minutes), proceed with the opening routine.

Co-Facilitator: *We hope you enjoyed your dinner. It is now time to begin our activities for tonight.*

Proceed with ritual planned by the group.

Refer to poster of rules and review.

Ask each family the following question: *So, is there anything going on right now that might get in the way of your family taking part in today's group?*

Co-Facilitator: *If you will look at that schedule now, I will tell you a little bit about tonight's group. This session focuses on the people who help you out and support your family.*

Proceed with introducing each activity briefly.

Note 1: Facilitators encourage and model appropriate conversation, sharing, and supervision of children. Facilitators try several methods to stimulate conversation, including joining the family and modeling or use of conversation prompts. A facilitator might stop at the table of a family and offer encouragement, praise, and suggestions for managing different situations (behavior management, cueing, discipline). Work with families on interactions/behaviors occurring "in the moment." Remember to be sensitive to and empowering of the parent(s).

Note 2: One facilitator should take on the role of process monitor making sure that the session runs smoothly and proceeds in a timely fashion. The process facilitator should encourage families to start finishing their dinner and cleaning up their tables after about 20 minutes to make sure that this activity is finished within 30 minutes and the group is ready to begin the next activity on time.

Module II

ACTIVITY 2: IDENTIFYING/EVALUATING RESOURCES

30 MINUTES

Goals

*   To increase awareness of how to identify and utilize social supports.
*   To prepare families for the subsequent exercise of creating a "network sculpture."

Materials

*   Play tunnel
*   Pens/crayons/markers
*   Paper

Handouts

*   Sociograms
*   People Help

Books

*   *Mrs. Katz and Tush* (with condensed version)
*   *So Much*

Instructions

Lead Facilitator: *Before we start the first activity tonight, I want to take time for families to share what you learned about the places that you called.*

Have participants briefly tell the group which organization they called. They can then be considered "experts" in that area and can be consulted during the family sculpture exercise regarding resources. Only spend about five minutes.

Lead Facilitator: *If you will hand in your completed sheets to me, we will put them together into a notebook for all families to share the information you collected. It is now time to break into smaller groups. Remember,*

Module II

each facilitator will take a different group, one for adults, one for teens, one for older children, one for younger children, and one for babies. Let's begin by forming those groups.

Facilitators gather their groups together. When the groups are formed and quiet, facilitators move one group at a time to their designated areas.

Lead Facilitator (Adult Group): Hand out the "Sociograms." *We are going to talk some about people who are important to you. On this handout, I want you to put the first names of everyone who you think belongs in each circle. Let's do the first group together. Write the names of everyone in your immediate family in this circle. Your immediate family includes your children and your partner, if you have one. Now, let's think about your extended family. Your extended family includes those people who you consider family, like your parents, sisters and brothers, aunt and uncles, and maybe others like godparents or really close family friends.*

Hand out "People Help." Each adult identifies a recent stressor and the social resources they used to cope with the stressor. Adults then think of additional resources that they: (1) could have used; and/or (2) wish were available to them. Remind the adults of the people they identified in the safety mapping exercise as someone who feels safe.

Co-Facilitator (Teen Group): Hand out the "Sociograms." *We are going to talk some about people who are important to you. On this handout, I want you to put the first names of everyone who you think belongs in each circle. Let's do the first group together. Write the names of everyone in your immediate family in this circle. Your immediate family includes your parents and your siblings, if you have some. Now, let's think about your extended family. Your extended family includes those people who you consider family, like your grandparents, aunt and uncles, and maybe others like godparents or really close family friends.*

Hand out "People Help." Each teen identifies a recent stressor and the social resources they used to cope with the stressor. Families then think of additional resources that they: (1) could have used; and/or (2) wish were available to them. Remind the teens of the people they identified in the safety mapping exercise as someone who feels safe.

Co-Facilitators (Older Child Group): Hand out the "Sociograms." *We are going to talk about some people who are important to you. On this handout, I want you to put the first names of everyone who you think belongs in each circle. Let's do the first group together. Write the names of everyone in your immediate family in this circle. Your immediate family includes your parents and your siblings, if you have some. Now, let's think about your extended family. Your extended family includes those people who you consider family, like your grandparents, aunt and uncles, and maybe others like godparents or really close family friends.*

Then children pick someone not in their immediate family who has helped them out or kept them safe and tell the story of that person and how they helped.

Module II

Co-Facilitator (Young Child Group): Read *Mrs. Katz and Tush*. Then children draw a picture of someone not in their immediate family who has helped them out or kept them safe and tell the story of that person and how they helped. *So Much* can be substituted for *Mrs. Katz and Tush* if more developmentally appropriate.

Co-Facilitator (Baby Group): Read *So Much*. Facilitators encourage babies to crawl through the tunnel using big smiles and warm hugs when they get to the end.

> *Note 1:* Facilitators for each group should start wrapping up the discussions or games after 25 minutes to allow three to four minutes to transition back to the family meeting room.

ACTIVITY 3: FAMILY SCULPTURES

 50 MINUTES

 Goals

- To increase each family's emotional processing and awareness of their network through social sharing with others.
- To increase awareness of how others support the family's coping with stress or threats.
- To facilitate family problem-solving through group discussion and sharing.
- To generate a problem-solving template and plan for action.

 Materials

- Pens
- Camera

 Books

- *Anansi the Spider: A Tale from the Ashanti*

Module II

People Resources

Handouts

- Facilitators Instructions and Questions
- Family Sculpture Outline and Action Plan

Instructions

Co-Facilitator: *Now, we are going to read a story about Anansi the Spider and his family. While I am reading, be sure to pay attention to each family member's special strengths in the story and their role in helping out during a difficult situation.*

Read the book *Anansi the Spider: A Tale from Ashanti*. Read from beginning through to the point where Anansi is rescued by his sons, ending with "They were very happy that spider family."

Lead Facilitator: *In the story we just finished about Anansi the Spider, we saw something bad happen to Anansi and he needed help. Each of his sons used their special strengths and skills to help save their dad and bring him back home. Just like the characters in the story, each of us has special strengths or skills, and important roles we play in our family. We also saw in the story that Anansi asked someone outside his family for help when he was having a tough time making a decision. In our breakout groups, we talked about some of the people outside your families who can help you or your family when you are having a hard time. Thinking about our own families, we are now going to make sculptures. Usually sculptures are made out of clay, marble, or wax, but we are going to make these sculptures out of people. It is something like acting in a play, too, because you will take the role of different people in each sculpture. Each family will get to make their own sculpture. But first, we are going to build a sculpture to show you what we mean. We each have different families, so we are going to use the story we just read about Anansi the Spider to build a sculpture about his family. We won't have enough people to do it ourselves, so we will need your help too.*

Proceed to build sculpture of Anansi's family. You can either direct the building of the sculpture or make the activity more interactive by eliciting input/suggestions from the families, depending on time constraints. Sculpture should include: Anansi (representing the center and foundation of his family) and each of his sons, See Trouble, Road Builder, River Drinker, Game Skinner, Stone Thrower, and Cushion. You can position each person representing a son equally around Anansi, as each was equally instrumental in saving him. Each person can also represent that character's role by positioning themselves in a way that reflects their skills (e.g., Road Builder—pretend to be hammering on ground).

Facilitator: *Now, it is your turn to make a sculpture of your family. And remember, like Anansi, we want you to include your family members AND people outside of your family that are resources for you. Now, we are going to break into two groups. Two facilitators will take each group, with two/three families in each group. Let's begin by forming those groups.*

Module II

Facilitators gather their groups together. When the groups are formed and quiet, facilitators move one group at a time to their designated areas.

Lead Sculpture Facilitators: Assist each family in building a "live sculpture" to represent their existing social resources, especially those people who support the family's sense of safety or help them cope under stressful circumstances. Use group members to represent members of the family's social network. Follow the Facilitator's Instructions for this exercise.

Give each family a total of 15 minutes. Each family will present their sculpture and answer questions about how they would like to change their social support resources in the future.

Take a picture of each family's sculpture.

During the last five minutes, have each family decide on a way to seek support during the next week. Hand out the "Family Sculpture Outline and Action Plan."

Facilitator: *Wow, we learned a lot about the people who are part of your family support network especially during times of stress. Please talk together and decide on one thing to do during the week to increase your social support.*

ACTIVITY 4: CLOSING

10 MINUTES

Goals

- To increase sense of group cohesion.
- To practice planning and implementation of rituals and routine.
- To assure continuity from one session to the next.

Handouts

- Phone Tree
- Contact Sheets
- Family Rating Form
- Participant Log
- Clinician Rating Form

Module II

 Instructions

Lead Facilitator: *We want to thank everyone for taking part in tonight's group. It is now time to finish this session and at the end of every group, we do a few things to end the group and to get ready for the next group.*

Co-Facilitator: *Is there anything that we still need to do to finish tonight's activities? I want to let each family know what a good job they did.*

Tell each family, or a family member, one thing that they did especially well.

Introduce and review the topic for next week.

Co-Facilitator: *Next week, we will talk about life choices, setting goals, and making decisions about how you want your life to go and then making it happen. Here are extra copies of your job chart and more stickers so that you can keep on working together to get everything done.*

Lead Facilitator: *We want to make sure that we stay in touch during the week, but we know that you are comfortable as a group and have gotten to know each other. So instead of a facilitator calling you, let's set up a system for you to call each other.*

Introduce Buddy System or Phone Tree.

Lead Facilitator: *Now, let's end by (closing rituals).*

Families share closing rituals, if desired. Cue families to acknowledge the end of group to other family members as well.

Lead Facilitator: *Please complete your family rating form now and hand it in. Thanks.*

Facilitators complete participant log and clinician rating form.

 Homework to be Assigned

- Seeking Support
- Contacting each other

Module II

Objectives

- To reinforce the notion of deliberate planning.
- To encourage families to model deliberate planning of life choices and to provide developmentally appropriate opportunities for deliberate planning.

Threads

- *Deliberateness*: This session focuses on deliberate planning across the family life cycle. It introduces skills related to goal setting, future thinking, and hope. This session includes another family storytelling activity focused on the potential for a brighter future for the family based on realistic goals that each family member can accomplish.
- *Connectedness*: Family members join together to construct a positive vision for their future.
- *Positive Affect, Memories, Meaning*: Families imagine possibilities for their future that include sharing and attaining their aspirations. Families who believe in their ability to succeed are more resilient.

Preparation

- Send out postcard to remind families of group.
- Prepare all materials.
- Food and facilities planning and preparation.
- Decide on facilitators' roles.
- Update on the status of each family in the group.
- Anticipate any problems that might arise during the session.

Homework Due

- Seeking Support

Session Overview

Activity 1	Family Meal	30 Minutes
Activity 2	Family Timeline	30 Minutes
Activity 3	Life Choices	30 Minutes
Activity 4	Into the Future	20 Minutes
Activity 5	Closing	10 Minutes

Homework to be Assigned

- Sources of Spiritual Support/Spiritual Assessment

Module II

Materials

- Tables (one for each family)
- Centerpieces
- Nameplates and session schedules (one for each family)
- Place settings/napkins
- Nutritious meal/drinks
- Dress up clothes for a mother, father, children, babies, grandparents or dollhouse with family of dolls, occupational hats, and accessories or doll house
- Chutes and Ladders
- Poster boards (one for each family)
- Rulers
- Pens/pencils/markers/crayons
- Paper
- Glue
- Tape recorders (one for each family)
- Labels, blank
- Job charts and star stickers (one pack for each family)

Handouts

Conversation Prompts	M2.S7.Prompts
The More Things Change	M2.S7.Things.Change
Family Timeline Example	M2.S7.Family.Timeline
Timeline Worksheet	M2.S7.Timeline.WS
Life Choices	M2.S7.Life.Choices
Life Choices—Adolescent	M2.S7.Life.Choices.Adoles
Path to My Future	M2.S7.Path.Future
Sources of Spiritual Support	M2.S7.Spiritual.Support
Spiritual Assessment	M2.S7.Spiritual.Assessment
Phone Tree	M2.S7.Phone.Tree
Family Rating Form	M2.S7.Feedback
Contact Sheets	M2.S7.Contact.Sheets
Participant Log	M2.S7.Log
Clinician Rating Form	Clinician.Measures

Posters

Rules Poster	Group.Rules.Poster

Module II

ACTIVITY 1: FAMILY MEAL

 30 MINUTES

 Goals

*   To facilitate an intimate family interaction.
*   To increase awareness of the importance of routine within each family.

 Materials

*   Tables (one for each family)
*   Centerpieces
*   Nameplates and session schedules (one for each family)
*   Place settings/napkins
*   Nutritious meal/drinks
*   Video camera, remote microphones, and tapes (research groups only)

 Handouts

*   Conversation Prompts

 Posters

*   Rules Poster

 Instructions

Facilitators prepare room by setting tables (one for each family). A simple centerpiece for each table is a nice touch. A nameplate and schedule for the session's activities are also placed on each table. Hang poster with group rules listed in a prominent place where all the families can see it.

Food should be pre-cooked and ready to serve. Food can be served buffet or family style.

Parent(s) gather their children around a table and share a meal together. Before serving the food:

Lead Facilitator: *We are so happy to have you back with us tonight. Let's begin. First, let's thank (name of cooks) for fixing this wonderful meal. Please help yourselves to some food. Parents, why don't you serve your children first and then make a plate for yourself.*

Module II

Life Choices

Parent(s) should be encouraged to serve their children and then themselves.

Lead Facilitator: *To help your family have a good time during dinner, you might want to ask each other these questions or talk about the ideas on these cards.*

Hand out conversation prompts.

After the families have eaten and cleaned up (20–25 minutes), proceed with the opening routine.

Co-Facilitator: *We hope you enjoyed your dinner.*

Proceed with ritual planned by the group.

Refer to poster of rules and review.

Ask each family the following question: *So, is there anything going on right now that might get in the way of your family taking part in today's group?*

Co-Facilitator: *It is now time to begin our activities for tonight. This session focuses on life choices, how we make them and follow through with them. If you will look at that schedule now, I will tell you a little bit about tonight's group.*

Proceed with introducing each activity briefly.

Co-Facilitator: *So, let's get started.*

Note 1: Facilitators encourage and model appropriate conversation, sharing, and supervision of children. Facilitators try several methods to stimulate conversation, including joining the family and modeling or use of conversation prompts. A facilitator might stop at the table of a family and offer encouragement, praise, and suggestions for managing different situations (behavior management, cueing, discipline). Work with families on interactions/behaviors occurring "in the moment." Remember to be sensitive to and empowering of the parent(s).

Note 2: One facilitator should take on the role of process monitor, making sure that the session runs smoothly and proceeds in a timely fashion. The process facilitator should encourage families to start finishing their dinner and cleaning up their tables after about 20 minutes to make sure that this activity is finished within 30 minutes and the group is ready to begin the next activity on time.

Module II

ACTIVITY 2: FAMILY TIMELINE

 30 MINUTES

 Goals

- To increase parents' knowledge of normal changes throughout the family life cycle.
- To improve understanding of how families adapt to the normal process of change.
- To improve understanding of transitions and loss.
- To help families track both normative and non-normative events that have affected their family.

 Materials

- Poster boards (one for each family)
- Paper
- Markers
- Glue
- Labels or postcards, blank

 Handouts

- The More Things Change
- Family Timeline Example

 Instructions

Lead Facilitator: *Before we start the first activity tonight, I want to find out about your successes at seeking support. Tell us about what you did and how it worked. Tell us about any support you received last week.* Let each family have an opportunity to share briefly.

Hand out "The More Things Change." Show the Family Timeline Example to let the families know what a timeline looks like. Each family constructs a Family Timeline starting with what lead up to the birth of the first child or when the parent(s) started planning a family. First, each family makes a list of important family events that have occurred on the labels or postcards. Family members make a small sign using the labels/postcards to represent each event. Families put these events on the poster board in order of their occurrence. Tell the families to put today about ¾ of the way across the poster, leaving room for the future.

Module II

Give the families about 20 minutes to complete their family timelines. A facilitator may want to join each family to record the events that the family lists.

Note 1: Facilitators who are not talking should spread around the room, monitoring families' reactions and level of participation. A facilitator might stop at the table of a family and offer encouragement, praise, and suggestions for managing different situations (behavior management, cueing, discipline). Work with families on interactions/behaviors occurring "in the moment." Remember to be sensitive to and empowering of the parent(s). Facilitators encourage families to discuss the ways in which their family has changed over the years, to think about the family life cycle, and to think about both positive and negative changes that have occurred.

ACTIVITY 3: LIFE CHOICES

 30 MINUTES

 Goals

- To have each developmental group conceptualize long-term planning about life choices.
- To understand the path between life scripts and what actually happens.

 Materials

- Pens
- Dress up clothes
- Chutes and Ladders

 Handouts

- Life Choices
- Life Choices—Adolescent Version
- Path to My Future

Module II

SESSION 7 *Life Choices*

Instructions

Lead Facilitator: *It is now time to break into smaller groups. Remember, each facilitator will take a different group, one for the adults, one for the teenagers, one for the older children, one for the younger children, and one for the babies. Let's begin by forming those groups.*

Facilitators gather their groups together. When the groups are formed and quiet, facilitators move one group at a time to their designated areas.

Lead Facilitator (Adult Group): Hand out "Life Choices." Parents learn about the importance of deliberate planning by discussing their own life choices and their satisfaction with their current family life. To encourage participation, you might ask each group member to tell what their life plans were at each stage of development. After about 15 minutes, hand out the "Path to My Future" worksheet and have the parents complete it. Using Chutes and Ladders as a metaphor, have the adults set a realistic goal and the steps that they would need to take to reach that goal. Also focus on the supports and obstacles to reaching their goal. For example, when they land on a ladder, they talk about something that might happen that might challenge them in getting to the next step. When they land on a chute, they talk about something that might happen that would make it harder to or delay reaching their goal. Facilitator should begin to wrap up this activity in about 25 minutes.

Co-Facilitator (Teen Group): Hand out "Life Choices—Adolescent Version." Adolescents talk about the importance of deliberate planning by discussing their own life choices and how they can make their plans actually happen. To encourage participation, you might ask each group member to tell what their life plans were at each stage of development. After about 15 minutes, hand out the "Path to My Future" worksheet and have the adolescents complete it as described for adults. Facilitator should begin to wrap up this activity in about 25 minutes.

Co-Facilitator (Older Child Group): Facilitator introduces "Chutes and Ladders" and explains the modified rules. Each child picks a goal that is relevant to them. This is the goal that represents the end of the game. The children write their goal on a postcard/Post-It Note that is placed at the top of the game board. While the children are playing, they focus on the supports and obstacles to reaching their goal. For example, when they land on a ladder, they talk about something that might happen that would help them reach their goal. When they land on a chute, they talk about something that might happen that would make it harder to or delay reaching their goal. The facilitator helps each child by suggesting realistic things that might happen. The game ends when all of the children reach their goal.

Co-Facilitator (Young Child and Baby Group): Show the children the box of dress up clothes, or show the children a doll house and let them have unstructured play time. You might want to comment that by

Module II   SESSION 7 Life Choices

pretending, they are learning about the way adults act and starting to decide what they might want to be when they grow up. Facilitator should begin to wrap up this activity in about 25 minutes.

Note 1: Facilitators for each group should start wrapping up the discussions or games after 25 minutes to allow three to four minutes to transition back to the family meeting room.

ACTIVITY 4: INTO THE FUTURE

 20 MINUTES

 Goals

- To illustrate the deliberate planning for the family's future.
- To share goals and steps for follow-through.

 Materials

- Timelines
- Rulers
- Markers
- Paper
- Glue
- Tape recorders (one for each family)

 Instructions

Co-Facilitator: *Before we start the next activity, let's take a moment to practice our relaxation.*

Give the families a two-minute relaxation activity.

Co-Facilitator: *Using ideas from tonight's activities, I want you to add your family's future to your timeline. Each person in the family should draw/create something to represent something you imagine will take place*

Module II

in your family's future such as the goals you set in the small groups. Add to your timeline the things you want for your family in the future.

You can write in the steps that each child will need to go through to get to that imagined future. After about 10 minutes hand out the tape recorders.

Co-Facilitator: *To end tonight's activity, let's tell another story. Tell a story that represents a "Vision Statement" for your family. Remember, this is what you imagine and can plan for yourselves in the future.*

Give the families about 20 minutes to complete.

ACTIVITY 5: CLOSING

 10 MINUTES

 Goals

- To increase sense of group cohesion.
- To practice planning and implementation of rituals and routine.
- To assure continuity from one session to the next.

 Handouts

- Sources of Spiritual Support
- Spiritual Assessment
- Phone Tree
- Contact Sheets
- Family Rating Form
- Participant Log
- Clinician Rating Form

 Instructions

Lead Facilitator: *We want to thank everyone for taking part in tonight's group. It is now time to finish this session and at the end of every group, we do a few things to end the group and to get ready for the next group.*

Module II

Co-Facilitator: *Is there anything that we still need to do to finish tonight's activities? I want to let each family know what a good job they did.*

Tell each family, or a family member, one thing that they did especially well.

Introduce and review the topic for next week.

Co-Facilitator: *Next week, we will start talking about spirituality. Also, think about if and how your sense of spirituality gives you comfort or support.*

Hand out "Sources of Spiritual Support."

Co-Facilitator: *Please fill out this handout while you are thinking about this. Your older children may also be interested in filling out one of these so I am giving each family several copies. Here are extra copies of your job chart and more stickers so that you can keep on working together to get everything done.*

Lead Facilitator: *We want to make sure that we stay in touch during the week, so let's continue to try the Buddy System or Phone Tree. Now, let's end by (closing rituals).*

Families share closing rituals, if desired. Cue families to acknowledge the end of group to other family members as well.

Lead Facilitator: *Please complete your family rating form now and hand it in. Thanks.*

Facilitators complete participant log and clinician rating form.

 ## Homework to be Assigned

- Sources of Spiritual Support/Spiritual Assessment

Module II — SESSION 8 — Spirituality and Values

Objectives

- To consider spirituality in a broader context—a philosophy of life, source of hope, self-actualization.
- To help families increase their awareness of a spiritual meaning to their lives.
- To aid families in evaluating their spirituality and looking at means for enriching their family experience.
- To aid family discussion and adoption of shared values.

Threads

- *Connectedness*: Co-construction of family stories and meanings are based on shared frames of reference and worldview. Helping families articulate this shared frame is an important building block for their family trauma narrative and for their ability to make genuine connections with one another. The banner/quilt and new routine help families communicate their shared beliefs.
- *Positive Affect, Memories, and Meaning*: Families often use their faith to help make sense of bad things that happen. Often, parents have a hard time talking with their children about this. This session helps provide structure and vocabulary for that communication.

Preparation

- Send out postcard to remind families of group.
- Prepare all materials.
- Print and cut out petals using Petal Template.
- Prepare Word Flower poster (see instructions in Activity 2).
- Food and facilities planning and preparation.
- Decide on facilitators' roles.
- Update on the status of each family in the group.
- Anticipate any problems that might arise during the session.

Homework Due

- Sources of Spiritual Support/Spiritual Assessment

Session Overview

Activity 1	Family Meal	30 Minutes
Activity 2	Spirituality Word Flower	15 Minutes
Activity 3	Values Assessment	65 Minutes
Activity 4	Closing	10 Minutes

Module II   SESSION 8 Spirituality and Values

 Homework to be Assigned

- None

 Materials

- Tables (one for each family)
- Centerpieces
- Nameplates and session schedules (one for each family)
- Place settings/napkins
- Nutritious meal/drinks
- Poster board (1)
- Yellow petals (five for each family) printed and cut out
- Pens/pencils/markers/crayons
- Glue/tape
- Songbook
- Musical instruments
- For Option 1: Banner materials (felt, fabric glue, wooden dowels, yarn or rope, decorative materials)
- For Option 2: Quilt materials (large rectangle of plain fabric cut to size of posterboard, small fabric squares in different prints cut to 8 ½ × 11, fabric glue, fabric scraps, fabric paint, decorative materials, pinking shears)
- Scissors
- Camera
- Job charts and star stickers (one pack for each family)

 Handouts

- Conversation Prompts   M2.S8.Prompts
- Sources of Spiritual Support   M2.S8.Spiritual.Support
- Spiritual Assessment   M2.S8.Spiritual.Assessment
- Spirituality Word Flower Instruction Sheet   M2.S8.Word.Flower
- Petal Template   M2.S8.Petal
- Our Family Values   M2.S8.Family.Values
- Phone Tree   M2.S8.Phone.Tree
- Family Rating Form   M2.S8.Feedback
- Contact Sheets   M2.S8.Contact.Sheets
- Participant Log   M2.S8.Log
- Clinician Rating Form   Clinician.Measures

 Posters

- Rules Poster   Group.Rules.Poster

Module II   SESSION 8   *Spirituality and Values*

ACTIVITY 1: FAMILY MEAL

 30 MINUTES

 Goals

- To facilitate an intimate family interaction.
- To increase awareness of the importance of routine within each family.

 Materials

- Tables (one for each family)
- Centerpieces
- Nameplates and session schedules (one for each family)
- Place settings/napkins
- Nutritious meal/drinks
- Video camera, remote microphones, and tapes (research groups only)

 Handouts

- Conversation Prompts

 Posters

- Rules Poster

 Instructions

Facilitators prepare room by setting tables (one for each family). A simple centerpiece for each table is a nice touch. A nameplate and schedule for the session's activities are also placed on each table. Hang poster with group rules listed in a prominent place where all the families can see it.

Food should be pre-cooked and ready to serve. Food can be served buffet or family style.

Parent(s) gather their children around a table and share a meal together. Before serving the food:

Lead Facilitator: *We are so happy to have you back with us tonight. First, let's thank (name of cooks) for fixing this wonderful meal. Please help yourselves to some food. Parents, why don't you serve your children first and then make a plate for yourself.*

Module II   SESSION 8 *Spirituality and Values*

Parent(s) should be encouraged to serve their children and then themselves.

Lead Facilitator: *To help your family have a good time during dinner, you might want to ask each other these questions or talk about the ideas on these cards.*

Hand out conversation prompts.

Lead Facilitator: *Let's begin.*

After the families have eaten and cleaned up (20–25 minutes), proceed with the opening routine.

Co-Facilitator: *We hope you enjoyed your dinner. It is now time to begin our activities for tonight.*

Proceed with ritual planned by the group.

Refer to poster of rules and review.

Ask each family the following question: *So, is there anything going on right now that might get in the way of your family taking part in today's group?*

Co-Facilitator: *This session focuses on what you believe in or your sense of spirituality. If you will look at the schedule now, I will tell you a little bit about tonight's group.*

Proceed with introducing each activity briefly.

Co-Facilitator: *So, let's get started.*

Note 1: Facilitators encourage and model appropriate conversation, sharing, and supervision of children. Facilitators try several methods to stimulate conversation, including joining the family and modeling or use of conversation prompts. A facilitator might stop at the table of a family and offer encouragement, praise, and suggestions for managing different situations (behavior management, cueing, discipline). Work with families on interactions/behaviors occurring "in the moment." Remember to be sensitive to and empowering of the parent(s).

Note 2: One facilitator should take on the role of process monitor making sure that the session runs smoothly and proceeds in a timely fashion. The process facilitator should encourage families to start finishing their dinner and cleaning up their tables after about 20 minutes to make sure that this activity is finished within 30 minutes and the group is ready to begin the next activity on time.

Module II SESSION 8 *Spirituality and Values*

ACTIVITY 2: SPIRITUALITY WORD FLOWER

 15 MINUTES

 Goals

• To expand the range of images associated with spirituality.

 Materials

• Poster board
• Yellow petals (five for each family)
• Markers
• Glue/tape

 Handouts

• Word Flower Instruction Sheet

 Instructions

Word Flower Activity:[1] A brainstorming activity in which the entire group identifies words associated with spirituality.

On a sheet of poster board, draw a large circle. Fill in or color the circle, if you want. In the middle of the circle, write the word "Spirituality." Hang the poster on the wall in a central location in the room. This can be done before the start of this session.

In yellow construction paper, cut out enough petals for each family to have five. Hand out five petals and a marker to each family.

Lead Facilitator: *It is time for our first activity. We are going to spend the session on spirituality. What we mean is "personal beliefs or values that give us a sense of being close to nature and the universe and that help us find meaning in things that happen." Maybe for you, spirituality includes a higher power or force that gives you strength and helps to guide you.*

Lead Facilitator: *Everyone has different ideas about what spirituality means. We want to start by finding out what spirituality means to each of you and to this group. Think a minute about your sense of spirituality. Talk with your family about it. Then write down five words, one on each of these petals, that you think of*

Module II   SESSION 8 *Spirituality and Values*

when you think about spirituality. When everyone has written down their words on the petals, we will add the petals to the word flower.

Give the families time to think, talk, and write.

Lead Facilitator: *Now, who wants to put the first petal on the flower? To you and your family, spirituality means (____). Great, let's tape that petal to the flower.*

Allow each family to tape all of their petals to the flower, saying the word as they put each one on.

NOTE

1. Adapted from Hopkins, E., Kelley, R., Bentley, K., & Murphy, J. (1995). *Working with Groups on Spiritual Themes.* Duluth, MN: Whole Person Associates.

ACTIVITY 3: VALUES ASSESSMENT

 65 MINUTES

 Goals

- To aid families in evaluating their spirituality and looking at means for enriching their family experience.
- To aid family discussion and adoption of shared values.
- To depict an aspect of the family's spirituality/values and to display this image.
- To help families put their shared values into action by developing traditions or routines that support their shared values.

 Materials

- Pens/pencils/markers/crayons
- Option 1: Banner materials (felt, fabric glue, wooden dowels, yarn or rope, decorative materials)
- Option 2: Quilt materials (large plain fabric cut to size of posterboard, small print fabric squares 8½ × 11, fabric glue, fabric scraps, fabric paint, decorative materials)
- Scissors or pinking shears (for quilt)
- Songbook
- Musical instruments
- Camera

Module II SESSION 8 *Spirituality and Values*

 Handouts

• Our Family Values

 Instructions

Note: For the activity, families have one of two options. Facilitators should decide which option will be available to families and only purchase materials for their selected option. Option 1 is to construct a family banner, while option 2 is to construct a family quilt.

Lead Facilitator: *Now we are going to spend some time talking about what spirituality and beliefs means to your family. This is a long activity so we will take the youngest children to another room for a sing-a-long. Please have your young children line up at the door.*

Lead Facilitator: *During the week, we asked you to talk together about how you practice your spirituality, fill out forms with the different ways marked, and bring them back with you tonight. Let each family who brought theirs back show the group by holding them up at their table for everyone to see.*

Lead Facilitator: *We have another way for you to talk about your spirituality and family values.*

Hand out "Our Family Values." Families talk about what they have learned about their spirituality and values. Each family decides on a list of values that they all believe in and can share. Families complete handouts, encouraging active participation by all.

Facilitator provides example and instructions. Allow about 15 minutes for this activity.

Option 1: Family Banner

Co-Facilitator: *Now that you have spent some time talking about your family's spirituality and values, you are going to make a banner celebrating it. We have all of the materials for you. First, you need to discuss and decide on a message for your banner.*

Each family discusses their banner message and design. Families proceed with task of banner production. Adults direct this task and ensure maximum participation by all.

Young children return to help finish and display banners. Take pictures of families with their banners. Families should be given 35 minutes to work on their banner.

Option 2: Family Quilt

Co-Facilitator: *Now that you have spent some time talking about your family's spirituality and values, you are going to make a quilt celebrating it. We have all of the materials for you. First, you need to discuss and decide on what values to include in your quilt.*

Module II SESSION 8 *Spirituality and Values*

Each family discusses which values to include and their quilt design. They can decorate the smaller squares to reflect specific values, which are then attached to the larger quilt, which may include a larger family message and/or the family name. Families proceed with task of quilt production. Adults direct this task and ensure maximum participation by all.

Young children return and help finish and display quilts. Take pictures of families with their quilts. Families should be given 35 minutes to work on their quilt.

Note: It is helpful to place a piece of posterboard under the quilt during construction to provide support. The quilt can be removed from the posterboard once it is fully dry (families usually take it home the following session).

After construction of banner quilt, all families should participate in the following.

Finally, have families look at "Family Values and Family Life." Families develop a ritual or routine that will help communicate or put into practice one of their shared family values. Each family uses the family planning tools to plan such an event. Give families 15 minutes to complete this activity.

Co-Facilitator (Young Child and Baby Group): *Today, we are going to make music and sing songs. Who has a favorite song that they would like to share? Is there a song that your family likes to sing together?*

Children can share favorite songs or important family songs. They can play instruments along with the singing. The children return to their families after 45 minutes.

ACTIVITY 4: CLOSING

 10 MINUTES

 Goals

- To increase sense of group cohesion.
- To practice planning and implementation of rituals and routine.
- To assure continuity from one session to the next.

 Handouts

- Phone Tree
- Contact Sheets

Module II SESSION 8 *Spirituality and Values*

- Family Rating Form
- Participant Log
- Clinician Rating Form

 Instructions

Lead Facilitator: *We want to thank everyone for taking part in tonight's group. It is now time to finish this session and at the end of every group, we do a few things to end the group and to get ready for the next group.*

Co-Facilitator: *Is there anything that we still need to do to finish tonight's activities?*

I want to let each family know what a good job they did. Tell each family, or a family member, one thing that they did especially well.

Co-Facilitator: *Introduce and review the topic for next week. Next week we will talk about things that get in the way of planned activities. Here are extra copies of your job chart and more stickers so that you can keep on working together to get everything done.*

Lead Facilitator: *We want to make sure that we stay in touch during the week, so let's continue to try the Buddy System or Phone Tree. Now, let's end by closing rituals.*

Families share closing rituals, if desired. Cue families to acknowledge the end of group to other family members as well.

Please complete your family rating form now and hand it in. Thanks.

Facilitators complete participant log and clinician rating form.

 Homework to be Assigned

- None

Module II   SESSION 9 *Things Get in the Way*

Objectives

- To facilitate discussion among family members around things that get in the way of planned activities.
- To allow parents and children to express emotions resulting from not carrying out planned family activities.
- To build problem-solving skills relevant to carrying out planned family activities.

Threads

- *Deliberateness*: We return again to deliberateness and to gaining control over daily life by planning and problem-solving. We want families to believe in themselves and their ability to follow through on what they have planned.
- *Co-Regulation*: We focus on identifying and modulating feelings of disappointment, frustration, anger, and sadness. It may be helpful to link the notion of feeling better with active coping and problem-solving.

Preparation

- Send out postcard to remind families of group.
- Prepare all materials.
- Print "Things Get in the Way" skit description cards on half fold cardstock, cut in half, laminate.
- Food and facilities planning and preparation.
- Decide on facilitators' roles.
- Update on the status of each family in the group.
- Anticipate any problems that might arise during the session.

Homework Due

- None

Session Overview

Activity 1	Family Meal with Experiential Disruption	30 Minutes
Activity 2	What Got in the Way?	20 Minutes
Activity 3	Carrying Out Activities	45 Minutes
Activity 4	Carrying it Out This Week	15 Minutes
Activity 5	Closing	10 Minutes

Homework to be Assigned

- Record of family activity carried out

Module II   SESSION 9 *Things Get in the Way*

 Materials

- Tables (one for each family)
- Centerpieces
- Nameplates and session schedules (one for each family)
- Place settings/napkins
- Nutritious meal/drinks
- Flipchart
- Movie clip from *When a Man Loves a Woman*
- Jack-in-the Box toys
- Sorting boxes/plastic rings (assortment of problem-solving skills and games for babies)
- Paper
- Pens/pencils/crayons/markers, including purple crayons
- Camera
- Disposable cameras (one for each family)
- Job charts and star stickers (one pack for each family)

 Handouts

Conversation Prompts	M2.S9.Prompts
"Things Get in the Way" skit description cards	M2.S9.TGW.Cards (half fold cards)
"Things Get in the Way" handout	M2.S9.TGW.Handout
FLIP the Problem	M2.S9.FLIP
Harold and the Purple Crayon (condensed)	M2.S9.Harold
Carrying it Out This Week	M2.S9.Carry.Out.Week
Phone Tree	M2.S9.Phone.Tree
Contact Sheets	M2.S9.Contact.Sheets
Family Rating Form	M2.S9.Feedback
Participant Log	M2.S9.Log
Clinician Rating Form	M2.S9.Clinic.Measures

 Posters

Rules Poster	Group.Rules.Poster

 Books

- *I Wish Daddy Didn't Drink So Much*
- *On Monday When it Rains*
- *Harold and the Purple Crayon (2)*

Module II   SESSION 9 *Things Get in the Way*

ACTIVITY 1: FAMILY MEAL WITH EXPERIENTIAL DISRUPTION

 30 MINUTES

 Goals

- To facilitate an intimate family interaction.
- To increase awareness of the importance of routine within each family.
- To illustrate the effects of routine disruption on family/group functioning.
- To share the psychological and emotional reactions of members to routine disruption.

 Materials

- Tables (one for each family)
- Centerpieces
- Nameplates and session schedules (one for each family)
- Place settings/napkins
- Nutritious meal/drinks
- Video camera, remote microphones, and tapes (research groups only)

 Handouts

- Conversation Prompts

 Posters

- Rules Poster

 Instructions

Facilitators prepare room by setting tables (one for each family). A simple centerpiece for each table is a nice touch. A nameplate and schedule for the session's activities are also placed on each table. Hang poster with group rules listed in a prominent place where all the families can see it.

Food should be pre-cooked and ready to serve. Food can be served buffet or family style.

Module II

SESSION 9 *Things Get in the Way*

Parent(s) gather their children around a table and share a meal together. Before serving the food:

Lead Facilitator: *We are so happy to have you back with us tonight. First, let's thank (name of cooks) for fixing this wonderful meal. Please help yourselves to some food. Parents, why don't you serve your children first and then make a plate for yourself. To help your family have a good time during dinner, you might want to ask each other these questions or talk about the ideas on these cards.*

Hand out conversation prompts.

Lead Facilitator: *Let's begin.*

After the families have eaten and cleaned up (20–25 minutes), proceed with the planned disruption.

Forget to proceed with ritual planned by the group. Forget to review rules, tonight's agenda, and check-in.

After about five minutes, start debriefing and processing of Disruption in Routine Exercise.

Co-Facilitator: *We did not start tonight's group the same way we usually do. How did it feel, what was liked/disliked, how similar/different was this to life at home, etc.?*

Review the rules, agenda, check-in.

Co-Facilitator: *This session focuses on what gets in the way. On your table, you will find a schedule for the activities we will be doing. So, let's get started.*

> *Note 1:* Facilitators who are not talking should initially just stand around and talk with one another. They should appear busy or preoccupied, rather than involved with the families. After the processing, spread around the room, monitoring families' reactions and level of participation. Facilitators encourage and model appropriate conversation, sharing, and supervision of children. Facilitators try several methods to stimulate conversation, including joining the family and modeling or use of conversation prompts. A facilitator might stop at the table of a family and offer encouragement, praise, and suggestions for managing different situations (behavior management, cueing, discipline). Work with families on interactions/behaviors occurring "in the moment." Remember to be sensitive to and empowering of the parent(s).

> *Note 2:* One facilitator should take on the role of process monitor, making sure that the session runs smoothly and proceeds in a timely fashion. The process facilitator should encourage families to start finishing their dinner and cleaning up their tables after about 20 minutes to make sure that this activity is finished within 30 minutes and the group is ready to begin the next activity on time.

Module II   **SESSION 9** *Things Get in the Way*

ACTIVITY 2: WHAT GOT IN THE WAY?

 20 MINUTES

 Goals

- To identify factors that "get in the way" of planned family activities.
- To facilitate interaction within and between families.

 Materials

- Flipchart
- Markers
- Camera

 Handouts

- "Things that Get in the Way" skit description cards.

 Instructions

Co-Facilitator: *Now, we want each family to get together and get comfortable. Parents, you might want to get your younger children to sit next to you or in your lap.*

Give each family a "Things that Get in the Way" skit card.

Co-Facilitator: *We want your family to act out what is on the card.*

Give the families about five minutes to practice.

Co-Facilitator: *Now, we would like you to share your skit with the other families. Don't tell us what you are acting out and we will try to guess. Which family would like to go first? Please, let's show our respect for each family, by listening to them.*

Encourage each family to take a turn. Give lots of praise to each family as they share. The facilitator lists "things that got in the way" on a flipchart. Pictures are taken of families during skits for family scrapbooks.

Module II _____ SESSION 9 Things Get in the Way

ACTIVITY 3: CARRYING OUT ACTIVITIES

 45 MINUTES

 Goals

- To identify situations in which activities have not been carried out in each family.
- To identify common factors that get in the way of carrying out activities for each family.
- To facilitate discussion about emotions associated with not carrying out planned family activities.
- To improve each family's skill in solving problems.

 Materials

- Pens/pencils/markers/crayons
- *When a Man Loves a Woman* DVD
- Purple crayons
- Jack-in-the-Box toys
- Sorting boxes/plastic rings (assortment of problem-solving skills and games for babies)

 Handouts

- Things Get in the Way
- FLIP the Problem
- *Harold and the Purple Crayon* (condensed)

 Books

- *I Wish Daddy Didn't Drink So Much*
- *On Monday When it Rains*
- *Harold and the Purple Crayon (2)*

 Instructions

Lead Facilitator: *It is now time to break into smaller groups. Remember, each facilitator will take a different group, one for adults, one for teens, one for older children, one for younger children, and one for babies.*

Module II   SESSION 9 *Things Get in the Way*

Let's begin by forming those groups. Facilitators gather their groups together. When the groups are formed and quiet, facilitators move one group at a time to their designated areas.

Lead Facilitator (Adult Group): Adults review "Things that Get in the Way." Facilitator asks parents to consider family activities that have not been carried out due to things getting in the way. Parents are asked to consider situations in which a variety of factors (parents, children, external factors) may have gotten in the way of successfully carrying out family activities. Parents should identify their own feelings and their children's feelings about not carrying out planned family activities. The facilitator uses these descriptions to teach about the importance of carrying out family activities.

Facilitator then teaches parents a problem-solving technique known as FLIP the problem (adapted from CBT for Relapse Prevention of Depression).

Lead Facilitator (Adult Group): *Everyone faces problems in life, whether with family, friends, teachers, or co-workers. Problems can include when things don't go as planned, as we were just talking about, and other situations as well. It is important to have a general way to solve these problems, so that they don't lead you to feel discouraged, hopeless, or even depressed. Today, I wanted us to talk about problem-solving, and how this skill might help you solve future problems, such as when things don't go as planned. First let's define a problem. What is a problem? A problem is a source of stress. Basically, a problem is any situation that causes you to be anxious, worried, or stressed out.*

Hand out FLIP the Problem.

Lead Facilitator (Adult Group): *Let's learn about FLIP. When you encounter a problem, FLIP the problem to look at all sides.*

F: Figure out what the problem is and what you want to happen. Sometimes when people are overwhelmed, everything becomes part of the problem. This often leads to more stress! In order to solve the problem, you need to figure out what the problem is.

L: List all possible solutions. Even adults often overlook this step in problem-solving. Most problems have many possible solutions. The trick is to brainstorm all of these possibilities before choosing one.

I: Identify the best solution. Once you have listed all possible options, you can fill in the positive consequences ("plusses") and negative consequences ("minuses") for each. After looking at the positives and negatives to each option, it often is easy to choose a solution—the one with the most "plusses"! If it is not obvious which solution is the best, then continue to brainstorm any "plusses" or "minuses" that you might have left off the list.

P: Plan what to do next. After choosing a solution, it is important to plan how to carry out this solution. Once you have acted on this solution, evaluate the effectiveness of your choice and learn from it!

Module II   SESSION 9   *Things Get in the Way*

Have the group help you apply FLIP to one of the problems raised, such as when things do not go as planned.

Co-Facilitator (Teen Group): Adolescents watch a short movie clip from *When a Man Loves a Woman* (start with the last two minutes of Chapter 2 and the first two minutes of Chapter 3—the scene starts with the dad coming home and the babysitter announcing that the mom did not come home. Talk about family dynamics when things get in the way. With remaining time, introduce problem-solving as one way of managing when things do not go as planned. Hand out and review FLIP the problem, as described in the adult group outline above. As an example, discuss "FLIP" technique for the family in the video clip, including identifying other ways they could have worked through their problem. Encourage adolescents to share common problems they experience and apply FLIP as a group.

Co-Facilitator (Older Child Group): Children read the story *I Wish Daddy Didn't Drink So Much,* and are asked to identify the main character's feelings when she did not get to go sledding, an activity that had been planned with her father. With remaining time, introduce problem-solving as one way of managing when things do not go as planned. Discuss as a group how the main character and her mom worked around events that did not go as planned (such as Christmas dinner). Introduce Harold (from *Harold and the Purple Crayon*) as someone who gets himself into a lot of problems with his crayon, but is also a great problem-solver. Read a story from *Harold and the Purple Crayon.* Hand out paper and purple crayons. Have children work individually or in pairs to solve some of Harold's problems. Suggested problems include: when Harold ends up in the water and cannot swim, when he climbs a steep mountain but has no way down, and/or when Harold goes on a long adventure, gets hungry, and realizes he has no food. Let the children work on these for about 10 minutes. Have each child/pair tell about how they solved Harold's problems. Give lots of encouragement and praise for working together, creativity, resourcefulness, quick thinking, trying, etc.

Co-Facilitator (Young Child Group): Read *On Monday When it Rains* and talk about disappointment.

Remember when you wanted to do something really, really badly, but did not get to do it. You probably felt disappointed.

Have each child draw a face that illustrates disappointment. Tell a story about a time when you felt disappointed. Children can draw a picture of their story. Discuss as a group how the disappointed child in the book could solve some of the problems that occurred when things did not work out the way they wanted (or from the stories children bring up).

Introduce Harold (from Harold and the Purple Crayon) as someone who gets himself into a lot of problems with his crayon, but is also a great problem-solver. Complete *Harold and the Purple Crayon* problem-solving activity as outlined above, in the older child group.

Co-Facilitator (Baby Group): Play with the toddlers and babies with Jack-in-the-Box toys. Use the toys to build expectations. Help the babies anticipate the action. The babies can also play with assorted sorting toys.

Module II   SESSION 9 *Things Get in the Way*

Note 1: Facilitators for each group should start wrapping up the discussions or games after 40 minutes to allow three to four minutes to transition back to the family meeting room.

ACTIVITY 4: CARRYING IT OUT THIS WEEK

 15 MINUTES

 Goals

- To encourage families to carry out one family activity in upcoming week.
- To encourage family problem solving around potential obstacles to family activities.
- To increase each family's self-efficacy related to carrying out family activities.

 Materials

- Pens
- Disposable cameras (one for each family)

 Handouts

- Carrying it Out This Week

 Instructions

Co-Facilitator: *Before we start the next activity, let's take a moment to practice our relaxation.*

Give the families a two-minute relaxation activity.

Hand out "Carrying it Out This Week" Each family identifies a family activity that they would like to carry out in the upcoming week. Activities should be "doable," and should include all family members. Some examples may be: family meal, family game, family outing/walk.

Each family should complete the handout, identifying potential obstacles to carrying out their activity, and ways to overcome obstacles. Each family decides on a way to record their activity to report back to the group

Module II — SESSION 9 — *Things Get in the Way*

(pictures, book/story, scrapbook, audiotape or videotape). Hand out disposable cameras for the families to take pictures while they carry out their event.

ACTIVITY 5: CLOSING

 10 MINUTES

 Goals

- To increase sense of group cohesion.
- To practice planning and implementation of rituals and routine.
- To assure continuity from one session to the next.

 Handouts

- Phone Tree
- Contact Sheets
- Family Rating Form
- Participant Log
- Clinician Rating Form

 Instructions

Lead Facilitator: *We want to thank everyone for taking part in tonight's group. It is now time to finish this session and at the end of every group, we do a few things to end the group and to get ready for the next group.*

Co-Facilitator: *Is there anything that we still need to do to finish tonight's activities? I want to let each family know what a good job they did.*

Tell each family, or a family member, one thing that they did especially well.

Co-Facilitator: *Remember to make a record of your family activity that you are going to carry out during the week.*

Introduce and review the topic for next week.

Module II

SESSION 9 *Things Get in the Way*

Co-Facilitator: *Next week, we will talk about the bad things that have happened to your family. We will do this in family groups. Here are extra copies of your job chart and more stickers so that you can keep on working together to get everything done.*

Lead Facilitator: *We want to make sure that we stay in touch during the week, so let's continue to try the Buddy System or Phone Tree. Now, let's end by (closing rituals).*

Families share closing rituals, if desired. Cue families to acknowledge the end of group to other family members as well.

Lead Facilitator: *Please complete your family rating form now and hand it in. Thanks.*

Facilitators complete participant log and clinician rating form.

 Homework to be Assigned

- Record of your family activity carried out last week!

Module II

SESSION HR 10 *Celebration!*

Objectives

- To highlight the role of positive affect (humor, laughter) in family interaction and in stress reduction.
- To carry out a planned celebration practicing the skills and concepts discussed in earlier sessions.
- To reinforce the notion of richness in family gatherings and celebrations.
- To review each family's goals and evaluate the group with respect to meeting those goals.
- To encourage deliberate planning of traditions/routines and endings (goodbyes).

Threads

- *Deliberateness*: Families leave group feeling like they have accomplished something by coming every week, planning and carrying out homework and family events, and learning valuable skills to keep their family close and safe.
- *Structure and Safety*: Families provide structure and protection for themselves.
- *Resource Seeking*: Families plan to stay connected with their new supports.
- *Positive Affect, Memories, Meaning*: This session helps the family frame their trauma history as something in the past and focus on making and celebrating positive choices and making positive memories.

Preparation

- Send out postcards to remind families of group.
- Prepare all materials.
- Print certificates for each family (fill in name, date, print on heavy stock paper).
- Food and facilities planning and preparation.
- Decide on facilitators' roles.
- Update on the status of each family in the group.
- Anticipate any problems that might arise during the session.

Homework Due

- Record of Family Activity Carried Out.

Session Overview

Activity 1	Family Meal Celebration	30 Minutes
Activity 2	Our Own Feel Good Book	25 Minutes
Activity 3	Making Us Laugh	25 Minutes
Activity 4	Getting Closure	25 Minutes
Activity 5	Closing Ceremony	15 Minutes

Module II   SESSION HR 10   Celebration!

Homework to be Assigned

- Follow through on their family ritual tree care plan!

Materials

- Tables (one for each family)
- Centerpieces
- Nameplates and session schedules (one for each family)
- Place settings/napkins
- Nutritious meal/drinks
- Materials for family scrapbook pages (paper, hole punch, decorating materials, glue)
- Apples to Apples or Don't Make Me Laugh, Senior version or Zobmondo: Questions
- Paper/construction paper/postcard card stock
- Phone and address cards
- Pens/colored pencils/crayons/markers
- Research folders and instruments (if being completed during this session)
- Camera
- Facilitator chosen parting gifts (optional)
- Frames (one for each family) (to fit certificates)
- Job charts and star stickers (one pack for each family)

Handouts

Laughing is Important	HRM2.S10.Laugh.Important
Laughing Through Life	HRM2.S10.Laughing.Life
Closure Questionnaire	HRM2.S10.Closure.Question
Family Ritual Tree Care	HRM2.S10.Tree.Care
Family Drawing	HRM2.S10.Family.Drawing
Certificates	HRM2.S10.Certificate
Family Rating Form	HRM2.S10.Feedback
Participant Log	HRM2.S10.Log
Clinician Rating Form	HRM2.S10.Clinic.Measures

Posters

Rules Poster	Group.Rules.Poster

Books

- *The FEEL GOOD Book*
- *I Love to Laugh! A Book of Fun and Giggles*

Module II  SESSION HR 10 Celebration!

ACTIVITY 1: FAMILY MEAL CELEBRATION

 30 MINUTES

 Goals

- To carry out a planned celebration practicing the skills and concepts discussed in earlier sessions.
- To reinforce the notion of richness in family gatherings and celebrations.

 Materials

- As planned by families

 Handouts

- Conversation Prompts

 Posters

- Rules Poster

 Instructions

Lead Facilitator: *We are so happy to have you back with us tonight for our last group. This session focuses on celebration and saying "Goodbye." So, let's get started and have a good time!*

Families carry out celebration dinner as planned.

After the families have eaten and cleaned up (20–25 minutes), proceed with the opening.

Lead Facilitator: *You decided to start the meal by (opening ritual), so let's begin that way.*

Proceed with ritual planned by the group.

Refer to poster of rules and review. Make link between group rules-group functioning with family rules (explicit, agreed upon, written down for review) with healthy family functioning.

Ask each family the following question: *So, is there anything going on right now that might get in the way of your family taking part in today's group?* Make link between checking in with family members to be sure

Module II — SESSION HR 10 — Celebration!

each person can participate (problem solving, helping with a task), or may be over burdened, with staying attuned to the mood and needs of all family members during other family activities.

ACTIVITY 2: OUR OWN FEEL GOOD BOOK

 25 MINUTES

 Goals

- To help families explore ways they can have fun together as a family.
- To encourage deliberate planning.
- To encourage a positive focus and valuing of family accomplishments.

 Materials

- Paper
- Pens
- Materials for scrapbook pages (paper, hole punch, glue)
- Decorating materials

 Books

- *The FEEL GOOD Book*

 Instructions

Lead Facilitator: *We hope you enjoyed your dinner. It is now time to begin our activities for tonight. If you will look at the schedule now, I will tell you a little bit about tonight's group.*

Proceed with introducing each activity briefly.

Co-Facilitator: *As we get started on our first activity tonight, I have a book to share with you.*

Read *The FEEL GOOD Book*. Encourage the families to share experiences that make them feel good. They can discuss experiences included in the book and add additional experiences as well. Encourage them to brainstorm, as a family, activities or experiences that make them all feel good.

Module II

 **SESSION HR 10** *Celebration!*

After families have had a chance to brainstorm, hand out scrapbook pages and materials. Ask families to create their own "Feel Good Book" scrapbook pages, including activities and experiences that make each family member and the entire family feel good. Families should also be encouraged to include activities that could make them feel good in the future. Give families about 20 minutes to complete this. Once finished, facilitators can encourage families to share their Feel Good scrapbook pages. Encourage the family to add these pages to their scrapbook.

ACTIVITY 3: MAKING US LAUGH

 25 MINUTES

 Goals

- To help family members understand why laughter is important and identify what makes them laugh.
- To encourage positive and fun interactions within the family's comfort zone related to expressing positive affect and laughter.

 Materials

- Paper
- Pens
- Teen Game: Apples to Apples, or Don't Make Me Laugh, senior version, or Zobmondo: Questions

 Handouts

- Laughter is Important!
- Laughing Through Life

 Books

- *I Love to Laugh! A Book of Fun and Giggles*

 Instructions

Lead Facilitator: *It's time to break into smaller groups. Remember, each facilitator will take a different group, one for the adults, one for teens, one for the older children, one for the younger children, and one for the babies. Let's begin by forming those groups.*

Module II   SESSION HR 10   Celebration!

Facilitators gather their groups together. When the groups are formed and quiet, facilitators move one group at a time to their designated areas.

Lead Facilitator (Adult Group): Hand out "Laughter is Important" and "Laughing Through Life," which outline the importance of laughter and developmental differences in humor. Discuss with parents why they think laughter is important. Discuss the importance of balancing positive experiences for families who have experienced trauma. Encourage parents to share examples of funny things their children have done or said. Ask parents what types of fun, laughter-promoting activities they do with their children now. What types of activities would they like to do more of? If needed, a few minutes can be taken at the end of the breakout group to discuss treatment planning for each family as the group draws to a close.

Co-Facilitator (Teen Group): Facilitate discussion with teens about why they think laughter is important. Discuss what makes them laugh. What activities do they enjoy to do with their peers? Lead teens in a game to promote fun and laughter. Facilitators can choose between Apples to Apples, Don't Make Me Laugh, senior version, or Zobmondo Questions.

Co-Facilitator (Older Child Group): Ask the children what fun things they like to do and what makes them laugh. After the discussion, encourage fun in the group by either singing silly songs together or playing "Sound and the Fury" game. Suggestions for songs are listed in the handout "Fun and Silly Songs." To play "Sound and the Fury," the facilitator and the children all stand in a circle. The facilitator starts by modeling a funny gesture with their whole body paired with a silly sound. Everyone else in the group has to imitate the movement and sound. The child standing to the right of the facilitator then models their own gesture paired with a silly sound. The group then imitates the first gesture and sound, followed by the new gesture and sound. Circle continues clockwise until all children have had a turn. Each round, the group will imitate all of the previous gestures and add the newly exhibited gesture and sound at the end.

Co-Facilitator (Young Child Group): Ask the children what fun things they like to do and what makes them laugh. After the discussion, encourage fun in the group by singing fun and silly songs with the children. Suggestions for silly songs are listed in the handout "Fun and Silly Songs." The children can also initiate singing their favorite silly songs.

Co-Facilitator (Baby Group): Read babies *I Love to Laugh! A Book of Fun and Giggles.* Play the included games and activities with the babies as you read the book, including Peek-A-Boo, Itsy Bitsy Spider, and Ring Around the Rosie.

Note 1: Facilitators for each group should start wrapping up the discussions or games after 20 minutes to allow three to four minutes to transition back to the family meeting room.

Module II

SESSION HR 10 — *Celebration!*

ACTIVITY 4: GETTING CLOSURE

 25 MINUTES

 Goals

- To encourage families to make long-term commitments to maintaining family traditions and routines.
- To predict how their family will have changed in six months.
- To bring closure to the group.
- To facilitate further communication between families, if desired.

 Materials

- Paper/construction paper/postcard card stock
- Phone and address cards
- Pens/colored pencils/crayons/markers
- Glue

 Handouts

- Closure Questionnaire
- Family Ritual Tree Care

 Instructions

Hand out "Closure Questionnaire" and "Family Ritual Tree Care."

Lead Facilitator: *I want you to complete this first sheet so that you can tell us what you liked and did not like about this group. What you thought was useful for you and your family and what you thought was not as helpful.*

Parent(s) complete the closure questionnaire with input from all family members. Ask families to share briefly their thoughts and feelings about what they learned and whether anything has changed. Make a copy of the questionnaire for the family.

After about 10–12 minutes: *Now on the other sheet, I want you to think about what traditions or routines that we have talked about or that you have thought about during the weeks that we have been meeting and that you would like your family to keep doing. Talk together about this and write down what you decide.*

Module II   SESSION HR 10   *Celebration!*

Families agree on what traditions and routines they want to continue to work on in the future. Ask families to share what they would like to continue to work on.

Co-Facilitator: Take all of the young children to another side of the room or another room. Alternatively, facilitators could circulate in the room and help young children (3+ years) at the tables so they can contribute to the family task. Help them make "Goodbye" cards.

ACTIVITY 5: CLOSING CEREMONY

 15 MINUTES

 Goals

- To reach closure, to model showing appropriate recognition and to engage in a rewarding goodbye.

 Materials

- Camera
- Facilitator chosen parting gifts (optional)
- Frames (one for each family) (to fit certificates)
- Job charts and star stickers (one pack for each family)

 Handouts

- Certificates (printed for each family)
- Family Rating Form
- Participant Log
- Clinician Rating Form

 Instructions

Facilitators work together to make this ceremonial. This could include calling each family up to the front of the room to present them with their certificate and a small memento of their time spent in group. As the family proceeds to the front of the room, facilitators could hum or play the Graduation March or other music. Take pictures of each family.

Module II

 **SESSION HR 10** *Celebration!*

Facilitators: *You have done a great job during this group and should be proud! We are proud of the work and the play you have done and would like to recognize you for that. We have a certificate that we would like to present to each family. Please come forward when we call your name to receive your certificate.*

Allow time for each facilitator to compliment the family members.

Facilitators: *Now it is time to say "Goodbye" for the last group. Let's end like we always have with our closing rituals.*

Families share closing rituals, if desired. Cue families to acknowledge the end of group with each other.

Facilitators: *Please complete your family rating form now and hand it in. Thanks.*

Facilitators complete participant log and clinician rating form.

 Homework to be Assigned

- Follow through on their family ritual tree care plan!

MODULE III
TRAUMA RESOLUTION AND CONSOLIDATION

This Module provides:

Family Trauma Work: The intervention model proposed here explores the role of constructive, naturally occurring family rituals as a vehicle for strengthening a family's protective function and for accomplishing many of the treatment objectives outlined in the literature on family trauma treatment (Allen & Bloom, 1994; Banyard et al., 2001; Davies et al., 1998; Miller, 1999; Temple, 1997). Specific areas for trauma work with families included in this module are working through the trauma, developing a shared sense of meaning, and using problem solving techniques for minimizing additional stresses.

Between Modules II and III, a treatment conference should be held between the primary therapist and the group facilitator who will be working with the family on their narrative. This meeting is important for planning the family work involved in Module III, including whether to build narration skills or talk directly about traumas, timing of the narrative, strategies for working with the family and with each individual family member, and communication of potential issues that might arise as the family moves through creation of a shared family trauma story. Group facilitators should discuss this information as a team as they plan the sessions in Module III.

MODULE OVERVIEW

Session Number

10	Telling About What Happened
11	When Bad Things Happen I
12	When Bad Things Happen II
13	Marking the Trauma
14	Good Things Happen Too!
15	Celebration!
Post-Session	Re-Evaluating Trauma and Family Functioning

Module III SESSION 10 *Telling About What Happened*

 Objectives

- To help families understand the importance of talking about the trauma.
- To educate about and evaluate any avoidance the family is experiencing regarding talking about what happened.
- To partner with families to decide whether or how to develop new narration skills or tell their trauma stories.
- To establish plans for dealing with any distress that families experience as they share their stories or talk about difficult issues.

 Threads

- *Structure and Safety:* With the family as the "expert" on how to proceed, a narrative process is planned that will not harm any family member.
- *Co-Regulations:* Each family uses the skill sets that they have learned and practiced to help them engage in a narrative process that is within their comfort zone.
- *Positive Affect, Memories, and Meaning:* Important components of this session include psychoeducation about trauma symptoms, education about family narrative skills, and trauma narratives. Families embark on the narrative process with hope for gaining a better understanding of their traumas and new skills for communication about difficult issues in the future.
- *Connectedness:* Family collaborative communication is stressed in the activity and the planning of the family narrative process.

 Preparation

- Send out postcard to remind families of group.
- Prepare all materials.
- Food and facilities planning and preparation.
- Decide on facilitators' roles.
- Update on the status of each family in the group.
- Anticipate any problems that might arise during the session.
- Treatment conference with each child's and family's primary therapist.
- Review the Narrative Guide.

 Homework Due

- Record of Family Activity Carried Out.

Module III Telling About What Happened

 Session Overview

Activity 1	Family Meal	30 Minutes
Activity 2	Communicating without Words	15 Minutes
Activity 3	Understanding Our Reactions	25 Minutes
Activity 4	Telling About Bad Things That Have Happened	40 Minutes
Activity 5	Closing	10 Minutes

 Homework to be Assigned

- Using Your Coping Resources

 Materials

- Tables (one for each family)
- Centerpieces
- Nameplates and session schedules (one for each family)
- Place settings/napkins
- Nutritious meal/drinks
- Tape recorders and tapes (one for each family)
- Wooden dowels (one for each member of each family)
- Blank postcards (set of 10 for each family)
- Envelopes for postcards (one for each family)
- Paper
- Pens/markers
- Job charts and star stickers (one pack for each family)

 Handouts

• Conversation Prompts	M3.S10.Prompts (Avery 5371)
• Narrative Guide	M3.S10.Narrative.Guide
• Using Your Coping Resources	M3.S10.Using.Coping.Resources
• Phone Tree	M3.S10.Phone.Tree
• Contact Sheets	M3.S10.Contact.Sheets
• Family Rating Form	M3.S10.Feedback
• Participant Log	M3.S10.Log
• Clinician Rating Form	M3.S10.Clinic.Measures

 Posters

• Rules Poster	Group.Rules.Poster

Module III   SESSION 10   *Telling About What Happened*

ACTIVITY 1: FAMILY MEAL

 30 MINUTES

 Goals

- To facilitate an intimate family interaction.
- To increase awareness of the importance of routine within each family.

 Materials

- Tables (one for each family)
- Centerpieces
- Nameplates and session schedules (one for each family)
- Place settings/napkins
- Nutritious meal/drinks
- Video camera, remote microphones, and tapes (research groups only)

 Handouts

- Conversation Prompts

 Posters

- Rules Poster

 Instructions

Facilitators prepare room by setting tables (one for each family). A simple centerpiece for each table is a nice touch. A nameplate and schedule for the session's activities are also placed on each table. Hang poster with group rules listed in a prominent place where all the families can see it.

Food should be pre-cooked and ready to serve. Food can be served buffet or family style.

Parent(s) gather their children around a table and share a meal together. Before serving the food:

Module III   SESSION 10   Telling About What Happened

Lead Facilitator: *We are so happy to have you back with us tonight. First, let's thank (name of cooks) for fixing this wonderful meal. Please help yourselves to some food. Parents, why don't you serve your children first and then make a plate for yourself.*

Parent(s) should be encouraged to serve their children and then themselves.

Co-Facilitator: *To help your family have a good time during dinner, you might want to ask each other these questions or talk about the ideas on these cards.*

Hand out conversation prompts.

After the families have eaten and cleaned up (20–25 minutes), proceed with the opening routine.

Co-Facilitator: *You decided to start the meal by (opening ritual), so let's begin that way.*

Proceed with ritual planned by the group.

Refer to poster of rules and review.

Ask each family the following question: *So, is there anything going on right now that might get in the way of your family taking part in today's group?*

Co-Facilitator: *This session focuses on the bad things that have happened to your family. So, let's get started.*

Note 1: Facilitators encourage and model appropriate conversation, sharing, and supervision of children. Facilitators try several methods to stimulate conversation, including joining the family and modeling or use of conversation prompts. A facilitator might stop at the table of a family and offer encouragement, praise, and suggestions for managing different situations (behavior management, cueing, discipline). Work with families on interactions/behaviors occurring "in the moment." Remember to be sensitive to and empowering of the parent(s).

Note 2: One facilitator should take on the role of process monitor, making sure that the session runs smoothly and proceeds in a timely fashion. The process facilitator should encourage families to start finishing their dinner and cleaning up their tables after about 20 minutes to make sure that this activity is finished within 30 minutes and the group is ready to begin the next activity on time.

Module III SESSION 10 Telling About What Happened

ACTIVITY 2: COMMUNICATING WITHOUT WORDS[1]

 15 MINUTES

 Goals

- To illustrate attunement and communication theory.
- To let families experience a collaborative communication process.

 Materials

- Wooden dowels (one for each member of each family)

 Instructions

Lead Facilitator: *We hope you enjoyed your dinner. It is now time to begin our activities for tonight. If you will look at that schedule now, I will tell you a little bit about tonight's group.*

Proceed with introducing each activity briefly.

Lead Facilitator: *Before we start the first activity tonight, I want us to take time for families to tell us about the activity that you carried out this week. We asked you to bring some kind of record of this back with you tonight.*

Let each family that brought theirs back show the group and tell about their activity. Ask the other families why they did not bring a record back. If they just forgot but carried out the activity, have them describe it. If they did not carry out the activity, ask what got in the way.

Hand out dowels (one for each family member).

Co-Facilitator: *This first activity for tonight is done in silence. It does not take any words for you to work together as a family and understand each other. First, divide up into pairs. On your table are wood sticks. Watch what we do with these.*

Two facilitators demonstrate by using the palms of their hands to hold the sticks between them. They can then demonstrate moving their hands around, watching each other to see how they move together. They can then use their fingertips to hold the sticks up between them. Finally, a third facilitator can join and show how multiple people can do this together.

Module III SESSION 10 Telling About What Happened

Co-Facilitator: *Now you try. We want you to work together to keep the sticks up, so don't let go.*

Let the pairs try this, and then instruct the families to try it with everyone all together. While the families do this activity ask them: *How are you letting each other know what you are going to do next? How are you working together to keep the sticks from falling? Who is taking the lead and can everyone be a leader?* etc. This activity should last about 12 minutes. Let the families know how good they are at communicating with each other and that communicating is an important skill for a family!

Note 1: Facilitators who are not talking should spread around the room, monitoring families' reactions and level of participation. A facilitator might stop at the table of a family and offer encouragement, praise, and suggestions for managing different situations (behavior management, cueing, discipline). Work with families on interactions/behaviors occurring "in the moment." Remember to be sensitive to and empowering of the parent(s).

Note 2: Families with babies can do this activity by placing the baby in the middle of circle created by the family. Toddlers can be part of this activity by holding the wood sticks in their fists.

NOTE

1. This activity was presented by the Cirque Du Monde in a workshop at the All Network Meeting of the National Child Traumatic Stress Network in March 2007 in Anaheim, CA.

Module III

ACTIVITY 3: UNDERSTANDING OUR REACTIONS

 25 MINUTES

 Goals

- To educate families about common reactions to trauma.

 Materials

- Paper
- Pens/markers

 Instructions

Facilitator: *It is now time to break into smaller groups. Remember, each facilitator will take a different group, only tonight each family is going to be a small group.*

Facilitators should join their assigned family at this time. Facilitators move one family at a time to their designated areas.

Family Facilitator: *First, let's spend some time talking about some common ways that people feel after bad things have happened.*

Talk about the word "trauma" and what it means. Use Van der Kolk's way of talking about it: An overwhelming, overstimulating, extremely painful and/or terrifying experience. During that experience, your usual ways of reacting while something bad is happening do not seem to work (coupled with an inability to employ the fight or flight response).

Explain to the family about anticipating that more bad things will happen, reminders of bad things that have happened and how people react to these reminders, re-experiencing what happened, avoidance, arousal/dysregulations, expectancies about self and the world, and problems with relationships/trust. Have family members talk about their own experiences with each of these reactions to make them real.

Talk about avoidance and how avoidance makes it hard to talk about what happened but is a common reaction. Anticipate their avoidance by letting the family know that they may not want to come back next week or for the two to three weeks that involve talking about what happened. Problem-solve by asking the family to come up with ways that they will work together to overcome their avoidance and come back each week.

Module III SESSION 10 *Telling About What Happened*

ACTIVITY 4: TELLING ABOUT BAD THINGS THAT HAVE HAPPENED

 40 MINUTES

 Goals

- To understand and plan the narrative process.
- To help the family construct a timeline that chronicles the traumas they have experienced.

 Materials

- Tape recorders and tapes (one for each family)
- Blank postcards (set of 10 for each family)
- Envelopes for postcards (one for each family)
- Paper
- Pens/markers

 Handouts

- Narrative Guide

 Instructions

Family Facilitator: *We have spent a lot of time over the past weeks getting ready for this activity. Talking together about the bad things that have happened to your family is an important and necessary step towards feeling better and coping. Now, you have a new set of skills for having this family conversation. Remember all of things that you have learned about talking together as a family, about sharing feelings, and about dealing with scared and anxious feelings. You are ready to do this.*

Before beginning this session, remind families about safety procedures that were discussed in the consent process and during earlier sessions including use of safety plans, confidentiality, and reporting responsibilities.

Provide information to the family about why telling their trauma story is important.

Talk about studies that have shown that talking or writing about what happened has been shown to help trauma survivors feel better and move on in a healthier manner.

Module III SESSION 10 *Telling About What Happened*

> *Note 1:* If the decision is made that the family is not ready to engage in a trauma narrative process, the facilitator and the family work to define a set of narrative skills that would help the family communicate effectively about difficult things that happen. Refer to Chapter 4 for additional instructions.

Use the Narrative Guide to help the family develop a plan regarding their narrative.

Talk to the family about their narrative style and about how families can talk to each other about difficult things that have happened. Work with the family to set some ground rules, such as who gets to talk, what the family is prepared to talk about, what the family is willing to talk about first, and whether the family wants to/needs to engage in a narrative process about communication or exposure.

Explain the process of developing the trauma story.

Family Facilitator: *First, you are going to make a list of all of the bad things that have happened. You can then use this list to talk about when things happened and which things were the least scary and which were the scariest. Second, as a family, you will tell your story about the bad thing(s) that happened. You will decide how you want to start your story, what bad things you want to talk about in what order, how much detail you want to include, how you want to record your story, and how you will know when to end your story. Remember that I am here to help you decide these things and make sure that you can tell your story in a way that everyone continues to feel safe. One thing to think about as you are telling your story is that everyone in your family has different experiences when bad things happen and every one of you may remember what happened differently. That's fine. It's just fine for each member of the family to have their own piece of the story.*

Each family constructs a family timeline about the different traumas that the family has experienced. First, each family writes on a blank postcard each traumatic event that has occurred. Families might want to order their list starting with mildly traumatic events and ending with the most traumatic events that have happened to them. The families should put the cards in chronological order after all the traumas are listed. Give the families about 20 minutes to complete their family trauma timelines. The families can store their trauma timeline in the envelope provided at the end of the session.

About 10 minutes before time to return to the group, the facilitator should assess where the family is in their trauma timeline. If the family is close to the end, the facilitator should do nothing. If the family is not near the end, the facilitator should help the family reach a stopping point and regain emotional balance before ending the session. It is important that the session ends with the family able to rejoin the group, continue to participate in the closing activities, and leave the group to go home in a healthy manner.

Module III　SESSION 10　Telling About What Happened

Facilitators should end by recapping the family's plan for telling their trauma story and remind the family that they have all of the skills necessary to do it.

Family Facilitator: *Talking about trauma is very difficult. Many times when families start to share about bad things that have happened, stress goes up. When stress levels go up, both children and adults can feel angry, irritable, sad, or can feel bad physically. We have worked a lot on things that you can do when this happens. Here is a sheet to help remind you of all the skills you have learned. You know that you can also always reach out to your therapist or one of group leaders if you are having trouble during the week. Because telling your trauma story is hard work, you may not want to come back every week. Remember that not wanting to talk about or think about what happened is a symptom of PTSD. But it is important that you do come back each week and that you work together as a family to make sure that happens.*

> *Note 2:* Facilitators should not become part of the family conversation but might want to gently encourage families to elaborate, to get everyone's point of view, to talk about how they felt at the time, etc.

ACTIVITY 5: CLOSING

 10 MINUTES

 Goals

- To increase sense of group cohesion.
- To practice planning and implementation of rituals and routine.
- To assure continuity from one session to the next.

 Materials

- Job charts and star stickers (one pack for each family).

Module III SESSION 10 *Telling About What Happened*

 Handouts

- Using Your Coping Resources
- Family Rating Form
- Participant Log
- Clinician Rating Form

 Instructions

Lead Facilitator: *We want to thank everyone for taking part in tonight's group. It is now time to finish this session and at the end of every group, we do a few things to end the group and to get ready for the next group.*

Co-Facilitator: *Is there anything that we still need to do to finish tonight's activities? I want to let each family know what a good job they did.*

Tell each family, or a family member, one thing that they did especially well.

Introduce and review the topic for next week.

Co-Facilitator: *Remember that this is hard work that you are doing. Use your coping skills during the week to take care of yourselves.*

Hand out "Using Your Coping Skills."

Co-Facilitator: *Reach out for support if it gets too hard.*

Lead Facilitator: *We want to make sure that we stay in touch during the week, so let's continue to try the Buddy System or Phone Tree. Now, let's end with our closing rituals.*

Families share closing rituals, if desired. Cue families to acknowledge the end of group to other family members as well.

Lead Facilitator: *Please complete your family rating form now and hand it in. Thanks.*

Facilitators complete participant log and clinician rating form.

 Homework to be Assigned

- Using Your Coping Resources

Module III — SESSION 11 — *When Bad Things Happen 1*

Objectives

- To increase the families' ability to share trauma stories or to talk about important family topics.
- To co-construct a shared trauma narrative.
- To express and share trauma pain.

Threads

- *Connectedness:* Overarching goal of this and the coming sessions is helping families with the process of talking about the trauma, as opposed to the goal of having a "finished" trauma narrative. This process can be a very slow one, and taking the time to comment on and discuss the family's process of talking about the trauma is at least as important as talking about the trauma itself. The activity reinforces the realization that everyone in the family is potentially impacted by trauma(s).
- *Co-Regulation:* The family shares difficult and potentially emotionally challenging interactions but works to do this while remaining within their comfort zone.
- *Positive Affect, Memories, and Meaning:* Module III is meant to use the skill sets that the family has learned and practiced to help them cope with and move beyond their trauma history.

Preparation

- Send out postcard to remind families of group.
- Prepare all materials.
- Food and facilities planning and preparation.
- Decide on facilitators' roles.
- Update on the status of each family in the group.
- Anticipate any problems that might arise during the session.

Homework Due

- Using Your Coping Resources.

Session Overview

Activity 1	Family Meal	30 Minutes
Activity 2	Gears	15 Minutes
Activity 3	Telling about the Trauma	65 Minutes
Activity 4	Closing	10 Minutes

Module III SESSION 11 *When Bad Things Happen 1*

Homework to be Assigned

- Using Your Coping Resources

Materials

- Tables (one for each family)
- Centerpieces
- Nameplates and session schedules (one for each family)
- Place settings/napkins
- Nutritious meal/drinks
- Gear sets (one for each family)
- Family trauma timelines (completed in Session 10)
- Tape recorders and tapes (one for each family)
- Paper
- Pens/markers/crayons
- Toys
- Job charts and packages of star stickers (one for each family)

Handouts

Conversation Prompts	M3.S11.Prompts
Using Your Coping Resources	M3.S11.Using.Coping.Resources
Phone Tree	M3.S11.Phone.Tree
Contact Sheets	M3.S11.Contact.Sheets
Family Rating Form	M3.S11.Feedback
Participant Log	M3.S11.Log
Clinician Rating Form	M3.S11.Clinic.Measures

Posters

Rules Poster	Group.Rules.Poster

Module III   SESSION 11   When Bad Things Happen 1

ACTIVITY 1: FAMILY MEAL

30 MINUTES

Goals

- To facilitate an intimate family interaction.
- To increase awareness of the importance of routine within each family.

Materials

- Tables (one for each family)
- Centerpieces
- Nameplates and session schedules (one for each family)
- Place settings/napkins
- Nutritious meal/drinks
- Video camera, remote microphones, and tapes (research groups only)

Handouts

- Conversation Prompts

Posters

- Rules Poster

Instructions

Facilitators prepare room by setting tables (one for each family). A simple centerpiece for each table is a nice touch. A nameplate and schedule for the session's activities are also placed on each table. Hang poster with group rules listed in a prominent place where all the families can see it.

Food should be pre-cooked and ready to serve. Food can be served buffet or family style.

Module III SESSION 11 *When Bad Things Happen 1*

Parent(s) gather their children around a table and share a meal together. Before serving the food:

Lead Facilitator: *We are so happy to have you back with us tonight. Let's begin. First, let's thank (name of cooks) for fixing this wonderful meal. Please help yourselves to some food. Parents, why don't you serve your children first and then make a plate for yourself. To help your family have a good time during dinner, you might want to ask each other these questions or talk about the ideas on these cards.*

Hand out conversation prompts.

After the families have eaten and cleaned up (20–25 minutes), proceed with the opening routine.

Co-Facilitator: *We hope you enjoyed your dinner. It is now time to begin our activities for tonight.*

Proceed with ritual planned by the group.

Refer to poster of rules and review.

Ask each family the following question: *So, is there anything going on right now that might get in the way of your family taking part in today's group?*

Co-Facilitator: *If you will look at that schedule now, I will tell you a little bit about tonight's group. This session focuses on helping each family explore ways to talk about bad things that have happened to them.*

Proceed with introducing each activity briefly.

Co-Facilitator: So, let's get started.

> *Note 1*: Facilitators who are not talking should spread around the room, monitoring families' reactions and level of participation. Facilitators encourage and model appropriate conversation, sharing, and supervision of children. A facilitator might stop at the table of a family and offer encouragement, praise, and suggestions for managing different situations (behavior management, cueing, discipline). Work with families on interactions/behaviors occurring "in the moment." Remember to be sensitive to and empowering of the parent(s).

> *Note 2*: One facilitator should take on the role of process monitor, making sure that the session runs smoothly and proceeds in a timely fashion. The process facilitator should encourage families to start finishing their dinner and cleaning up their tables after about 20 minutes to make sure that this activity is finished within 30 minutes and the group is ready to begin the next activity on time.

Module III SESSION 11 When Bad Things Happen 1

ACTIVITY 2: GEARS

 15 MINUTES

 Goals

- To illustrate family systems theory.
- To educate about trauma and its effects.

 Materials

- Gear sets (one for each family).

 Instructions

Lead Facilitator: *We hope you enjoyed your dinner. It is now time to begin our activities for tonight. If you will look at that schedule now, I will tell you a little bit about tonight's group.*

Proceed with introducing each activity briefly.

Hand out gear sets.

Co-Facilitator: *On your table is a game that involves gears. We want you to work together to build something with the gears. Build something so that when you turn the handle all of the gears work together.*

This activity should last about 10 minutes.

Co-Facilitator: *Now, I want you to take out one of the gears. Now turn the handle and see what happens. Do all the gears turn? Take out another gear. Do all the gears turn? Now put the gear back. Now add a gear some place and see what happens. Do all the gears turn? Your family works something like the gears. When something happens, no matter if it is something good or bad, it affects everyone. Something really bad, a trauma, could happen to any one member of the family sending ripples throughout the family. This is called indirect trauma when the trauma experienced by only one family member creates distress or a traumatic stress reaction in other family members. "Family trauma" also happens when trauma is experienced directly by the whole family. A traumatized family reacts as a unit even though not everyone in the family will have the same reaction.*

Also, reactions to bad things that happen change over time. The way you or your family responds right after the event or disclosure of the trauma may not be the same as the way you or your family responds after some

Module III SESSION 11 When Bad Things Happen 1

time has passed. Whole families can develop trauma-related symptoms and these symptoms can last for a year or longer. Even after that, trauma-related symptoms may re-occur or get worse when your family is under a lot of stress or when things in the family are changing. Families who are dealing with multiple events or always thinking that something bad might happen may have a hard time knowing what they are reacting to and have a harder time adjusting.

> *Note 1*: Facilitators who are not talking should spread around the room, monitoring families' reactions and level of participation. A facilitator might stop at the table of a family and offer encouragement, praise, and suggestions for managing different situations (behavior management, cueing, discipline). Work with families on interactions/behaviors occurring "in the moment." Remember to be sensitive to and empowering of the parent(s).

ACTIVITY 3: TELLING ABOUT THE TRAUMA

 65 MINUTES

 Goals

- To help families track non-normative events that have affected their family.
- To assist the family in the co-construction of their trauma story.
- To allow the family to share the pain of the trauma under safe conditions.

 Materials

- Family trauma timelines (completed in Session 10)
- Tape recorders and tapes (one for each family)
- Paper
- Pens/markers/crayons
- Toys

Module III   SESSION 11   *When Bad Things Happen 1*

 Instructions

Facilitator: *It is now time to break into smaller groups. Remember, each facilitator will take a different group, only tonight each family is going to be a small group.*

Facilitators should join their assigned family at this time. Facilitators move one family at a time to their designated areas.

Family Facilitator: Avoidance Check-in. Ask the family, "*Did you feel reluctant to come today like I talked about last week?*" Have them rate reluctance on a scale from 1 to 10. Ask them, "*Why did you feel reluctant?*" and "*What did you do to overcome it?*" Praise the family for their ability to overcome their reluctance. From PPT Scheeringa (2003).

Before beginning this session, remind families about safety procedures that were discussed in the consent process and during earlier sessions, including use of safety plans, confidentiality, and reporting responsibilities.

As a family, tell your story about the bad thing(s) that happened. The facilitator should name the trauma or traumas that the family is dealing with using the words that the family uses to talk about it. Remember to help the family choose a trauma to start talking about that they are prepared to discuss without getting overly distressed. *One thing to think about as you are telling your story is that everyone in your family has different experiences when bad things happen and every one of you may remember what happened differently. That's fine. It's just fine for each member of the family to have their own piece of the story.*

Ask if someone in the family would like to write down the story as it is being told.

Young children in the family may want to draw the story as it is being told. Having some toys available for them to play quietly is also helpful.

Facilitators should monitor the level of family members' stress and anxiety closely. Facilitators should cue family members to use SIT skills if needed during the narrative.

After about 40 minutes, the facilitator should assess where the family is in their conversation about the trauma(s). If the family is close to the end of the story, the facilitator should do nothing. If the family is nowhere near the end, the facilitator should help the family reach a stopping point and regain emotional balance before ending the session. Remember, it is not important that the family reach the end of the narrative or reach some form of coherence during this session. It is important that the session ends with the family able to rejoin the group, continue to participate in the closing activities, and leave the group to go home in a healthy manner.

Module III SESSION 11 *When Bad Things Happen 1*

Wow, what an incredible story you are sharing with each other. Even though it is sometimes hard to talk about bad things that happen, you did a great job. You listened, heard each other, and learned something important about how you as a family experience hard things that happen.

Facilitators should describe the family's process and reflect on what the family learned, not content but the process of telling the family story.

> *Note 1:* Facilitators should not become part of the family conversation, but might want to gently encourage families to elaborate, to get everyone's point of view, to talk about how they felt at the time, etc. Each family will process their narrative at different rates. Some families may need only three sessions while others may need more. Be sensitive to the pace of the family more so than the structure of the group.

ACTIVITY 4: CLOSING

 10 MINUTES

 Goals

- To increase sense of group cohesion.
- To practice planning and implementation of rituals and routine.
- To assure continuity from one session to the next.

 Materials

- Job charts and packages of star stickers (one for each family).

 Handouts

- Using Your Coping Resources
- Phone Tree
- Contact List

Module *III* SESSION 11 *When Bad Things Happen 1*

- Family Rating Form
- Participant Log
- Clinician Rating Form

 Instructions

Lead Facilitator: We want to thank everyone for taking part in tonight's group. It is now time to finish this session and at the end of every group, we do a few things to end the group and to get ready for the next group.

Co-Facilitator: *Is there anything that we still need to do to finish tonight's activities? Talking about trauma is very difficult. Many times when families start to share about bad things that have happened, stress goes up. When stress levels go up, both children and adults can feel angry, irritable, sad, or can feel bad physically. We have worked a lot on things that you can when this happens. Here is a sheet to help remind you of all the skills you have learned. You know that you can also always reach out to your therapist or one of the group leaders if you are having trouble during the week. I want to let each family know what a good job you did.*

Tell each family, or a family member, one thing that they did especially well.

Introduce and review the topic for next week.

Co-Facilitator: *Next week, we will continue to talk about the bad things that your family has experienced.*

Lead Facilitator: *Make sure to continue to contact each other during the week. Now, let's end by (closing rituals).*

Families share closing rituals, if desired. Cue families to acknowledge the end of group to other family members as well.

Lead Facilitator: *Please complete your family rating form now and hand it in. Thanks.*

Facilitators complete participant log and clinician rating form.

 Homework to be Assigned

- Using Your Coping Resources

Module III SESSION 12 When Bad Things Happen II

 Objectives

- To increase the families' ability to share trauma stories or to talk about important family topics.
- To co-construct a shared trauma narrative.
- To express and share trauma pain.
- To help families understand the cumulative impact of multiple traumas on the family.

 Threads

- *Connectedness*: Overarching goal of this and the coming sessions is helping families with the process of talking about the trauma, as opposed to the goal of having a "finished" trauma narrative. This process can be a very slow one, and taking the time to comment on and discuss the family's process of talking about the trauma is at least as important as talking about the trauma itself.
- *Co-Regulation*: The family shares difficult and potentially emotionally challenging interactions but works to do this while remaining within their comfort zone.
- *Positive Affect, Memories, and Meaning*: Module III is meant to use the skill sets that the family has learned and practiced to help them cope with and move beyond their trauma history.

 Preparation

- Send out postcard to remind families of group.
- Prepare all materials.
- Food and facilities planning and preparation.
- Decide on facilitators' roles.
- Update on the status of each family in the group.
- Anticipate any problems that might arise during the session.

 Homework Due

- Using Your Coping Resources.

 Session Overview

Activity 1	Family Meal	30 Minutes
Activity 2	Jenga	15 Minutes
Activity 3	SIT Reinforcement	10 Minutes
Activity 4	Telling the Family Trauma Story	55 Minutes
Activity 5	Closing	10 Minutes

Module III   SESSION 12   When Bad Things Happen II

 Homework to be Assigned

- Using Your Coping Resources

 Materials

- Tables (one for each family)
- Centerpieces
- Nameplates and session schedules (one for each family)
- Place settings/napkins
- Nutritious meal/drinks
- Jenga (one for each family)
- Family trauma timelines (completed in Session 10)
- Tape recorders and tapes (one for each family)
- Paper
- Pens/markers/crayons
- Toys
- Job charts and star stickers (one pack for each family)

 Handouts

Conversation Prompts	M3.S12.Prompts
Using Your Coping Resources	M3.S12.Using.Coping.Resources
Phone Tree	M3.S12.Phone.Tree
Contact Sheets	M3.S12.Contact.Sheets
Family Rating Form	M3.S12.Feedback
Participant Log	M3.S12.Log
Clinician Rating Form	M3.S12.Clinic.Measures

 Posters

- Rules Poster   Group.Rules.Poster

 Books

- *Cool Cats, Calm Kids*

Module III SESSION 12 *When Bad Things Happen II*

ACTIVITY 1: FAMILY MEAL

 30 MINUTES

 Goals

- To facilitate an intimate family interaction.
- To increase awareness of the importance of routine within each family.

 Materials

- Tables (one for each family)
- Centerpieces
- Nameplates and session schedules (one for each family)
- Place settings/napkins
- Nutritious meal/drinks
- Video camera, remote microphones, and tapes (research groups only)

 Handouts

- Conversation Prompts

 Posters

- Rules Poster

 Instructions

Facilitators prepare room by setting tables (one for each family). A simple centerpiece for each table is a nice touch. A nameplate and schedule for the session's activities are also placed on each table. Hang poster with group rules listed in a prominent place where all the families can see it.

Food should be pre-cooked and ready to serve. Food can be served buffet or family style.

Parent(s) gather their children around a table and share a meal together. Before serving the food:

Lead Facilitator: *We are so happy to have you back with us tonight. Let's begin. First, let's thank (name of cooks) for fixing this wonderful meal. Please help yourselves to some food. Parents, why don't you serve your*

Module III   SESSION 12   *When Bad Things Happen* II

children first and then make a plate for yourself. To help your family have a good time during dinner, you might want to ask each other these questions or talk about the ideas on these cards.

Hand out conversation prompts.

After the families have eaten and cleaned up (20–25 minutes), proceed with the opening routine.

Co-Facilitator: *We hope you enjoyed your dinner. It is now time to begin our activities for tonight.*

Proceed with ritual planned by the group.

Refer to poster of rules and review.

Ask each family the following question: *So, is there anything going on right now that might get in the way of your family taking part in today's group?*

Co-Facilitator: *If you will look at that schedule now, I will tell you a little bit about tonight's group. This session continues to focus on helping each family explore ways to talk about bad things that have happened to them.*

Proceed with introducing each activity briefly.

Co-Facilitator: *So, let's get started.*

Note 1: Facilitators encourage and model appropriate conversation, sharing, and supervision of children. Facilitators try several methods to stimulate conversation, including joining the family and modeling or use of conversation prompts. A facilitator might stop at the table of a family and offer encouragement, praise, and suggestions for managing different situations (behavior management, cueing, discipline). Work with families on interactions/behaviors occurring "in the moment." Remember to be sensitive to and empowering of the parent(s).

Note 2: One facilitator should take on the role of process monitor making sure that the session runs smoothly and proceeds in a timely fashion. The process facilitator should encourage families to start finishing their dinner and cleaning up their tables after about 20 minutes to make sure that this activity is finished within 30 minutes and the group is ready to begin the next activity on time.

Module III SESSION 12 When Bad Things Happen II

ACTIVITY 2: JENGA

 15 MINUTES

 Goals

- To illustrate family systems theory.
- To educate about trauma and its effects.

 Materials

- Jenga (one for each family)

 Instructions

Lead Facilitator: *It is now time to begin our activities for tonight. If you will look at that schedule now, I will tell you a little bit about tonight's group.*

Proceed with introducing each activity briefly.

Hand out Jenga.

Co-Facilitator: *Tonight we are going to talk more about trauma and how it affects you and your family. On your table is a game called Jenga. This is a game where you take turns removing pieces of wood from the puzzle. Go ahead and start. Just go around your family and give everyone a turn at taking out a piece.*

After a few turns, stop the families and have them look at their Jenga structures.

Co-Facilitator: *What will happen if you keep taking pieces away? The whole thing will collapse.*

Make a connection between Jenga and the effects of chronic trauma and what families need to keep from collapsing.

> *Note 1*: Facilitators who are not talking should spread around the room, monitoring families' reactions and level of participation. A facilitator might stop at the table of a family and offer encouragement, praise, and suggestions for managing different situations (behavior management, cueing, discipline). Work with families on interactions/behaviors occurring "in the moment." Remember to be sensitive to and empowering of the parent(s).

Module **III**   SESSION 12   *When Bad Things Happen* 11

ACTIVITY 3: SIT REINFORCEMENT

 10 MINUTES

 Goals

- To practice relaxation skills.
- To prepare family members for co-constructing trauma narrative.

 Books

- *Cool Cats, Calm Kids*

 Instructions

Lead Facilitator: *We know you have been practicing your relaxation routines. We would like to give you another idea about a way to relax.*

Introduce *Cool Cats, Calm Kids* relaxation activity. Have participants either sit or stand and stretch like a cat. Remind participants of the benefits of relaxation.

ACTIVITY 4: TELLING THE FAMILY TRAUMA STORY

 55 MINUTES

 Goals

- To assist the family in the co-construction of their trauma story.
- To allow the family to share the pain of the trauma under safe conditions.

Materials

- Family trauma timelines (completed in Session 10)
- Tape recorders and tapes (one for each family)

Module III   SESSION 12   When Bad Things Happen II

- Paper
- Pens/markers/crayons
- Toys

 Instructions

Facilitator: *It is now time to break into smaller groups. Remember, each facilitator will take a different group, only tonight each family is going to be a small group.*

Facilitators should join their assigned family at this time. Facilitators move one family at a time to their designated areas.

Family Facilitator: Avoidance Check-in. Ask the family: *"Did you feel reluctant to come today like I talked about last week?"* Have them rate reluctance on a scale from 1 to 10. Ask them, *"Why did you feel reluctant?"* and *"What did you do to overcome it?"* Praise the family for their ability to overcome their reluctance. From PPT Scheeringa (2003).

Remember, talking together about the bad things that have happened to your family is an important and necessary step towards feeling better and coping. Remember all of the things that you have learned about talking together as a family, about sharing feelings, and about dealing with scared and anxious feelings. You can use all of these skills as you continue to tell your trauma story today.

As a family, tell your story again about the bad thing(s) that happened.

The facilitator should name the trauma or traumas that the family is dealing with using the words that the family uses to talk about it.

Facilitators should monitor the level of family members' stress and anxiety closely. Facilitators should cue family members to use SIT skills if needed during the narrative.

If it was decided that the narrative was to be used as an exposure technique, at some point in the telling of the trauma story, facilitators ask the family to talk together about the worst moment/memory/part of the traumatic event. Encourage the family to tell about this including as much detail as possible. Each family member will probably have a different worst moment and this is fine. Encourage the family to hear each person's recollections.

Young children in the family may want to draw the story as it is being told. Having some toys available for them to play quietly is also helpful.

After about 40 minutes, the facilitator should assess where the family is in their conversation about the trauma(s). If the family is close to the end of the story, the facilitator should do nothing. If the family is nowhere near the end, the facilitator should help the family reach a stopping point and regain emotional

Module III SESSION 12 When Bad Things Happen II

balance before ending the session. Remember, it is not important that the family reach the end of the narrative or reach some form of coherence during this session. It is important that the session ends with the family able to rejoin the group, continue to participate in the closing activities, and leave the group to go home in a healthy manner.

If the family is not close to finishing the narrative, a separate family session should be scheduled with the family prior to the next group.

> *Note 1*: Facilitators should not become part of the family conversation but might want to gently encourage families to elaborate, to get everyone's point of view, to talk about how they felt at the time, etc. Each family will process their narrative at different rates. Some families may need only three sessions while others may need more. Be sensitive to the pace of the family more so than the structure of the group.

ACTIVITY 5: CLOSING

 10 MINUTES

 Goals

- To increase sense of group cohesion.
- To practice planning and implementation of rituals and routine.
- To assure continuity from one session to the next.

 Materials

- Job charts and packages of star stickers (one for each family)

 Handouts

- Using Your Coping Resources
- Phone Tree

Module III

SESSION 12 — *When Bad Things Happen II*

- Contact List
- Family Rating Form
- Participant Log
- Clinician Rating Form

 Instructions

Lead Facilitator: *We want to thank everyone for taking part in tonight's group. It is now time to finish this session and at the end of every group, we do a few things to end the group and to get ready for the next group.*

Co-Facilitator: *Is there anything that we still need to do to finish tonight's activities?*

Talking about trauma is very difficult. Many times when families start to share about bad things that have happened, stress goes up. When stress levels go up, both children and adults can feel angry, irritable, sad, or can feel bad physically. We have worked a lot on things that you can do when this happens. Here is a sheet to help remind you of all the skills you have learned. You know that you can also always reach out to your therapist or one of the group leaders if you are having trouble during the week.

I want to let each family know what a good job you did.

Tell each family, or a family member, one thing that they did especially well.

Lead Facilitator: *We want to make sure that we stay in touch during the week, so continue with the Buddy System or Phone Tree. Now, let's end by closing rituals.*

Families share closing rituals, if desired. Cue families to acknowledge the end of group to other family members as well.

Please complete your family rating form now and hand it in. Thanks.

Facilitators complete participant log and clinician rating form.

 Homework to be Assigned

- Using Your Coping Resources

Module III

SESSION 13 *Marking the Trauma*

Objectives

- To complete a shared, coherent co-constructed family trauma narrative or to finish with narrative skill development to allow the family to discuss difficult issues more successfully.
- To increase the family's ability to attach some positive meaning to their experience.

Threads

- *Connectedness:* Overarching goal of this and the coming sessions is helping families with the process of talking about the trauma, as opposed to the goal of having a "finished" trauma narrative. This process can be a very slow one, and taking the time to comment on and discuss the family's process of talking about the trauma is at least as important as talking about the trauma itself. The activity reinforces the realization that everyone in the family is potentially impacted by trauma(s).
- *Co-Regulation:* The family shares difficult and potentially emotionally challenging interactions but works to do this while remaining within their comfort zone.
- *Positive Affect, Memories, and Meaning:* Module III is meant to use the skill sets that the family has learned and practiced to help them cope with and move beyond their trauma history.

Preparation

- Send out postcard to remind families of group.
- Prepare all materials.
- Food and facilities planning and preparation.
- Decide on facilitators' roles.
- Update on the status of each family in the group.
- Anticipate any problems that might arise during the session.

Homework Due

- Using Your Coping Resources

Session Overview

Activity 1	Family Meal	30 Minutes
Activity 2	Processing the Trauma	50 Minutes

Module III

SESSION 13 *Marking the Trauma*

| Activity 3 | Enduring Traditions | 30 Minutes |
| Activity 4 | Closing | 10 Minutes |

Homework to be Assigned

- Things to Celebrate!

Materials

- Tables (one for each family)
- Centerpieces
- Nameplates and session schedules (one for each family)
- Place settings/napkins
- Nutritious meal/drinks
- Tape recorders and tapes (one for each family)
- Paper
- Pen/markers/crayons
- Toys
- Safety maps (created by families in Session 5)
- Job charts and star stickers (one pack for each family)

Handouts

Conversation Prompts	M3.S13.Prompts
Things to Celebrate!	M3.S13.Things.Celebrate
Safety Mapping Labels	M3.S13.Safety.Map.Labels (print on Avery #5163)
Enduring Traditions	M3.S13.Enduring.Traditions
Phone Tree	M3.S13.Phone.Tree
Contact Sheets	M3.S13.Contact.Sheets
Family Rating Form	M3.S13.Feedback
Participant Log	M3.S13.Log
Clinician Rating Form	M3.S13.Clinic.Measures

Posters

Rules Poster	Group.Rules.Poster

Module III   SESSION 13   *Marking the Trauma*

ACTIVITY 1: FAMILY MEAL

 30 MINUTES

 Goals

- To facilitate an intimate family interaction.
- To increase awareness of the importance of routine within each family.

 Materials

- Tables (one for each family)
- Centerpieces
- Nameplates and session schedules (one for each family)
- Place settings/napkins
- Nutritious meal/drinks
- Video camera, remote microphones, and tapes (research groups only)

 Handouts

- Conversation Prompts

 Posters

- Rules Poster

 Instructions

Facilitators prepare room by setting tables (one for each family). A simple centerpiece for each table is a nice touch. A nameplate and schedule for the session's activities are also placed on each table. Hang poster with group rules listed in a prominent place where all the families can see it.

Food should be pre-cooked and ready to serve. Food can be served buffet or family style.

Parent(s) gather their children around a table and share a meal together. Before serving the food:

Module III

SESSION 13 *Marking the Trauma*

Lead Facilitator: *We are so happy to have you back with us tonight. Let's begin. First, let's thank (name of cooks) for fixing this wonderful meal. Please help yourselves to some food. Parents, why don't you serve your children first and then make a plate for yourself. To help your family have a good time during dinner, you might want to ask each other these questions or talk about the ideas on these cards.*

Hand out conversation prompts.

After the families have eaten and cleaned up (20–25 minutes), proceed with the opening routine.

Co-Facilitator: *We hope you enjoyed your dinner. It is now time to begin our activities for tonight.*

Proceed with ritual planned by the group.

Refer to poster of rules and review.

Ask each family the following question: *So, is there anything going on right now that might get in the way of your family taking part in today's group?*

Co-Facilitator: *If you will look at that schedule now, I will tell you a little bit about tonight's group. This session focuses on finding ways to move beyond the bad things that have happened to your family.*

Proceed with introducing each activity briefly.

Co-Facilitator: *So, let's get started.*

> *Note 1*: Facilitators encourage and model appropriate conversation, sharing, and supervision of children. Facilitators try several methods to stimulate conversation, including joining the family and modeling or use of conversation prompts. A facilitator might stop at the table of a family and offer encouragement, praise, and suggestions for managing different situations (behavior management, cueing, discipline). Work with families on interactions/behaviors occurring "in the moment." Remember to be sensitive to and empowering of the parent(s).

> *Note 2*: One facilitator should take on the role of process monitor making sure that the session runs smoothly and proceeds in a timely fashion. The process facilitator should encourage families to start finishing their dinner and cleaning up their tables after about 20 minutes to make sure that this activity is finished within 30 minutes and the group is ready to begin the next activity on time.

Module III

Marking the Trauma

ACTIVITY 2: PROCESSING THE TRAUMA

50 MINUTES

Goals

- To improve planning for and coping with non-normative family changes.
- To reinforce the role of ritual in creating stability for family members during times of trauma.

Materials

- Tape recorders and tapes (one for each family)
- Paper
- Pen/markers/crayons
- Toys
- Safety maps

Handouts

- Safety Mapping Labels

Instructions

Lead Facilitator: *It is now time to break into smaller groups. Remember, each facilitator will take a different group, only tonight each family is going to be a small group.*

Facilitators should join their assigned family at this time. Facilitators move one family at a time to their designated areas.

Family Facilitator: Avoidance Check-in.

Today we will finish telling your family's trauma story. Remember all of the things that you have learned about talking together as a family, about sharing feelings, and about dealing with scared and anxious feelings. You can use all of these skills as you continue to tell your trauma story today.

As a family, tell your story again about the bad thing(s) that happened.

Module III

SESSION 13 *Marking the Trauma*

The facilitator should name the trauma or traumas that the family is dealing with using the words that the family uses to talk about it.

Facilitators should monitor the level of family members' stress and anxiety closely. Facilitators should cue family members to use SIT skills if needed during the narrative.

Young children in the family may want to draw the story as it is being told. Having some toys available for them to play quietly is also helpful.

Facilitators should help the family identify any false or unhelpful beliefs that have arisen due to the trauma(s). These may include thoughts of guilt, responsibility, blame, retribution, or thoughts about their family and the world. Using cognitive processing techniques, help the family identify these thoughts and understand the impact of these thoughts on their family. Help them work through these thoughts to replace them with more helpful ones.

After the family finishes their trauma story, facilitators ask the family to think about ways in which the trauma(s) has changed their family; how their family is different now from when the traumatic events started. Ask the family about what they have learned about themselves individually and as a family. Perhaps they have learned things that they think would be helpful for other families who experience trauma.

Ask the family if they want to make any changes to their narrative as a result of their processing it.

After about 40 minutes, the facilitator should assess where the family is in their processing of the trauma(s). If the family is close to the end of the story, the facilitator should do nothing. If the family is nowhere near the end, the facilitator should help the family reach a stopping point and regain emotional balance before ending the session. Remember, it is not important that the family finish processing the narrative during this session. It is important that the session ends with the family able to rejoin the group, continue to participate in the closing activities, and to leave the group to go home in a healthy manner.

If the family is not finished processing the narrative, a separate family session should be scheduled with the family prior to the next group.

If appropriate to wind up the processing of the trauma, have each family update their safety map.

Since you drew this map, your family has spent a lot of time practicing safety routines, learning relaxation skills, and talking about the bad things that have happened. Let's see whether you feel any differently about the places you go during your week?

> Note 1: Facilitators should not become part of the family conversation but might want to gently encourage families to elaborate, to get everyone's point of view, to talk about how they felt at the time, etc.

Module III SESSION 13 Marking the Trauma

ACTIVITY 3: ENDURING TRADITIONS

 30 MINUTES

 Goals

- To improve planning for and coping with non-normative family changes.
- To reinforce the role of ritual in creating stability for family members during trauma.

 Materials

- Pens

 Handouts

- Enduring Traditions

 Instructions

Lead Facilitator: *We have spent lots of time talking about how families deal with bad things, and how these bad things changed your family. We have also talked about how traditions connect families to the past no matter how many changes have occurred.*

Hand out "Enduring Traditions."

Talk about how you are the same and make a list of the rituals or routines that you still do regardless of the changes. Is there a tradition that you would like to start to help you get through or mark these changes and still feel connected to your past?

Module III

SESSION 13 *Marking the Trauma*

ACTIVITY 4: CLOSING

 10 MINUTES

 Goals

- To increase sense of group cohesion.
- To practice planning and implementation of rituals and routine.
- To assure continuity from one session to the next.

 Handouts

- Things to Celebrate!
- Phone Tree
- Contact Sheets
- Family Rating Form
- Participant Log
- Clinician Rating Form

 Instructions

Lead Facilitator: *We want to thank everyone for taking part in tonight's group. It is now time to finish this session and at the end of every group, we do a few things to end the group and to get ready for the next group.*

Co-Facilitator: *Is there anything that we still need to do to finish tonight's activities? I want to let each family know what a good job they did.*

Tell each family, or a family member, one thing that they did especially well.

Introduce and review the topic for next week.

Co-Facilitator: *Next week, we will talk about planning celebrations. To get ready for this session, we would like your family to have a meeting during the week. At this meeting, talk about things that your family has to feel good about and to celebrate. Think about special times that are coming up. Think about things you have done either as a family or individually. Think about any big changes that might be happening in your family that you would like to mark. It doesn't have to be anything big; many small things are worth celebrating. While you are talking, fill out this handout listing all of the things, both big and small, that you can come up with.*

Module III

SESSION 13 *Marking the Trauma*

Lead Facilitator: *We want to make sure that we stay in touch during the week, so let's continue to try the Buddy System or Phone Tree. Now, let's end by (closing rituals).*

Cue families to acknowledge the end of group to other family members as well.

Please complete your family rating form now and hand it in. Thanks.

Facilitators complete participant log and clinician rating form.

 Homework to be Assigned

- Things to Celebrate!

Module III — SESSION 14 — Good Things Happen Too!

Objectives

- To encourage deliberate planning of fun family activities and celebrations.
- To teach the skills involved in planning and carrying out a successful family celebration.
- To reinforce the skills and lessons taught in the early sessions, such as setting expectations, planning, making special meaning of events, etc.
- To highlight the role of positive affect (humor, laughter) in family interaction and in stress reduction.

Threads

- *Connectedness*: The role of positivity is highlighted as families make memories of good time shared together. Playing together brings the family closer and strengthens their sense of belonging.
- *Co-Regulation*: Families are encouraged to explore their comfort zone related to expressing positive affect and laughter.
- *Positive Affect, Memories, and Meaning*: This session helps the family frame their trauma history as something in the past and focus on making and celebrating positive choices and making positive memories.

Preparation

- Send out postcard to remind families of group.
- Prepare all materials.
- Food and facilities planning and preparation.
- Decide on facilitators' roles.
- Update on the status of each family in the group.
- Anticipate any problems that might arise during the session.

Homework Due

- Things to Celebrate!

Session Overview

Activity 1	Family Meal	30 Minutes
Activity 2	Our Own Feel Good Book	30 Minutes
Activity 3	Making Us Laugh	30 Minutes
Activity 4	What to Celebrate? And How?	20 Minutes
Activity 5	Closing	10 Minutes

Module III SESSION 14 Good Things Happen Too!

Homework to be Assigned

- None

Materials

- Tables (one for each family)
- Centerpieces
- Nameplates and session schedules (one for each family)
- Place settings/napkins
- Nutritious meal/drinks
- Materials for family scrapbook pages (paper, hole punch, decorating materials, glue)
- Apples to Apples or Don't Make Me Laugh, senior version, or Zobmondo: Questions
- Paper
- Pens/crayons/markers
- Cards/postcards (blank)
- Video camera, remote microphones, and tapes (research groups only)
- Job charts and star stickers (one pack for each family)

Handouts

- Conversation Prompts M3.S14.Prompts
- Laughing is Important M3.S14.Laugh.Important
- Laughing Through Life M3.S14.Laughing.Life
- Things to Celebrate! M3.S14.Things.Celebrate
- Planning to Celebrate M3.S14.Planning.Celebrate
- Making It Special M3.S14.Making.Special
- Phone Tree M3.S14.Phone.Tree
- Contact Sheets M3.S14.Contact.Sheets
- Family Rating Form M3.S14.Feedback
- Participant Log M3.S14.Log
- Clinician Rating Form M3.S14.Clinic.Measures

Posters

- Rules Poster Group.Rules.Poster

Books

- *The FEEL GOOD Book*
- *I Love to Laugh! A Book of Fun and Giggles*

Module III SESSION 14 Good Things Happen Too!

ACTIVITY 1: FAMILY MEAL

 30 MINUTES

 Goals

- To facilitate an intimate family interaction.
- To increase awareness of the importance of routine within each family.

 Materials

- Tables (one for each family)
- Centerpieces
- Nameplates and session schedules (one for each family)
- Place settings/napkins
- Nutritious meal/drinks
- Video camera, remote microphones, and tapes (research groups only)

 Handouts

- Conversation Prompts

 Posters

- Rules Poster

 Instructions

Facilitators prepare room by setting tables (one for each family). A simple centerpiece for each table is a nice touch. A nameplate and schedule for the session's activities are also placed on each table. Hang poster with group rules listed in a prominent place where all the families can see it.

Food should be pre-cooked and ready to serve. Food can be served buffet or family style.

Parent(s) gather their children around a table and share a meal together. Before serving the food:

Module III   SESSION 14   *Good Things Happen Too!*

Lead Facilitator: *We are so happy to have you back with us tonight. First, let's thank (name of cooks) for fixing this wonderful meal. Please help yourselves to some food. Parents, why don't you serve your children first and then make a plate for yourself. To help your family have a good time during dinner, you might want to ask each other these questions or talk about the ideas on these cards.*

Hand out conversation prompts.

After the families have eaten and cleaned up (20–25 minutes), proceed with the opening routine.

Co-Facilitator: *We hope you enjoyed your dinner. It is now time to begin our activities for tonight.*

Proceed with ritual planned by the group.

Refer to poster of rules and review.

Ask each family the following question: *So, is there anything going on right now that might get in the way of your family taking part in today's group?*

Co-Facilitator: *It is now time to begin our activities for tonight. This session focuses on making time to celebrate special events and family accomplishments. If you will look at that schedule now, I will tell you a little bit about tonight's group.*

Proceed with introducing each activity briefly.

Co-Facilitator: *So, let's get started.*

Note 1: Facilitators encourage and model appropriate conversation, sharing, and supervision of children. Facilitators try several methods to stimulate conversation, including joining the family and modeling or use of conversation prompts. A facilitator might stop at the table of a family and offer encouragement, praise, and suggestions for managing different situations (behavior management, cueing, discipline). Work with families on interactions/behaviors occurring "in the moment." Remember to be sensitive to and empowering of the parent(s).

Note 2: One facilitator should take on the role of process monitor, making sure that the session runs smoothly and proceeds in a timely fashion. The process facilitator should encourage families to start finishing their dinner and cleaning up their tables after about 20 minutes to make sure that this activity is finished within 30 minutes and the group is ready to begin the next activity on time.

Module III   SESSION 14   Good Things Happen Too!

ACTIVITY 2: OUR OWN FEEL GOOD BOOK

 30 MINUTES

 Goals

- To help families explore ways they can have fun together as a family.
- To encourage deliberate planning of fun.
- To encourage a positive focus and valuing of family accomplishments.

 Materials

- Paper
- Pens
- Materials for scrapbook pages (paper, hole punch, glue)
- Decorating materials

 Books

- *The FEEL GOOD Book*

 Instructions

Co-Facilitator: *As we get started on our first activity tonight, I have a book to share with you.*

Read *The FEEL GOOD Book*. Encourage the families to share experiences that make them feel good. They can discuss experiences included in the book and add additional experiences as well. Encourage them to brainstorm, as a family, activities or experiences that make them all feel good.

After families have had a chance to brainstorm, hand out scrapbook pages and materials. Ask families to create their own "Feel Good Book" scrapbook pages, including activities and experiences that make each family member and the entire family feel good. Families should also be encouraged to include activities that could make them feel good in the future. Give families about 20 minutes to complete this. Once finished, facilitators can encourage families to share their Feel Good scrapbook pages. Encourage the family to add these pages to their scrapbook.

Module III *Good Things Happen Too!*

ACTIVITY 3: MAKING US LAUGH

 30 MINUTES

 Goals

- To help family members understand why laughter is important and identify what makes them laugh.
- To encourage positive and fun interactions.

 Materials

- Paper
- Pens
- Teen Game: Apples to Apples or Don't Make Me Laugh, senior version, or Zobmondo: Questions

 Handouts

- Laughter is Important!
- Laughing Through Life

 Books

- *I Love to Laugh! A Book of Fun and Giggles*

 Instructions

Lead Facilitator: *It's time to break into smaller groups. Remember, each facilitator will take a different group, one for the adults, one for teens, one for the older children, one for the younger children, and one for the babies. Let's begin by forming those groups.*

Facilitators gather their groups together. When the groups are formed and quiet, facilitators move one group at a time to their designated areas.

Lead Facilitator (Adult Group): Hand out "Laughter is Important!" and "Laughing Through Life," which outline the importance of laughter and developmental differences in humor. Discuss with parents why they think laughter is important. Discuss the importance of balancing positive experiences for families who have

Module III

Good Things Happen Too!

experienced trauma. Encourage parents to share examples of funny things their children have done or said. Ask parents what types of fun, laughter-promoting activities they do with their children now. What types of activities would they like to do more of? If needed, a few minutes can be taken at the end of the breakout group to discuss treatment planning for each family as the group draws to a close.

Co-Facilitator (Teen Group): Facilitate discussion with teens about why they think laughter is important. Discuss what makes them laugh. What activities do they enjoy to do with their peers? Lead teens in a game to promote fun and laughter. Facilitators can choose between Apples to Apples, Don't Make Me Laugh, senior version, or Zobmondo: Questions.

Co-Facilitator (Older Child Group): Ask the children what fun things they like to do and what makes them laugh. After the discussion, encourage fun in the group by either singing silly songs together or playing "Sound and the Fury" game. Suggestions for songs are listed in the handout "Fun and Silly Songs." To play "Sound and the Fury," the facilitator and the children all stand in a circle. The facilitator starts by modeling a funny gesture with their whole body paired with a silly sound. Everyone else in the group has to imitate the movement and sound. The child standing to the right of the facilitator then models their own gesture paired with a silly sound. The group then imitates the first gesture and sound, followed by the new gesture and sound. Circle continues clockwise until all children have had a turn. Each round, the group will imitate all of the previous gestures and add the newly exhibited gesture and sound at the end.

Co-Facilitator (Young Child Group): Ask the children what fun things they like to do and what makes them laugh. After the discussion, encourage fun in the group by singing fun and silly songs with the children. Suggestions for silly songs are listed in the handout "Fun and Silly Songs." The children can also initiate singing their favorite silly songs.

Co-Facilitator (Baby Group): Read babies *I Love to Laugh! A Book of Fun and Giggles.* Play the included games and activities with the babies as you read the book, including Peek-A-Boo, Itsy Bitsy Spider, and Ring Around the Rosie.

Note 1: Facilitators for each group should start wrapping up the discussions or games after 25 minutes to allow three to four minutes to transition back to the family meeting room.

Module III SESSION 14 Good Things Happen Too!

ACTIVITY 4: WHAT TO CELEBRATE? AND HOW?

 20 MINUTES

 Goals

- To encourage a positive focus and valuing of family accomplishments.
- To encourage deliberate planning.
- To help families explore ways that they can make family events memorable.

 Materials

- Paper
- Pens
- Crayons/markers
- Cards/postcards (blank)

 Handouts

- Things to Celebrate
- Planning to Celebrate
- Making it Special

 Instructions

Co-Facilitator: *We asked you to complete a page during the week listing some things that your family has to celebrate.*

Hand out additional copies of "Things to Celebrate!" to those families who did not bring one back. Hand out copies of "Planning to Celebrate."

Co-Facilitator: *If you have not already done so, please talk with your family now and list some of the things that your family has to celebrate. If you have already listed all the things that your family has to celebrate, review that list and pick one thing on the list that you want to plan and carry out an actual celebration for. Make some plans for celebrating. Decide when you will have this celebration, who will take part, etc. You can write down your plans on "Planning to Celebrate." On the back page, you can talk about how you will share the jobs for getting ready for your celebration.*

Module III SESSION 14 *Good Things Happen Too!*

Give families about 10 minutes to complete this.

Co-Facilitator: *Part of any celebration is making it special. There are lots of ways to make any event special.*

Hand out "Making it Special."

Co-Facilitator: *Think about what you are going to celebrate and look over the list of ways to make it special. Pick some ways that you would like to use. You don't have to pick any of the ones that are on the list; you can use your own ideas too.*

Give families about five minutes to complete this.

Co-Facilitator: *Even when something is well planned, things can still go wrong. For the last part of our activity tonight we will spend a few minutes problem solving so that you can think about what might go wrong and how you would fix it.*

Refer families back to "Planning to Celebrate" worksheet. Have each family list all of the things that they can think of that might go wrong. Then have each family come up with solutions.

If time allows, encourage families to share their celebration choices with the group.

Co-Facilitator: *Please, tell us some of the things on your list to celebrate and the one that you decided on. Also, please tell us some of the things you plan to do to make your family celebration special.*

Encourage each family to take a turn. Give lots of praise to each family as they share.

Younger children can be kept occupied with making invitations to the celebration for each family member.

ACTIVITY 5: CLOSING

 10 MINUTES

 Goals

- To increase sense of group cohesion.
- To practice planning and implementation of rituals and routine.
- To assure continuity from one session to the next.

Module III   SESSION 14   *Good Things Happen Too!*

 ## Handouts

- Phone Tree
- Contact Sheets
- Family Rating Form
- Participant Log
- Clinician Rating Form

 ## Instructions

Lead Facilitator: *We want to thank everyone for taking part in tonight's group. It is now time to finish this session and at the end of every group, we do a few things to end the group and to get ready for the next group.*

Co-Facilitator: *Is there anything that we still need to do to finish tonight's activities? I want to let each family know what a good job they did.*

Tell each family, or a family member, one thing that they did especially well.

Introduce and review the topic for next week.

Co-Facilitator: *Next week, we will finish this program on family traditions and say "goodbye." Is there any special activity you would like to add to the final session (i.e., potluck dinner)?*

Lead Facilitator: *We want to make sure that we stay in touch during the week, so let's continue to try the Buddy System or Phone Tree. Now, let's end by (closing rituals).*

Families share closing rituals, if desired. Cue families to acknowledge the end of group to other family members as well.

Lead Facilitator: *Please complete your family rating form now and hand it in. Thanks.*

Facilitators complete participant log and clinician rating form.

 ## Homework to be Assigned

- Celebrating (if the family's celebration is planned for this week)

Module III

Celebration!

 ## Objectives

- To carry out a planned celebration practicing the skills and concepts discussed in earlier sessions.
- To reinforce the notion of richness in family gatherings and celebrations.
- To review group concepts, activities, skills, and ideas, making explicit links to family life and experience.
- To review each family's goals and evaluate the group with respect to meeting those goals.
- To encourage deliberate planning of the family's traditions and routines and endings (goodbyes).
- To encourage families to think about the ways memories are stored and retrieved.

 ## Threads

- *Deliberateness*: Families leave group feeling like they have accomplished something by coming every week, planning and carrying out homework and family events, and learning valuables skills to keep their family close and safe.
- *Structure and Safety*: Families provide structure and protection for themselves.
- *Resource Seeking*: Families plan to stay connected with their new supports.
- *Positive Affect, Memories, and Meaning*: Families have gained the skills and the strength to overcome bad things that happen to them.

 ## Preparation

- Send out postcard to remind families of group.
- Prepare all materials.
- Print certificates for each family (fill in name, date, print on heavy stock paper).
- Food and facilities planning and preparation.
- Decide on facilitators' roles.
- Update on the status of each family in the group.
- Anticipate any problems that might arise during the session.

 ## Homework Due

- None

 ## Session Overview

| Activity 1 | Family Meal Celebration | 45 Minutes |
| Activity 2 | Getting Closure | 40 Minutes |

Module III

SESSION 15 *Celebration!*

Activity 3   Who We Are Now and in Six Months   20 Minutes

Activity 4   Closing Ceremony   15 Minutes

 Homework to be Assigned

- Follow through on their family ritual tree care plan!

 Materials

- Tables (one for each family)
- Centerpieces
- Nameplates and session schedules (one for each family)
- Place settings/napkins
- Nutritious meal/drinks
- Paper/construction paper/postcard card stock
- Phone and address cards
- Pens/colored pencils/crayons/markers
- Glue/tape
- Research folders and instruments (if being completed during this session)
- Camera
- Facilitator chosen parting gifts (optional)
- Frames (one for each family) (to fit certificates)
- Job charts and star stickers (one pack for each family)

 Handouts

Closure Questionnaire	M3.S15.Closure.Question
Family Ritual Tree Care	M3.S15.Tree.Care
Certificates	M3.S15.Certificate
Family Rating Form	M3.S15.Feedback
Participant Log	M3.S15.Log
Clinician Rating Form	M3.S15.Clinic.Measures

 Posters

Rules Poster	Group.Rules.Poster

Module III

ACTIVITY 1: FAMILY MEAL CELEBRATION

 45 MINUTES

 Goals

* To help families carry out an event as planned.

 Materials

* As planned by families

 Handouts

* Conversation Prompts

 Posters

* Rules Poster

 Instructions

Facilitators prepare room by setting tables (one for each family). A simple centerpiece for each table is a nice touch. A nameplate and schedule for the session's activities are also placed on each table. Hang poster with group rules listed in a prominent place where all the families can see it.

Parent(s) gather their children around a table and share a meal together. Before serving the food:

Lead Facilitator: *We are so happy to have you back with us tonight for our last group.*

Families carry out celebration dinner as planned.

Lead Facilitator: *Have a good time!*

After the families have eaten and cleaned up (35–40 minutes), proceed with the opening routine.

Co-Facilitator: *You decided to start the meal by (opening ritual), so let's begin that way.*

Proceed with ritual planned by the group.

Module III

Celebration!

Refer to poster of rules and review. Make link between group rules, group functioning with family rules (explicit, agreed upon, written down for review), and family functioning.

Ask each family the following question: *So, is there anything going on right now that might get in the way of your family taking part in today's group?*

Make link between checking in with family members to be sure each person can participate (problem-solving, helping with a task) or may be over burdened, staying attuned to the mood and needs of all family members during other family activities.

Co-Facilitator: *This session focuses on celebration and saying "Goodbye." So, let's get started.*

ACTIVITY 2: GETTING CLOSURE

 40 MINUTES

 Goals

- To encourage families to make long-term commitments to maintaining family traditions and routines.
- To bring closure to the group.
- To facilitate further communication between families, if desired.

 Materials

- Paper/construction paper/postcard card stock
- Phone and address cards
- Pens/colored pencils/crayons/markers
- Glue

 Handouts

- Closure Questionnaire
- Family Ritual Tree Care

Module III

SESSION 15 *Celebration!*

 Instructions

Hand out "Closure Questionnaire" and "Family Ritual Tree Care."

Lead Facilitator: *I want you to complete this first sheet so that you can tell us what you liked and did not like about this group. What you thought was useful for you and your family and what you thought was not as helpful.*

Parent(s) complete the closure questionnaire with input from all family members.

After about 15 minutes, invite families (one at a time) to go through the closure questionnaire, sharing the family's answers. A facilitator should be taking notes of the family's answers. Consider asking to make a copy of the questionnaire. Have families discuss the group feedback and give suggestions/comments. Have the families talk about what they learned and whether anything has changed.

Lead Facilitator: *Now on the other sheet, I want you to think about what traditions or routines that we have talked about or that you have thought about during the weeks that we have been meeting and that you would like your family to keep doing. Talk together about this and write down what you decide.*

Families agree on what traditions and routines they want to continue to work on in the future. Ask families to share what they would like to continue to work on.

Co-Facilitator: Take all of the young children to another side of the room or another room. Alternatively, facilitators could circulate in the room and help young children (3+ years) at the tables so they can contribute to the family task. Help them make "Goodbye" cards.

ACTIVITY 3: WHO WE ARE NOW AND IN SIX MONTHS

 20 MINUTES

 Goals

- To think about what the family has accomplished during group.
- To reflect on how these changes can be maintained in the future.
- To predict how their family will have changed in six months.

Module III

SESSION 15 *Celebration!*

 ## Materials

- Paper/construction paper/postcard cards (blank)
- Phone and address cards
- Pens/colored pencils/crayons/markers
- Glue/tape
- Research folders and instruments (if being completed during this session)

 ## Instructions

If collecting instruments during this session, give parents and adolescents instruments from the folder. Offer to read each instrument to them, if they would like.

The children can make goodbye cards.

Collect all of the completed instruments and return them to the research folder. Note any concerns that you have about the validity of the answers.

If *not* collecting instruments, have family work together to draw a picture of the family doing something together six months from now that reflects what they have learned from participating in the SFCR group. Invite each family to share the drawing. Have a facilitator write down what is said and give the card to the family to keep with the drawing. Allow time for other families to comment/share their thinking.

ACTIVITY 4: CLOSING CEREMONY

 15 MINUTES

 ## Goals

- To reach closure, to model showing appropriate recognition and to engage in a rewarding goodbye.

Module III

Celebration!

Materials

- Camera
- Facilitator chosen parting gifts (optional)
- Frames (one for each family) (to fit certificates)
- Job charts and star stickers (one pack for each family)

Handouts

- Certificates (printed for each family)
- Family Rating Form
- Participant Log
- Clinician Rating Form

Instructions

Facilitators work together to make this ceremonial. This could include calling each family up to the front of the room to present them with their certificate and a small memento of their time spent in group. As the family proceeds to the front of the room, facilitators could hum or play the Graduation March or other music. Take pictures of each family.

Facilitators: *You have done a great job during this group and should be proud! We are proud of the work and the play you have done and would like to recognize you for that. We have a certificate that we would like to present to each family. Please come forward when we call your name to receive your certificate.*

Allow time for each facilitator to compliment the family members.

Facilitators: *Now it is time to say "Goodbye" for the last group. Let's end like we always have with our closing rituals.*

Families share closing rituals, if desired. Cue families to acknowledge the end of group with each other.

Facilitators: *Please complete your family rating form now and hand it in. Thanks.*

Facilitators complete participant log and clinician rating form.

Homework to be Assigned

- Follow through on their family ritual tree care plan!

Module III POST-SESSION   *Re-evaluating Trauma and Family Functioning*

Objectives

- To evaluate the effectiveness of SFCR.
- To help the family understand their future treatment needs, if any.

Threads

- *Resource Seeking*: Evaluation helps provide both the family and the team with important information to support treatment recommendations for further strengthening of the families coping abilities.

Preparation

- Schedule a convenient time to meet with the family for about two hours.
- Prepare all materials.
- Prepare research folder with copies of standardized measures of family functioning labeled with subject number, informant code, and date of administration.

Session Overview

Activity 1   Assessing Trauma Symptoms and Measuring Family Functioning   120 minutes

Materials

- Pens/pencils
- Paper
- Assessment measures, including satisfaction forms
- Research folder

Module III **POST-SESSION** *Re-evaluating Trauma and Family Functioning*

ACTIVITY 1: RE-ASSESSING TRAUMA SYMPTOMS AND MEASURING FAMILY FUNCTIONING

 120 MINUTES

 Goals

- To assess current symptoms.
- To collect additional standardized measures of family functioning.

 Materials

- Pens/pencils
- Paper
- Assessment measures, including initial satisfaction form
- Research folder

 Instructions

Interviewer: *Thanks for agreeing to meet with me today. Your family just completed a program that looks at family traditions and helping families use their traditions to strengthen their family life and to cope with bad things that happen. Before we started that program, you met with a researcher and provided information on how the trauma has affected your family's life. Today, we will be doing a follow-up interview to see how your family is currently doing.*

Give caregiver(s) and identified child (children) instruments from the folder. Offer to read each instrument to them, if they would like.

Collect all of the completed instruments and return them to the research folder. Note any concerns you have about the validity of the answers.

Interviewer: *Thanks for taking time to meet with me today. I hope that you enjoyed the program about family traditions.*

INDEX

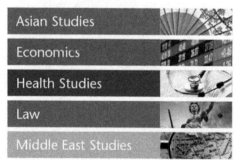

CPSIA information can be obtained
at www.ICGtesting.com
Printed in the USA
LVHW061753081119
636674LV00010BA/470/P